®

References for the Rest of Us! ®

COMPUTER BOOK SERIES FROM IDG

D0607650

Are you intimidated and confused by computers? Do you find that traditional manuals are overloaded with technical details you'll never use? Do your friends and family always call you to fix simple problems on their PCs? Then the *...For Dummies*® computer book series from IDG Books Worldwide is for you.

...For Dummies books are written for those frustrated computer users who know they aren't really dumb but find that PC hardware, software, and indeed the unique vocabulary of computing make them feel helpless. *...For Dummies* books use a lighthearted approach, a down-to-earth style, and even cartoons and humorous icons to diffuse computer novices' fears and build their confidence. Lighthearted but not lightweight, these books are a perfect survival guide for anyone forced to use a computer.

Already, hundreds of thousands of satisfied readers agree. They have made *...For Dummies* books the #1 introductory level computer book series and have written asking for more. So, if you're looking for the most fun and easy way to learn about computers, look to *...For Dummies* books to give you a helping hand.

™

IDG BOOKS
WORLDWIDE

THE
WORLD WIDE WEB
FOR
TEACHERS™

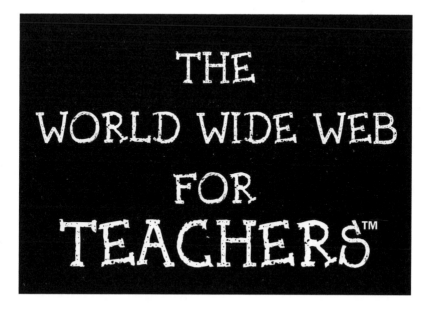

THE
WORLD WIDE WEB
FOR
TEACHERS™

by Bard Williams

IDG Books Worldwide, Inc.
An International Data Group Company

Foster City, CA ♦ Chicago, IL ♦ Indianapolis, IN ♦ Braintree, MA ♦ Southlake, TX

The World Wide Web For Teachers™

Published by
IDG Books Worldwide, Inc.
An International Data Group Company
919 E. Hillsdale Blvd.
Suite 400
Foster City, CA 94404

Library of Congress Catalog Card No.: 95-81813

ISBN: 1-56884-604-5

Printed in the United States of America

10 9 8 7 6 5 4 3 2

1A/RU/QV/ZW/IN

Distributed in the United States by IDG Books Worldwide, Inc.

Distributed by Macmillan Canada for Canada; by Computer and Technical Books for the Caribbean Basin; by Contemporanea de Ediciones for Venezuela; by Distribuidora Cuspide for Argentina; by CITEC for Brazil; by Ediciones ZETA S.C.R. Ltda. for Peru; by Editorial Limusa SA for Mexico; by Transworld Publishers Limited in the United Kingdom and Europe; by Al-Maiman Publishers & Distributors for Saudi Arabia; by Simron Pty. Ltd. for South Africa; by IDG Communications (HK) Ltd. for Hong Kong; by Toppan Company Ltd. for Japan; by Addison Wesley Publishing Company for Korea; by Longman Singapore Publishers Ltd. for Singapore, Malaysia, Thailand, and Indonesia; by Unalis Corporation for Taiwan; by WS Computer Publishing Company, Inc. for the Philippines; by WoodsLane Pty. Ltd. for Australia; by WoodsLane Enterprises Ltd. for New Zealand.

For general information on IDG Books Worldwide's books in the U.S., please call our Consumer Customer Service department at 800-762-2974. For reseller information, including discounts and premium sales, please call our Reseller Customer Service department at 800-434-3422.

For information on where to purchase IDG Books Worldwide's books outside the U.S., contact IDG Books Worldwide at 415-655-3021 or fax 415-655-3295.

For information on translations, contact Marc Jeffrey Mikulich, Director, Foreign & Subsidiary Rights, at IDG Books Worldwide, 415-655-3018 or fax 415-655-3295.

For sales inquiries and special prices for bulk quantities, write to the address above or call IDG Books Worldwide at 415-655-3200.

For information on using IDG Books Worldwide's books in the classroom, or ordering examination copies, contact the Education Office at 800-434-2086 or fax 817-251-8174.

For authorization to photocopy items for corporate, personal, or educational use, please contact Copyright Clearance Center, 222 Rosewood Drive, Danvers, MA 01923, or fax 508-750-4470.

is a trademark under exclusive license to IDG Books Worldwide, Inc., from International Data Group, Inc.

About the Author

Bard Williams

Bard Williams' friends wonder why he's always smiling. He tells us that it's because he's so happy to know so many great people and because he believes that there are no more powerful tools in the hands of an educator than a computer, the Internet, and some great ideas.

Bard is an educator, writer, and an educational technology consultant. He's also the author of IDG's *The Internet For Teachers*. He likes to present (you'll find him at educational conferences) and to write (he is the author of many articles including the "Online News" column in Turner Educational Services *T3: Technology, Teaching and Television* magazine).

Recently, Dr. Williams left a job as Instructional Technology Specialist for the Gwinnett County School system in Gwinnett County, Georgia, to join Apple Computer, Inc., as an Education Technology Consultant. Bard now spends his time helping teachers, administrators, school board members, and politicians understand and harness the power of the world's leading educational computer. In his spare time, he mines the Internet for new resources, helps college students with their homework, and answers truckloads of e-mail. (E-mail Bard at williams6@applelink.apple.com).

Welcome to the world of IDG Books Worldwide.

IDG Books Worldwide, Inc., is a subsidiary of International Data Group, the world's largest publisher of computer-related information and the leading global provider of information services on information technology. IDG was founded more than 25 years ago and now employs more than 7,700 people worldwide. IDG publishes more than 250 computer publications in 67 countries (see listing below). More than 70 million people read one or more IDG publications each month.

Launched in 1990, IDG Books Worldwide is today the #1 publisher of best-selling computer books in the United States. We are proud to have received 8 awards from the Computer Press Association in recognition of editorial excellence and three from Computer Currents' First Annual Readers' Choice Awards, and our best-selling ...For Dummies® series has more than 19 million copies in print with translations in 28 languages. IDG Books Worldwide, through a joint venture with IDG's Hi-Tech Beijing, became the first U.S. publisher to publish a computer book in the People's Republic of China. In record time, IDG Books Worldwide has become the first choice for millions of readers around the world who want to learn how to better manage their businesses.

Our mission is simple: Every one of our books is designed to bring extra value and skill-building instructions to the reader. Our books are written by experts who understand and care about our readers. The knowledge base of our editorial staff comes from years of experience in publishing, education, and journalism — experience which we use to produce books for the '90s. In short, we care about books, so we attract the best people. We devote special attention to details such as audience, interior design, use of icons, and illustrations. And because we use an efficient process of authoring, editing, and desktop publishing our books electronically, we can spend more time ensuring superior content and spend less time on the technicalities of making books.

You can count on our commitment to deliver high-quality books at competitive prices on topics you want to read about. At IDG Books Worldwide, we continue in the IDG tradition of delivering quality for more than 25 years. You'll find no better book on a subject than one from IDG Books Worldwide.

John J. Kilcullen

John Kilcullen
President and CEO
IDG Books Worldwide, Inc.

IDG Books Worldwide, Inc., is a subsidiary of International Data Group, the world's largest publisher of computer-related information and the leading global provider of information services on information technology. International Data Group publishes over 250 computer publications in 67 countries. Seventy million people read one or more International Data Group's publications each month. International Data Group's publications include: **ARGENTINA:** Computerworld Argentina, GamePro, Infoworld, PC World Argentina; **AUSTRALIA:** Australian Macworld, Client/Server Journal, Computer Living, Computerworld, Digital News, Network World, PC World, Publishing Essentials, Reseller; **AUSTRIA:** Computerwelt, PC TEST; **BELARUS:** PC World Belarus; **BELGIUM:** Data News; **BRAZIL:** Annuário de Informática, Computerworld Brazil, Connections, Super Game Power, Macworld, PC World Brazil, Publish Brazil, SUPERGAME; **BULGARIA:** Computerworld Bulgaria, Networkworld/Bulgaria, PC & MacWorld Bulgaria; **CANADA:** CIO Canada, ComputerWorld Canada, InfoCanada, Network World Canada, Reseller World; **CHILE:** Computerworld Chile, GamePro, PC World Chile; **COLUMBIA:** Computerworld Colombia, GamePro, PC World Colombia; **COSTA RICA:** PC World Costa Rica/Nicaragua; **THE CZECH AND SLOVAK REPUBLICS:** Computerworld Czechoslovakia, Elektronika Czechoslovakia, PC World Czechoslovakia; **DENMARK:** Communications World, Computerworld Danmark, Macworld Danmark, PC World Danmark, PC World Danmark Supplements, TECH World; **DOMINICAN REPUBLIC:** PC World Republica Dominicana; **ECUADOR:** PC World Ecuador, GamePro; **EGYPT:** Computerworld Middle East, PC World Middle East; **EL SALVADOR:** PC World Centro America; **FINLAND:** MikroPC, Tietoverkko, Tietoviikko; **FRANCE:** Distributique, Golden, Info PC, Le Guide du Monde Informatique, Le Monde Informatique, Reseaux & Telecoms; **GERMANY:** Computer Business, Computerwoche, Computerwoche Extra, Computerwoche Focus, Electronic Entertainment, GamePro, I/M Information Management, Macwelt, PC Welt; **GREECE:** GamePro, Macworld & Publish; **GUATEMALA:** PC World Centro America; **HONDURAS:** PC World Centro America; **HONG KONG:** Computerworld Hong Kong, PCWorld Hong Kong, Publish in Asia; **HUNGARY:** ABCD CD-ROM, Computerworld Szamitastechnika, PC & Mac World Hungary, PC-X Magazine; **INDIA:** Computerworld India, PC World India, Publish in Asia; **INDONESIA:** InfoKomputer PC World, Komputek Computerworld, Publish in Asia; **IRELAND:** ComputerScope, PC Live!; **ISRAEL:** PC World 32 BIT, People & Computers; **ITALY:** Computerworld Italia, Computerworld Italia Special Editions, Lotus Italia, Macworld Italia, Networking Italia, PC Shopping, PC World Italia, PC World/Walt Disney; **JAPAN:** Macworld Japan, Nikkei Personal Computing, SunWorld Japan, Windows World Japan; **KENYA:** East African Computer News; **KOREA:** Hi-Tech Information/Computerworld, Macworld Korea, PC World Korea; **MACEDONIA:** PC World Macedonia; **MALAYSIA:** Computerworld Malaysia, PC World Malaysia, Publish in Asia; **MEXICO:** Computerworld Mexico, GamePro, Macworld, PC World Mexico; **MYANMAR:** PC World Myanmar; **NETHERLANDS:** Computable, Computer! Totaal, LAN Magazine, Macworld, Net Magazine; **NEW ZEALAND:** Computer Buyer, Computerworld New Zealand, MTB, Network World, PC World New Zealand; **NICARAGUA:** PC World Costa Rica/Nicaragua; **NIGERIA:** PC World Africa; **NORWAY:** Computerworld Norge, Computerworld Privat, CW Rapport Klient/Tjener, CW Rapport Nettverk & Telecom, CW Rapport Offentlig Sektor, IDG's KURSGUIDE, Macworld Norge, Multimedia World, PC World Ekspress, PC World Nettverk, PC World Norge, PC World's Produktguide, Windows Spesial; **PAKISTAN:** Computerworld Pakistan, PC World Pakistan; **PANAMA:** GamePro, PC World Panama; **PARAGUAY:** PC World Paraguay; **P. R. OF CHINA:** China Computerworld, China Infoworld, Computer & Communication, Electronic Product World, Electronics Today, Game Camp, PC World China, Popular Computer Week, Software World, Telecom Product World; **PERU:** Computerworld Peru, GamePro, PC World Profesional Peru, PC World Peru; **POLAND:** Computerworld Poland, Computerworld Special Report, Macworld, Networld, PC World Komputer; **PHILIPPINES:** Computerworld Philippines, PC Digest, Publish in Asia; **PORTUGAL:** Cerebro/PC World, Correio Informático/Computerworld, Mac•In/PC•In Portugal; **PUERTO RICO:** PC World Puerto Rico; **ROMANIA:** Computerworld Romania, PC World Romania, Telecom Romania; **RUSSIA:** Computerworld Rossiya, Network World Russia, PC World Russia; **SINGAPORE:** Computerworld Singapore, PC World Singapore, Publish in Asia; **SLOVENIA:** MONITOR; **SOUTH AFRICA:** Computing S.A., Network World S.A., Software World; **SPAIN:** Computerworld España, COMUNICACIONES WORLD, Dealer World, Macworld España, PC World España; **SWEDEN:** CAP&Design, Computer Sweden, Corporate Computing, MacWorld, Maxi Data, MikroDatorn, Nätverk & Kommunikation, PC/Aktiv, PC World, Windows World; **SWITZERLAND:** Computerworld Schweiz, Macworld Schweiz, PCtip; **TAIWAN:** Computerworld Taiwan, Macworld Taiwan, PC World Taiwan, Publish Taiwan, Windows World; **THAILAND:** Thai Computerworld, Publish in Asia; **TURKEY:** Computerworld Monitör, MACWORLD Turkiye, PC WORLD Turkiye; **UKRAINE:** Computerworld Kiev, Computers & Software Magazine, PC World Ukraine; **UNITED KINGDOM:** Acorn User, Amiga Action, Amiga Computing, Amiga, Appletalk, CD Powerplay, CD-ROM Now, Computing, Connexion, GamePro, Lotus Magazine, Macaction, Macworld, Open Computing, Parents and Computers, PC Home, PC Works, The WEB; **UNITED STATES:** Cable in the Classroom, CD Review, CIO Magazine, Computerworld, Computerworld Client/Server Journal, Digital Video Magazine, DOS World, Electronic, InfoWorld, I-Way, Macworld, Maximize, MULTIMEDIA WORLD, Network World, PC World, PUBLISH, SWATPro Magazine, Video Event, WebMaster; **URUGUAY:** PC World Uruguay; **VENEZUELA:** Computerworld Venezuela, GamePro, PC World Venezuela; and **VIETNAM:** PC World Vietnam   10/17/95

Dedication

This book is dedicated to those teachers who make the time to learn and take the time to care and to my family — Joan (Hi, Mom!) and Tom Doyle; Brevard S. Williams, Jr. (Great genes, Dad); Susan (Love ya, Sis!), Doug, Ashley, and Jordan Cook; and Laura (Love ya, other Sis!), Bill, and Joshua Wilson — for their support, understanding, love, and encouragement.

Publisher's Acknowledgments

We're proud of this book; send us your comments about it by using the Reader Response Card at the back of the book or by e-mailing us at feedback/dummies@idgbooks.com. Some of the people who helped bring this book to market include:

Acquisitions, Development, & Editorial

Project Editor: Bill Helling

Assistant Acquisitions Editor: Gareth Hancock

Product Development Manager:
Mary Bednarek

Editor: Diana R. Conover

Technical Reviewer: Tommy Hann

Editorial Managers: Kristin A. Cocks,
Mary C. Corder

Editorial Assistants: Constance Carlisle,
Chris Collins, Kevin Spencer

Production

Project Coordinator: J. Tyler Connor

Layout and Graphics: Cameron Booker,
Kerri Cornell, Angela F. Hunckler,
Todd Klemme, Jill Lyttle, Jane Martin,
Mark Owens, Carla Radzikinas, Gina Scott

Proofreaders: Kathleen Prata, Joel Draper,
Christine Meloy Beck, Gwenette Gaddis,
Dwight Ramsey, Robert Springer

Indexer: Liz Cunningham

General & Administrative

IDG Books Worldwide, Inc.: John Kilcullen, President & CEO; Steven Berkowitz, COO & Publisher

Dummies, Inc.: Milissa Koloski, Executive Vice President & Publisher

Dummies Technology Press & Dummies Editorial: Diane Graves Steele, Associate Publisher; Judith A. Taylor, Brand Manager; Myra Immell, Editorial Director

Dummies Trade Press: Kathleen A. Welton, Vice President & Publisher; Stacy S. Collins, Brand Manager

IDG Books Production for Dummies Press: Beth Jenkins, Production Director; Cindy L. Phipps, Supervisor of Project Coordination; Kathie S. Schnorr, Supervisor of Page Layout; Shelley Lea, Supervisor of Graphics and Design

Dummies Packaging & Book Design: Erin McDermitt, Packaging Coordinator; Kavish+Kavish, Cover Design

♦

The publisher would like to give special thanks to Patrick J. McGovern, without whom this book would not have been possible.

♦

Acknowledgments

Projects like this just don't happen without the help of many friends and colleagues. I'm fortunate to have had the wisdom of many (with and without techno-weenie propeller-beanies) for this project. I apologize, in advance, for any I may have missed.

Tommy Hann, a Senior Systems Engineer for Apple Computer, did the technical editing of this book. I am convinced that you will find nobody with more troubleshooting and Net skills (and a bigger grin on his face) than Tommy.

Another Apple buddy, Craig Wall, helped put together the zillions of Web resources on *The World Wide Web For Teachers CD-ROM*. Between Black and Tans and bits and bytes, Craig's got the market pretty well cornered.

Now that I'm a *seasoned* author with IDG (seasoned means "been there, done that" at least once), I got to choose my editing team, and of course I chose the best! Bill Helling is the kindest, most competent editor I've ever encountered. Diana Conover helped my writing become more readable in my post-dissertation chaos. Mary Bednarek championed the software and worked long hours so that you could have great stuff on your CD-ROM. Megg Bonar, who has since left IDG, was my contract hero. (My accountant thanks you, Megg!) Jim Kelly is IDG's education guru. He's great at getting to the heart of education. And finally Judi Taylor — a marketing whiz whose smile and manner kept me rocking and rolling on the book when things got nuts.

One of the things that makes this book special is the CD. I want to especially thank IDG's own Kevin Spencer for his hard work getting the disc together. Rob Carroll and his people at Access Technology did a super job turning out the finished CD.

Extra-special thanks go to my America Online friend Gayle Keresey who played media specialist by day and sent me hundreds of cool Web addresses by night. To Scott Tyson and my other brothers at Phi Kappa Theta who kept me busy when I wasn't writing. To Nita Seng who is the best cheerleader on the planet. And to my friends Brice Vorderbrug, Jim Mansou, Leni Donlan, and Emery Roth for contributing both physically and mentally to the completion of this work.

Kudos to Robert Best whose *WebWeaver* got me interested in Web-page creation, to my Internet provider, Mindspring (http:www.mindspring.com) for an awesome gateway to the Net, and to the good folks at e-World and AOL who were happy to share information about their services and the Net with a struggling author.

And last, but not least, my friend Michelle Robinette, *Mac goddess* (move over David Pogue!), friend, and teacher, who kicked me one day and said, "You should do a book." This is my second (the first was *The Internet For Teachers*, IDG Books Worldwide, Inc.) Thank you, Michelle, and may your books, *Macs For Teachers* and *Mac Multimedia For Teachers*, be on every teacher's must-read list!

Contents at a Glance

Cartoons at a Glance

By Rich Tennant

page 255

page 72

page 73

page 199

page 115

page 221

page 9

page 214

Table of Contents

Chapter 23: Ten Web Sites for Parents and Kids 229

Chapter 24: Ten Web Sites for Teachers 233

Foreword

*T*here used to be an ice-harvesting industry in New England. Companies would go out to frozen lakes and ponds and cut out blocks of ice. Then they would ship blocks of ice all over the world.

The ice-harvesting companies, however, were put out of business by the ice-making companies. These innovators figured out that people wanted ice during the entire year and at a lower cost than ice shipped in from New England. Thus, they built mechanical ice-making factories in cities all around the United States.

The ice-making companies were put out of business by the refrigerator companies. It was great to have a local ice-making company, but it was even better to have a PDC (Personal Desktop Chiller, as someone in the personal computer industry undoubtedly would have named it) in your home.

There are close parallels between the personal chilling industry and the personal computer industry. Our ice-harvesting stage was when hardware was the key: disk drives, monitors, keyboards, etc. Our ice-making stage occurred when we started to duke it out on system software: Windows versus Macintosh.

We are just entering the refrigeration stage: access and distribution of information on the Internet. More and more, the Internet is defining the personal computer experience. One major consequence of this development is that people need a strong knowledge of the World Wide Web, and teachers need it even more because they are the intellectual beacons of our communities.

Enter *The World Wide Web For Teachers*. Should you read this book? Let me be subtle. How many people do you know who teach how to cut blocks of ice out of ponds and lakes? Of all people, teachers should be leading our youth into the adoption of new paradigms like the World Wide Web — and this book is indispensable for them.

Though I understand the need for market segmentation (because yet-another Internet book would get lost in a morass of junk), the title of this book understates its true value. *The World Wide Web For Teachers* is a great book for *anyone* eager to learn about the World Wide Web.

Guy Kawasaki

Apple Fellow

Author of *How to Drive Your Competition Crazy*

Introduction

· ·

Welcome to *The World Wide Web For Teachers*. This book is written for educators who have stuck their ears to the ground, have heard all the traffic on the information superhighway, and have realized that the time to get a learner's permit has long passed.

Never fear! You'll be happy to know that, from the very beginnings of the Internet, educators like you and me took the lead in developing strategies for applying the amazing technology of telecommunications to the real world. You'll be even happier to know that you have three things many non-educators don't have that will get you out *ahead* of the other folks on the infobahn very quickly:

🗸 You are a lifelong learner.

🗸 You know enough about learning and teaching to teach yourself.

🗸 You work with hyperactive, growing brains every day.

The first two of these three factors probably got you to buy this book. (Thank you!) The third factor will keep you hopping and will allow you to leapfrog all the snails on the information superhighway sooner than you think. Relax and enjoy the ride.

If you're like many educators, your mind keeps racing well after the lights go out and you're snug in your bed. You're thinking about grading periods, dissertations in progress, convincing the world that Johnny can really read and won't admit it, and (of course) all the other zillion things going on in your life. If you have any problems at all going to sleep, do *not* read this book just before you've scheduled a date with the sandman. You shouldn't read this book at that time of night because it may give you ideas. (You know, those special ideas that start as little twitches in your head and blossom so quickly that their growth is almost scary.) You may find yourself lying awake all night long because you are so excited about the prospects of trying out the ideas the next day with your students! Sorry. It's a tough job, but someone's got to do it. <grin>

Many books about the Internet are available today, but precious few of those books view the Net from the unique perspective of an educator. Whether you're an assistant professor in one of our nation's colleges or universities or an equally frustrated preschool teacher who just got access to your first computer, this book will help you understand and apply one of the most exciting Internet tools ever — the World Wide Web — to the teaching/learning process and to your everyday life.

Inside *The World Wide Web For Teachers,* you can find information about how to get the most out of Web access, how to jump over hurdles such as parental concern, and how you and your students can become producers and online publishers with your classroom's word processor.

So, here it is in plain English. All the technobabble has been stripped away, and here are *just the facts* that tell you how to get started using the Web, how to do some cool things after you get online, and how you can harness the power of the Internet in your classroom.

About This Book

This book is designed for use by anyone who is working on acquiring, or already has access to, an Internet connection and wants to know more about accessing Internet resources through the World Wide Web (also known as *the Web*). Just jump right into any chapter, get what you need, and jump back to the real world.

In *The World Wide Web For Teachers,* you'll find handy information that answers the following questions (and many, many more):

- ✔ What is the World Wide Web?
- ✔ Why should I learn about the Web (and the Internet)?
- ✔ What do I need to get started?
- ✔ How do I get connected to the Internet?
- ✔ How do I use a Web browser?
- ✔ How do I keep up with all the information that my students and I collect?
- ✔ How do I publish information on the Internet?
- ✔ How can I manage students if I have only one computer?
- ✔ What can I do to help other educators learn about the Internet and the World Wide Web?
- ✔ Where are the best places to begin on a journey through the Web?

How to Read This Book

Grab this book when you need a quick reference. Glance at the Table of Contents, peruse the Index, and zip right to the page that has the answer you need.

The World Wide Web For Teachers has been written so that each chapter pretty much stands alone. This book is great for those five-minute (two-minute?) reading breaks between classes.

Conventions

I've done some things to make your life easier. Watch for them.

When you have to type something, it appears in **boldface** type, unless it's an Internet address. Internet addresses (sometimes called *URLs*) and the commands for writing your own Web pages look like this:

```
http://www.mindspring.com/~bardw/bard.html
```

Type the address in, just as it appears, capitalization and all, and then press the Return or Enter key on your keyboard. When you make a boo-boo, just type the address again. Sometimes the keyboard gremlin is active (kind of like the gremlin that steals your grade book and car keys now and then). Just be patient. It'll work.

When you use your World Wide Web browser, you need to use commands from the menu bar. I used *Netscape Navigator's* Mac version when writing this book (and my screen shots are from this version), but the version for Windows is just about the same. To avoid having to give separate commands for Mac and Windows users, I've often combined them like this:

File⇨Open Location (⌘+O)

This means that from the menu bar you simply choose Open Location from the File menu. The underlined letters are *hot keys* for Windows users who can just press Alt+F and then O instead of using the mouse. You can see the underlined letters on the Windows version of the browser. And the *command key* symbol in parentheses is for Mac users who can use this sequence instead of using the mouse.

Finally, I've italicized program names (such as *Eudora*, for example) so that they stand out just a little bit from the text.

Who am I talking to? (also known as: To whom am I speaking?)

In preparing this book for you, I've assumed the following:

- ✔ You have (or would like to have) access to the Internet.

- ✔ You intend to get access to the Internet through a direct network connection, through an online service, or through an Internet service provider.

- ✔ You are an educator who is wondering how you can learn about the Internet and the World Wide Web and how you can use them in what you do every day.

✔ You are responsible for arranging to bring the Internet into your school or your school system.

✔ You have heard everyone on the planet talking about the Internet, you've seen Internet URLs all over television and in the newspapers, and the Internet is driving you crazy. You want to learn more about it.

Whether you're a Macintosh user or one who's a Windows guru, I've got you covered. *The World Wide Web For Teachers CD-ROM* that comes with this book is equipped with America Online client software (for Mac or Windows users) that allows you to browse the Web at will — and maybe pick up other great Internet software.

In addition, hundreds of clickable Web links to keep you busy for at least a year are included on the CD-ROM; and for you Macintosh users, I have included a great Web-page-creation tool called *Web Weaver.* Or check out the *Internet Assistant* tool, a tool for PC users.

By the way, if you want to know more about the Internet as a whole and things such as FTP, IRC, Gopherspace, and telnetting for fun and profit, grab a copy of *The Internet For Teachers* (IDG Books Worldwide, Inc.). The author's a great friend of mine. ; -)

(That "thing" at the end of the last paragraph is called a *smiley* or *emoticon.* You're likely to see many of those as you telecommunicate. In case you missed it, turn your head sideways to the left, and I'm winking at you.)

How this book is organized

This book has five parts. The parts are designed to be read either in sequence or on their own. You can jump in anywhere you like, but I recommend that you peek at Part I so that you'll know a bit about the Internet before you take the plunge.

Here are the parts of the book and what they contain:

Part I: Say Hello to the Web

In this part, you can take a quick journey into the Web, find out what all the hoopla is about, discover some compelling reasons for you and your students to surf the Net, and zip through a pre-surf checklist that can make your first trip on the Net as successful as possible.

Part II: Riding Your Web Surfboard

In this part, you can get your feet wet learning about surfing the Web with the powerful *Netscape Navigator* Web browser — although you can use the browser of your choice. This part covers beginning to advanced uses of *Netscape Navigator* and even talks a bit about what may be in store for the future of the World Wide Web. By the way, in Chapter 7 I'll tell you how to get *Netscape Navigator* — free!

Part III: Creating Your Own Web Page

This part is for when you and your students are ready to move up the food chain from being information *consumers* to being information *producers*. Part III walks you, step-by-step, through the process of planning, designing, and scripting your own Web page by using only a word processor or the Web-scripting tools included on *The World Wide Web For Teachers CD-ROM.* Creating a Web page is not sleight of hand. (It's really easy; I promise!)

Part IV: The Web Meets the Classroom

Here's a survival guide for using the Web in the classroom. This is the part where I tackle the tough stuff, such as what you can do if you have one Internet connection and 30 (or more) students, what you can do when the inevitable "what about the questionable content" call comes from a parent, and what you can do to help fellow educators become Web-literate.

Part V: The Part of Tens: Places to Go, Things to Do

Buckle your seat belts. This part contains lots and lots of Web places for you to go and features a few activities to get you started on your journey. Each of these Web sites is certified as "kid-and-teacher tested" to help ensure that it is worth the trip.

Part VI: Appendixes

Here you can find a glossary that's been exorcised of all technobabble, a summary of *HTML* (Web-scripting language) commands, and a couple of great samples of acceptable use policies should your school want to use a safety net when it begins flying on the Web trapeze.

Icons Used in This Book

Here are the pretty pictures that can make your life easier:

Learning Link

Learning Link icons indicate opportunities for you and your students to participate in Internet-related educational activities.

On the CD

This icon points out programs that are on *The World Wide Web For Teachers CD-ROM*, which is included with this book.

Teacher Approved

This icon highlights an item or an activity that I think is a "must use" in your classroom.

Techno Terms

The Techno Terms icon points out vocabulary items that the teacher (you!) should know in order to be a *true* Net surfer.

Tip

The Tip icon points out handy things that you should watch for or things that can make your life easier. These tips are time savers and frustration savers.

Warning!

A danger sign. Hold the mouse!

Cool Web Site

My favorite icon! This icon alerts you to useful and/or fun Web addresses that you can use in your classroom.

Just Do It!

Repeat after me:

"I can do this."

"It's easier than the entrance exam for graduate school."

"This is more meaningful than the last memo I received from the district office."

"It's worth my time to learn this stuff because I want to have all the advantages that I can get when I walk through the door and face the raging hormones in fifth-period science class."

Whatever your reason, you've gone so far as to buy this book and read this introduction. As you delve further into this book, you'll find that your journey onto the Net and the World Wide Web will be *a piece of cake*. Have a great meal!

Feedback!

I really, really want to know what you think about *The World Wide Web For Teachers*.

Send feedback to:

IDG Books Worldwide, Inc.
7260 Shadeland Station, Suite 100
Indianapolis, IN 46256

Or (even better) show us that you've learned something by sending an e-mail message (see Chapter 10) to IDG Books at **feedback@idgbooks.com**.

Part I
Say Hello to the Web

"You weren't kidding when you said the teachers were excited about surfing the Web."

In this part . . .

As educators, we experience many "mysterious" things. You know, those things that happen during a school day that seem inexplicable. For example: Why is there never any chalk in the chalk tray when you just put out a whole box yesterday? Or why do class periods seem to get longer as the school year nears its end? Hmm . . . maybe chalk pieces are like socks that get lost in the wash. I know! Someday you'll walk into a mini-mall and see a whole store selling nothing but little stubby pieces of chalk and unmated socks, all at an unbelievably low price!

The World Wide Web (also known as *the Web*) might seem like a mysterious thing, but it really isn't. This part of the book will help demystify the Web (and a few other parts of the Internet), will suggest some great reasons why your Internet access in classrooms should be as vital as access to pen and paper, and will give you a heads-up on what you'll need before you and your students jump onto your Web surfboards and take off.

Chapter 1

An Internet Primer

· ·

In This Chapter

▶ Learning the Net: a primer

▶ Dissecting the Web

▶ Webbing in education

▶ Exploring other Internet resources

▶ Preparing your surfboard

· ·

*R*emember your first day in the classroom? Years of preparation and student teaching couldn't possibly have prepared you for what you were to face on Day One.

Teaching, as you're well aware, is one of those wonderful professions that is vastly more difficult than it appears. It's not enough that you have to master a convoluted curriculum. You've also got to know what to do when Sally falls over backwards in her chair ("I told you so" is no longer an appropriate response), when Johnny doesn't come to school for three weeks (truant officers are hard to come by these days), or when you get a jargon-filled memorandum from the superintendent proclaiming the introduction of a new "outcome-based, interactive, collaborative, learner-centered, whole-language" science curriculum.

You jumped that first hurdle, though; and even though you were excited and nervous on that first day (on about three hours sleep?), you knew that you could sift through the complexities of classroom life and get on with the art of teaching. For me, my first introduction to telecommunications (and later to the Internet) gave me the same feeling.

The Net seemed really complex (of course, so did operating a purple ditto machine, at first), and the Net had its own jargon standing in the way of understanding. It took far less time than I had imagined, however, to get through the basics and realize that the Internet could be a valuable personal and classroom resource that, with a little practice, could help me transform my classroom into an information-rich learning environment.

I think that you'll find that learning the Internet is worth the effort. And it is tons easier than your first day in the classroom.

The Bus Stops Here

Okay. Time to get on the bus and head out for your journey on the information superhighway. Remember to keep your arms and heads inside the windows at all times and keep your hand on your mouse. For our first stop, I share with you a brief primer on the structure of the Internet and help you see where the World Wide Web (also known as *the Web*) fits in. Don't worry. Reading this guidebook to the infobahn will be much easier than grading 50 essays or writing "works well with others" on 125 report cards! Step carefully, please!

It's a bird. It's a plane! It's a network?

The *Internet* is really just a collection of computer networks linked together so that users can share vast data resources. To get onto the Internet, all you have to do is make arrangements to link your computer to an online service (such as e-World or America Online), a local area network with Internet connections, or a commercial Internet service provider (such as AT&T) that offers Internet access.

Of course, you can't *touch* the Internet — the Internet isn't a place at all. *Internet* is just a name for the union (get out your math books and turn to page 27) of many data sources. This "intangibility" confuses many beginning users. The Internet is about *how* resources are linked and *what* resources are available — and many, many resources are available.

How many resources? There are millions of computers that provide data on the Net, and that number is growing hourly. Colleges and universities, research organizations, government entities, and businesses are all rushing to find ways to connect to (and exploit) Internet resources. Schools are no exception. As of mid-1995, more than 30,000 schools had access to the Internet; and many schools were not only *consuming* information, but *producing* it. Figure 1-1 shows a Web page created by students and teachers at Auckland, New Zealand's Pakuranga College (really a high school). (See Part III for information about how *your* school can build its own Web page.)

Big computers and bunches of wire

The Internet began with nothing more than a bunch of wire, a telephone network, a few blinking behemoth computers, and an idea that people needed better ways to communicate. In 1969, the Department of Defense (DOD) funded a project to link DOD engineers with civilian research contractors, including a large number of universities that were doing military-funded research. The resulting interconnection of computers (in the beginning, there were only three), a network known as *ARPANET* (Advanced Research Projects Administration Network), formed the basis for future work in information exchange and data storage.

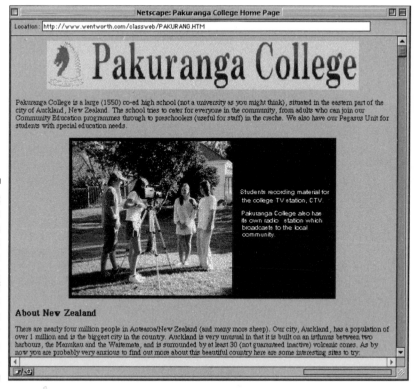

Figure 1-1:
Thousands
of schools
have access
to the
Internet;
many of
these
schools
have their
own Web
site.

Educators, it turns out, were a major force in helping the Internet idea spread like wildfire. In the early days, universities began to shift from centralized computing to a distributed workstation architecture. In plain English, that means their mainframe computers (big iron) got overwhelmed with byte-chomping insignificant traffic (electronic mail, also known as *e-mail*), and the gurus of silicon decided that computing power could be spread over many computers to free up the mainframes for more important tasks, like calculating pi to the 10,000th significant digit.

Electronic mail, in fact, was how the Internet spread through colleges and universities. Nowadays, virtually every institution of higher education offers free Internet access (or at least e-mail access) to every student and employee. Colleges, universities, and research institutions (such as the CDC and NASA) began to exchange information, and soon the Net was entrenched — as valuable a tool as chalk or pencil.

Not too much later (in the late '80s), the Internet (as it existed then) became overwhelmed with traffic. Enter the commercial Internet providers who saw a profit potential and who, with larger, faster, less-expensive computers and faster transmission (telephone) lines, quickly expanded Internet resources to clear the information logjam.

Today, there are thousands of Internet on-ramps (*nodes*) and millions of users. K-12 education, as you might expect, is one of the fastest-growing populations of new users. It's up to us educators to assess the value and determine the use of Internet resources with our kids.

A Web is born

The World Wide Web (an interactive, graphical presentation of information on the Internet) is a relative newcomer on the Internet timeline. The Father of the Web is generally thought to be Tim Berners-Lee of the European Particle Physics Laboratory. Lee developed the Web concept in 1989 as a means for building communication bridges between scientists throughout an organization of physicists called CERN. (Trivia: CERN stands for Conseil Européen pour Recherche Nucleaire. Now you know why they use an acronym.)

Web browsers (software tools used to access the World Wide Web) didn't appear until late 1990. Developers latched onto what was certainly a great idea and began to develop and expand the capabilities of the early Web software. As the developers worked, they developed a set of rules that, when followed by others, assures that software and computer systems work together peacefully. These rules are referred to in techno-speak as *protocols*.

The Web got its name from its ability to create a virtually infinite number of interconnections, called *links,* between different types of data at different locations. Whether the resource is a scientific report from Rome, Italy or a book report from a third grader in Rome, Georgia, the data can be interconnected using clickable text (called *hypertext*).

What Is the World Wide Web?

If you're familiar with *HyperStudio, HyperCard,* or *LinkWay*, you have a great reference point for learning about the World Wide Web (also known as the *Web*). The aforementioned "hyper-programs" present users with *cards* which are linked together with clickable *buttons*. The buttons on the cards can do different things in the hyper-world: they can launch programs, play sounds, show digital movies, or display simple animation. Put a bunch of cards together in *HyperStudio* or *HyperCard,* and we call them a *stack*.

In the world of the Web, cards become *pages,* buttons become *hypertext links,* and stacks become *Web sites*. Got it? *Web pages* are online documents that feature clickable hypertext links that transport you to documents, graphics, or other Web pages; or they connect you to other kinds of Internet resources such as *file transfer (FTP)* or *newsgroups (electronic bulletin boards).*Get all that? If so, you've got a pretty good operational definition of the Web. (See Figure 1-2.)

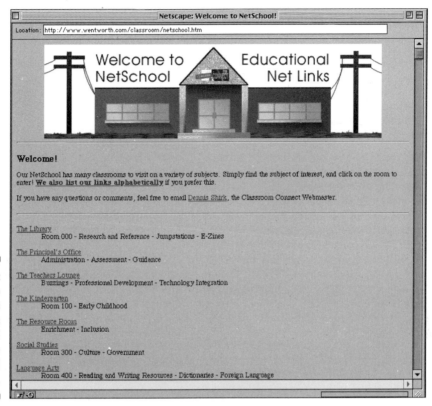

Location: http://www.wentworth.com/classroom/netschool.htm

Welcome to NetSchool — Educational Net Links

Welcome!

Our NetSchool has many classrooms to visit on a variety of subjects. Simply find the subject of interest, and click on the room to enter! We also list our links alphabetically if you prefer this.

If you have any questions or comments, feel free to email Dennis Shirk, the Classroom Connect Webmaster.

The Library
    Room 000 - Research and Reference - Jumpstations - E-Zines

The Principal's Office
    Administration - Assessment - Guidance

The Teachers Lounge
    Buzzings - Professional Development - Technology Integration

The Kindergarten
    Room 100 - Early Childhood

The Resource Room
    Enrichment - Inclusion

Social Studies
    Room 300 - Culture - Government

Language Arts
    Room 400 - Reading and Writing Resources - Dictionaries - Foreign Language

Figure 1-2:
The Web features pages connected by clickable text called hypertext.

Take a breath and go back and re-read that third sentence in the preceding paragraph. The keywords are "other kinds of Internet resources." People especially like the programs used to view Web pages, called *Web browsers,* because these programs are kind of the Swiss Army knife of Internet tools. In the beginning of Internet access, folks used a separate program to access file transfer (using a program such as *Fetch*), another to view newsgroups (using a program called a *newsreader*), and another to search computer databases (with a program called *telnet*). Most Web browsers available today allow you to do all those things, and more, from within one program.

Before you get too excited about this Mother of All Internet Tools, I'll give you one caution. The tools that I mentioned previously (newsreaders, *Fetch*, and such) do only one thing, but they do it very well — and with lots of bells and whistles. Web browsers typically do many things, but they're primarily designed to display Web pages, so you'll still likely find the need to access the other programs if you want to do something quickly or access the Internet without going through the Web.

Are you hyper yet?

The Web offers users an adventure in hypermedia, fueled by hypertext and hyperlinks. It's a truly hyper place that's perfect for hyper students (and teachers).

Hypermedia is a term used to describe the union of hypertext and multimedia. The term *hypertext*, coined by techno-culture guru Ted Nelson, describes text that, when selected with the click of a mouse, zips the user to another source of related information. For example, clicking on the hyper-linked word "projects" in the sentence "There are many online projects that NASA offers to students," might whisk you away to another site (residing on another computer halfway across the globe) that offers a list of specific projects and information about how to participate.

Multimedia refers to the union of different data types, such as text, graphics, sound, and sometimes movies. Hypermedia connects these data types together. With hypermedia, highlighted and linked text, called *hyperlinks* (or just *links*), allows a user to move between data in a nonlinear manner. You're just as likely to hear a sound when clicking on a hyperlinked word when browsing a hypermedia file, for example, as you are to view a picture.

The language that Web programs use to create hyperlinks is called *HyperText Transfer Protocol (HTTP)*. This set of rules allows any users to create their own Web pages and post them to the Internet and ensures that the files will be readable by Web browsers. When you enter a WWW (World Wide Web) address, you'll enter the following text before the Web address:

`http://`

The prefix tips off the Internet that the *URL* (*Uniform Resource Locator* — an Internet resource address) that you're looking for is a WWW address rather than a Gopher or FTP site. So, in the address `http://www.idg.com/`, the `http://` tells you, and the Net, that the site you seek is on the Web.

To help you remember to add the prefix, we've appended the `http://` prefix to WWW addresses in this book. Be sure to type the prefix before all of the Web addresses, or your browser will get confused.

Your School Supplies

Time for your yearly trip to the store to get all the goodies you'll need for school. This year, whip out your American Express card and get ready to spend — but gaining Internet access will likely cost you far less than you think. Using the Web requires only a computer, modem, Internet connection, and a software program called a *Web browser*. The Internet connection can be through a stand-alone service provider, your own Internet server, or an online service, such as America Online, CompuServe, or e-World.

If you're already a graduate of the "Web Browsers Institute" and are ready to create your own Web page, you'll need to add a word processor (or a Web-creation program such as the ones included on *The World Wide Web For Teachers CD-ROM* that comes with this book!) to your list. You'll also need a little knowledge about how to use an amazingly simple and powerful scripting language called *HTML (HyperText Markup Language)*. In Part III of this book, I give you all the mental tools you'll need to get your own Web page up and running in no time.

I'm sure that there are lots of teachers out there like me that are visual learners, so here is a handy diagram that illustrates exactly what you'll need to make an Internet connection.

The diagram in Figure 1-3 shows the "big five" items that you need: hardware, software, a modem, a phone line, and an Internet account.

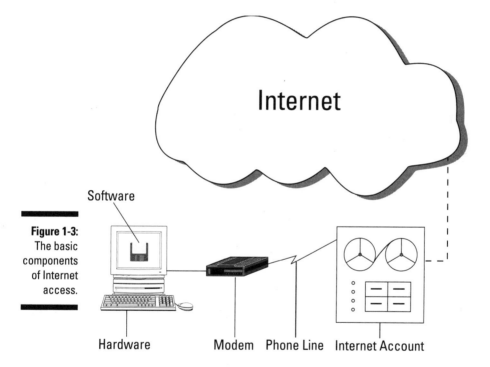

Figure 1-3:
The basic
components
of Internet
access.

You'll find an extended explanation about exactly what color of notebooks and what kind of lead for your pencils you will need, as well as specifics on the afore-mentioned hardware and software accoutrements, in Chapter 5. Happy shopping!

How Will We Pay for This?

I know what you're thinking. This Web thing is great, but how in the world will I ever pry enough money out of the school coffers to fund access? It once took me an entire school year to convince a principal that the school should supply each teacher with his or her own *personal* 5 ¹/₄-inch floppy disk — floppies that cost a whopping $.50 each. (This event occurred back in the Dark Ages when we had 50 Apple IIs and no supply budget. Now we have a bunch of Macintoshes, a few PCs, and a mammoth $50 per year for supplies.)

How much you need to budget for Web access (and other telecommunications) depends, largely, on the deal you strike with your Internet service provider. If you're connecting to the Internet through an online service such as America Online or CompuServe, you'll pay a bit more, but you'll get an easy all-in-one interface. If you purchase time through an Internet service provider, you'll have to consider how much time you'll use each month or get an unlimited-time account. If your school is in a rural area, you may also have to contend with long-distance charges from the school to the nearest Internet service provider.

The best way to estimate your budget costs is to try to find a school that's already connected and ask them how much they spend. In my school system, one school that's connected through a *PPP account* (PPP stands for Point-to-Point Protocol — one type of Internet connection) to an Internet provider pays $40.00 per month for a dedicated phone line and $35.00 per month for unlimited access time for one account (and that's in addition to a separate, free account donated through the good graces of a large local service provider). Don't be afraid to approach local providers or your school's business partner and make a case for a free account for school use. This kind of deal is good for *their* business.

Commercial online service access fees can range from $25 to more than $80 per month, depending on usage and the deal you get when you sign up. Shop carefully!

If your school chooses to get a direct connection and purchase a leased (high-speed) line, expect monthly charges to top $1,000. Remember, however, that with a leased line, many users can connect simultaneously using the same single line, so your *cost per line* may actually be less expensive. There's a great chapter in *The Internet For Teachers* (IDG Books Worldwide, Inc.) that explains how to raise big bucks for telecommunications support; but if you don't want to shell out the $20 for that wonderful resource, just post a message on an online service in the education forum and watch the ideas grow.

Speaking of Money

Throughout this book, I'll be sharing lots of great places to visit on the Web. Because we're talking about money, here's a list of sites that'll help you learn about grants available to fund Internet access. Don't worry if you don't under-stand what to do with the Internet address yet; just stick a mental bookmark here and remember it for later.

Here's a short list of just a few of the places on the Internet packed with useful information about how to get other folks to give you lots of money for your Internet habit:

```
http://galaxy.einet.net/galaxy/Reference_and_Interdisciplinary_
Information/Grants.html

http://infoserv.rttonet.psu.edu/gweb.htm

http://www.cs.virginia.edu/~seas/resdev/sponsors.html

http://deimos.ucsd.edu/space_grant/NASAspacegrant.html

http://timon.sir.arizona.edu/govdocs/grants/ED.HTM

http://www.yahoo.com/Education/Grants
```

or use the Keyword: **Grants** on America Online.

Internal Internet?

What's hot these days in networking? It's not the Internet — it's the *intranet.* Schools are finding out that the Web metaphor of browsers, links, and cross-platform communication works as well as an internal method of spreading information as it works for sharing information with the world.

Basically, the concept is that you take information (student handbooks, teacher's manuals, and so on) and place them on Web pages that reside on a Web server in your school's network but aren't connected to the Internet or accessible by outside sources. Using the Web internally jumps over such pesky questions as:

✔ What if I don't have the same kind of computer? (The Web is blind to platform and works well with virtually any kind of hardware.)

✔ How do I keep information within our school safe from naughty hackers? (An internal network not connected to the outside world is inherantly safer than connecting to all 23 million or so users on the Net.)

✔ How can we post calendars, timelines, schedules, and other information to every person in our school regardless of how they're connected to the Net? (Intranet's the way!)

So...yet another use of the Net's technology. It's inexpensive, it's easy for people to develop their own content, and it's a great first step to publishing information to the world on the Web.

Chapter 2

Dissecting the World Wide Web

*G*ood things seem to happen in threes. Get three Xs in a row, and it's tic-tac-toe; run three bases, and you're home free; get through three class periods, and it's downhill toward the end of the day. Because three seems to be a lucky number (we'll just breeze on past that three-strikes-and-you're-out rule), breaking down the seemingly complicated World Wide Web into three parts seems sensible. Maybe that's why fellow IDG author Paul Hoffman (author of *Netscape and the World Wide Web For Dummies,* IDG Books Worldwide, Inc.) and others suggested that the Web has three parts: client software, servers, and content. I like those neat little categories, so let's take a stab at seeing how they fit together.

The Big Three

It all boils down to three. When you set about to dissect the Web (my apologies to anyone allergic to formaldehyde), three basic parts emerge:

- ✓ Clients (your computer running client software)
- ✓ Servers (the machine on which the Web page resides)
- ✓ Content (the information delivered via the Web page)

Now, click your heels together *three* times and say "clients, servers, content." Feel better? The following is a quick peek at what these three body parts really do in relation to the whole Internet frog.

Students are our clients

You're probably a client of someone right now. Perhaps you're a doctor's client or a lawyer's client. Technically, your students (and their parents) are *your* clients. Clients typically call upon someone and request a service. Client software for the Internet is no different.

In order to access information from the Internet, your computer needs software that can communicate with the information source (the *server*). In the case of the World Wide Web, you'll need software categorized as a *Web client* or (as it is more commonly known) a *Web browser*. (You'll note that I use *client* and *browser* interchangeably in this book — mostly *browser*.)

Most computers that you may encounter can run popular Web browsers (a.k.a. Web clients, remember?). Whether you're sitting in front of a Macintosh, PC, or UNIX computer, Web browsers work pretty much the same way. The major difference in client software is found in the level of support for graphics. People who use Macintosh and PCs running Windows can see all the wonderful pictures, fancy backgrounds, and colorful text floating 'round the Internet. Some people accessing the Web using dial-up UNIX systems, such as those systems often found at colleges and universities, can sometimes only run a *text-based* browser called *Lynx*. Figure 2-1 shows a typical GUI browser and Figure 2-2 shows what the *Lynx* folks may see at the same site.

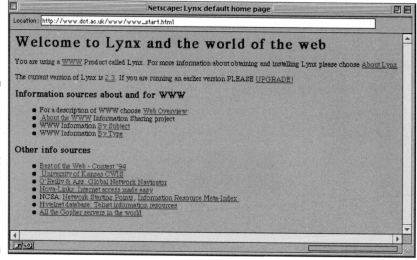

Figure 2-1:
Most people use Web browsers (clients) that support graphical user interfaces (GUIs).

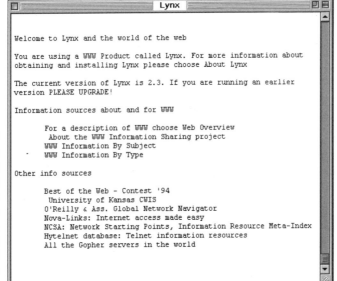

```
┌─────────────────────────────────────────────────┐
│ ▫          Lynx                          ▣ ▤    │
├─────────────────────────────────────────────────┤
│                                              ▲  │
│  Welcome to Lynx and the world of the web       │
│                                                 │
│  You are using a WWW Product called Lynx. For more information about │
│  obtaining and installing Lynx please choose About Lynx │
│                                                 │
│  The current version of Lynx is 2.3. If you are running an earlier │
│  version PLEASE UPGRADE!                        │
│                                                 │
│  Information sources about and for WWW          │
│                                                 │
│          For a description of WWW choose Web Overview │
│           About the WWW Information Sharing project │
│          WWW Information By Subject             │
│     ·    WWW Information By Type                │
│                                                 │
│  Other info sources                             │
│                                                 │
│          Best of the Web - Contest '94          │
│           University of Kansas CWIS             │
│          O'Reilly & Ass. Global Network Navigator │
│          Nova-Links: Internet access made easy  │
│          NCSA: Network Starting Points, Information Resource Meta-Index │
│          Hytelnet database: Telnet information resources │
│          All the Gopher servers in the world    │
│                                              ▼  │
└─────────────────────────────────────────────────┘
```

Figure 2-2:
Some folks
are stuck
with
text-only
browsers,
such as this
one, called
Lynx.

Web browsers allow you to do more than just browse around the Internet. Most fully-featured Web browsers, such as *Netscape, Mosaic, MacWeb,* and others, allow you to:

✔ Download and view software, sound files, graphics, and even digitized movies

✔ View Web pages created using *HTML* (HyperText Markup Language)

✔ Send e-mail

✔ Launch "helper applications" that allow you to begin telnet sessions, visit newsgroups, access databases, and more

✔ Save and print on-screen text and graphics

✔ View the HTML source code (the programming language that differentiates a Web page from a plain old text document)

✔ Save the location of your favorite spots for later use

✔ Display lots of nifty and colorful text, graphics, fonts, and backgrounds

Remember that you also need some sort of TCP/IP software (such as *MacTCP,* which is included with System 7.5 on your Macintosh) before your browser can actually "talk" with the Internet.

Serving up Web pages

Before you read this section about servers, know that you can be one heckuva Web surfer without ever knowing anything about where the information comes from. However, if you're like most educators who subscribe to the "lifelong learning" concept, knowing a bit about how the surfboard was made may satisfy your curiosity.

A *server* is a computer that makes content available to the Internet. That content is read by client software (see the preceding section) running on our computers. Servers are sometimes referred to as *Web servers* or *host computers*. Different kinds of Internet servers do pretty much the same thing.

Internet (or Web) servers used to be huge computers buried in the basements of university computing centers. Nowadays, a server could be the Macintosh sitting on the table next to the coffee machine in the teachers' lounge. As with most technology, the hardware needed to serve up the Internet is smaller, faster, cheaper, and easier to maintain than ever. (See Figure 2-3.)

Figure 2-3:
Nowadays, a Web server can be set up in just a few minutes, and for far less money than ever before.

Naming names

When one of my nephews was born, my sister and brother-in-law named him Jordan. If Jordan had been born an Internet server (I know — this is a reach, indulge me!), his name might have been `www.jordan.edu` or `123.233333.101.0`. Servers, then, like my wonderful baseball-whackin', mommy-huggin', little, future President, have names. *Server names* are also called *domain names*. Server names allow each server to be seen as a unique entity on the Internet, and these names allow us to find servers in nanoseconds.

Domain names for Web servers usually begin with the letters _www (lowercase)_ and end with a three-letter extension. These extensions, comprised of letters such as _gov_ (government), _edu_ (education), _org_ (organizations), and _com_ (commercial), indicate something about the owner of the server. A Web server at the University of Georgia, for example, may have a name like `www.uga.edu`.

In actuality, the alphabetic names for servers, such as the ones described previously, are only aliases for the exact techno-speak designation of computers on the Net, a series of four sets of numbers called a _dotted quad_. I'm sure glad that, when I call Jordan in from jumping on the neighbor's flowers, I don't have to scream, "Come inside 130. 94.283.0!"

Meet URL

URL (pronounced _earl_ or _U-R-L_) stands for _Uniform Resource Locator_. URLs list the exact location (address) of virtually any Internet resource, such as a Web page, a Gopher site, or a newsgroup. In most URLs, you can usually see the domain name (server name) hiding inside.

URLs look like this:

Resource Type	Example
A WWW page	`http://www.apple.com/education/`
A picture file	`ftp://fabercollege.edu/graphics/flounder.gif`
A newsgroup	`news:news.lists`
A Gopher site	`gopher://gopher.tc.umn.edu`
A telnet session	`telnet://ibm.com`

The first part of the URL, the junk preceding the colon, tells your Web browser or other Internet software what method to use to access the file. The part of the URL following the colon indicates the address of a host computer and the pathway to get to the desired resource.

What's in it for me?

You may be thinking right about now about why anyone would go to the expense of putting together an Internet server. Server providers couldn't possibly make money because access to Web servers is free (except for the fee that _you_ pay your online service or Internet service provider for _your_ online access). So what's in it for the server provider?

There are basically four reasons to build your own server:

- Because you have some valuable information that you'd like to share with the planet (educational institutions)

- Because you have a product to sell, support, or advertise (commercial servers)

- Because you want to publish information for use within your own school (the "intranet"!?)

- Because it is fun — fun to know that (potentially) millions of people are accessing your ideas, sharing your information, or enjoying your creativity

Sooner or later, we'll be paying for access to some Web pages, I suspect, because today's altruism will give way to the quest for the mighty dollar. Just hope that most server providers will continue to supply information to the world because they *can* and because they believe in contributing to the body of human knowledge.

Content: The Heart of the Matter

How many times have you reviewed textbooks and noted that, while content was essentially the same, there were differences in the presentation, organization, or visual attractiveness of each text series? Ultimately, we all tend to succumb to the "more pictures" and "more attractive layout" monster. The reason we review and purchase textbooks is for *content*. Part of the content is clearly presentation, but most teachers would agree that presentation is not the most important thing. Pretty pictures are nice *if* they back up or extend solid content.

Examining sites on the Web is similar, in many ways, to evaluating textbooks. Essentially, the pages you see will be presented: some may have more glitz and flash than others; some may have more substance. The heart of the matter is whether the content is accurate, easy to navigate, and usable to meet the objectives in your classroom.

What content can we find?

Asking what content is available on the Web is a little like asking a classroom full of high school students what they were thinking about during your last American History class. You may get as many answers as you have students. (Unfortunately, few of the students were probably thinking about history.) Because folks are always thinking up new Internet sites and are adding them to the Net practically once every minute, developing any kind of directory for the Net is impossible. With respect to content, the Web has moved (in two short years) from having only a few topics to having virtually any topic you could find in print.

Gettin' fuzzy

I wish I could tell you that all content on the Web is neatly categorized so as to be found and used easily. Nope. Things are a bit more confusing than that. Basically three categories of Web pages are available:

- ✔ Reference pages (libraries of data, pictures [images], search tools, telnet links, and so on)
- ✔ Personal pages (personal information about the author, favorite links, and so on)
- ✔ Commercial pages (designed by a business to be their "presence" on the Web)

Here's where things get a bit fuzzy. These three categories of Web pages aren't discrete; that is, you can certainly have reference works on your personal page (Wanna see mine? Try `http://www.mindspring.com/~bardw/bard.html`) and personal stuff on a commercial page. It's kind of like that file drawer that you've got marked "Miscellaneous." While most of the stuff in that file drawer is neatly categorized, some of the stuff is, well, just uncategorizable.

You can find reference materials such as online encyclopedias, lists of frequently asked questions *(FAQs)*, online manuals for software programs, and the complete works of Shakespeare, all mixed in with personal information, or, yes, a word from your sponsor. (Flip a page and glance at Yahoo's incredible education topics, seen in Figure 2-4.)

The medium is the message

If you want to teach reading, the Web is a great place to begin. The vast majority of what you'll find on the Web is text — most of which is plainly formatted and displayed in bulleted lists or in paragraph form. You will, however, find that (because Web browsers have become more sophisticated and connection speeds are increasing) several other types of media are jumping onto Web pages at an ever-increasing rate. You're likely to find many Web resources on education-related pages, too, including:

- Pictures (photographs, clip art, icons)
- Full-motion digital video (able to be downloaded and played back through your Mac or PC)
- CD-quality sound (more than one Generation-X rock group has released its music through the Web *before* the CD or cassette could be bought in stores)
- Animation (crude and slow, but pretty cool, nevertheless)

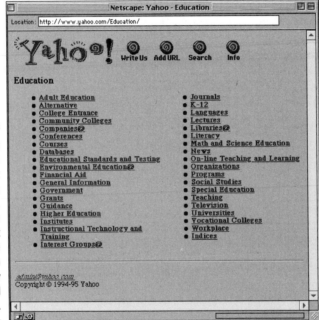

Figure 2-4: Content on the Internet varies wildly. Here's one site that wrote the book on quality educational content.

For a look at what the future may hold on the Web, look no further than the prognostications in Chapter 10. Nobody really knows what the future of the Web may be, but that future is fun to think about.

A word from our sponsor

Don't be surprised when you learn that some of the most popular sites are full of advertising. Corporate America jumped on the Web bandwagon early by hiring *Webmasters* to create a *Web presence*, complete with high-dollar, custom artwork and lots of neat things to click. From Coca-Cola (Figure 2-5, `http://www.cocacola.com/`) to Land's End, you can shop till you drop on the Internet.

Figure 2-5:
"The Real
Thing" —
on the Net.

Lucky for you and me (and our students), the vast majority of the content on the Web is still free; that is, there are no additional costs beyond the cost of your Internet connection. The number of sites requiring password access is increasing, however, and gue$$ how you get a pa$$word?

This is also a good time to remind you that you shouldn't transmit your credit card numbers via electronic mail or through forms on Web pages unless you know that you've logged into a secure site. How do you know? You don't. Recent strides in data encryption make secure Internetting a near-term reality, but until things get a bit more stable, I recommend that you use the good old toll-free telephone number for all your catalog shopping. Fair warning!

Sewing It All Together

Now that I've dissected the Web, I'll sew it all back together so that you can see what the Web really is. Basically, your computer and the Web browser program that you're running are *clients* that seek information from computers called *Web servers*. You're connected to these servers via a worldwide telephone network called the *Internet*.

While on the Web, you request and receive *content* from Web servers via clickable links (*hypertext*). The content varies from reference material (including databases and text documents), to personal information, to commercial resources.

As educators and students we can assume the role of:

- ✔ Information consumers (by personally and professionally accessing the Web as clients)
- ✔ Information producers (by creating our own Web pages and/or servers at school)

The best part about being consumers is that you and your students can jump from site to site collecting information. The not-so-good part is that some of that information may be inaccurate. That's why it's very important to discuss how to evaluate the *quality* of information you view or collect and to make a decision to use it based upon your best estimate of the credibility of that information. In other words (and you should write this on your chalkboard), *just because it's on the Internet doesn't make it correct.*

As an information producer, you and your students can share information with the entire planet. Opening your ideas and creativity to others helps increase the value of the Internet. Being an Internet information producer is kind of like publishing your own book, except that you have 3,000,000 or so potential readers the nanosecond that you publish your Web page. In Part IV of this book, you learn that you and your students can be Web producers in no time. I promise.

Chapter 3
The Web in Education

● ●

In This Chapter
▶ Webbing in the classroom
▶ Eight reasons to take the Net plunge
▶ Moving beyond the Web

● ●

*D*uring my fifth year as a middle school teacher, I was matched with a wonderful new teaching partner. We worked well together. I was the one that broke up the fights; she was the one that taught me how to braid a lanyard for use with our compasses in our orienteering activity. I was the one who showed her how to use a computer grade book; she taught me a nifty new way to handle classroom discipline. We were a great team.

We were decidedly different in one major way, however: I was a *drawer* person, and she was a *pile* person.

Drawers and Piles

A casual observer would think that my science classroom was immaculate: each piece of lab equipment in its place — lots of clean lab tables and seemingly organized shelves. Those who knew me, however, knew that I was an expert at hiding my messes. Opening my file cabinet took a crowbar, and the cabinets in the science workroom were filled with boxes marked "Bard's junk." I knew, of course, which drawer held each paper or piece of equipment, and I often amazed students as I extracted their Fall Quarter science projects from a drawer to give to them as they left for the summer. My teammate used to giggle that she'd probably come into class one day and find me asleep in a drawer.

Peek into my teammate's classroom and you'd immediately realize that she was different — she was a *pile* person. Now, before you snicker too much, think about your own classroom (or your home). You are a pile person if you look around and see virtually every flat surface festooned with a pile of books, papers, folders, or boxes. As a pile person, she knew exactly which pile contained the exact paper/project/assignment sheet at all times. A glimpse into her file cabinets (not that I glimpsed there) revealed very neat and organized trays and material organizers, but those cabinets weren't packed full like mine were. Everything in her piles was in plain sight and easy for her to locate.

The fact is that, no matter what our organizational methodology, we always knew where to find things. Using the Internet is no different. With zillions of bytes of information floating around on the Information Superhighway, knowing where to find things is perhaps the most important skill (next to knowing what to do with the things that we find). The fact is, whether you're a pile person, or a drawer person, you'll find a tool or strategy that can help you explore Internet resources in a way that makes you and your students comfortable.

The World Wide Web (*Web*) offers order to the chaos of the Internet. Using the Web in your school will help students (some of whom are *pile* or *drawer* people as well) settle into a knowledge-navigation scheme that is comfortable for them.

The Web: Good for Education?

What can the Web offer to your classroom? That depends, for the most part, on your teaching style and how you think. A famous puzzle challenges you to connect a matrix of nine dots with four single, straight, unbroken lines. If you haven't seen the puzzle, here's your chance:

```
     *    *    *


     *    *    *


     *    *    *
```

The answer to the puzzle, like the answer as to whether the Internet will be effective in your classroom, lies in your willingness to think "out of the box." As educators, we're conditioned to be locked into a standard set of materials that supports a curriculum: traditional things such as textbooks, workbooks, calculators, and computers. It's taken us quite a bit of time to become comfortable with computers in the classroom (we still have a long way to go on this one), and becoming comfortable with the Internet-tool is no different. Be a risk-taker. Be curious. Explore with your students. Learn together. If you are willing to think "out of the box" and experiment with new ways to do new things, you'll no doubt be successful.

Want the solution to the matrix puzzle? The answer lies in the first sentence of the preceding paragraph. The puzzle can be solved. Try it!

Welcome, Webmasters!

The Web offers access to more information resources than you can imagine. Web pages created by *Webmasters* offer a way to organize the Web's content and make access to that content easier and more efficient. The Web can also be your access point for many different types of Internet resources. For example, as Web surfers, you and your students will have the opportunity to:

- Exchange information via global communication links
- Retrieve information "just in time" for use in the classroom (or anywhere else)
- Send and receive files, including programs, graphics, sounds, and movies
- Log in and search remote databases
- Add to the body of human knowledge (Whoa! Think about the potential of being able to publish instantly to millions of people. Kind of gives you chills, doesn't it?)
- Have a lot of fun browsing the ideas, thoughts, and creations of others

In case you need specific education-related reasons to jump onto the information superhighway, here they are....

Eight Great Reasons to Jump onto the Information Superhighway

It takes a bit of imagination, but imagine that you've just opened a box containing the first piece of Velcro you've ever seen. At first glance, Velcro seems useful, but you're not sure of its purpose. Show your piece of Velcro to a few friends, and soon you'll stumble onto hundreds of uses. The day will come when that odd connection of tiny hooks and loops will be invaluable.

The Internet is like Velcro. The more you think about the resources that are out there on the Internet, the more ideas you'll generate for its use. The time we spend with our students is precious, so the "because it is there" rationale doesn't really cut it when we're talking about using the Net in a classroom. The fact is that there are some pretty compelling reasons to access the Internet, including a few reasons that may strongly appeal to you.

In *The Internet For Teachers* (IDG Books Worldwide, Inc.), I wrote about "Six Great Reasons to Get Your Class on the Information Superhighway." With the help of lots of other teachers who have attended several staff development activities that I've taught, I've added a couple more.

These eight reasons for logging onto the Net come from lots of conversations, both electronic and face-to-face, with people such as you who are pondering the Net's possibilities.

The Internet presents real-world examples of integrated knowledge

The Internet provides a bunch of electronic information that's organized in different ways and represents many different topics. You'll rarely see a Web page that features information on only one specific subject for one specific purpose. If students access the Web site at the Centers for Disease Control in Atlanta (`http://www.cdc.gov`), for example, they may expect to see information limited only to the science of virology or biology. Instead they'll see that the CDC maintains geographic information about landforms and climate as well as medical databases (see Figure 3-1). For the scientists and researchers who use the site on a daily basis, this integration of science, geography, and mathematical information makes their work more efficient.

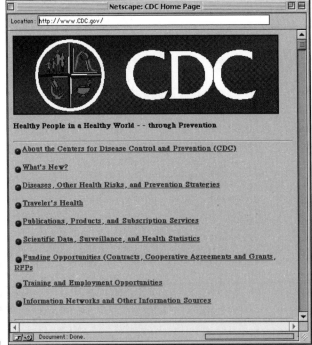

Figure 3-1:
The CDC site
is a great
example of
an inter-
disciplinary
collection of
information.

At NASA's Web site, students will see much more than just information about rockets and the sciences: libraries packed with technical writing, graphics, and newsletters describing the design and specifications of the latest shuttle payloads. NASA's Web site contains an elegant combination of writing, science, and mathematics. The site also has links to many Internet sites that support or extend the work of NASA's wondermakers. As with the CDC, the crafters of the NASA Web pages decide what knowledge to present and how to link that knowledge together. The result is truly interdisciplinary (NASA's URL is: `http://www.nasa.gov`).

In time, you and your students may create your own Web page, giving them an opportunity to link interdisciplinary resources that they believe are useful and important. The Internet is a place where electronic tools can form the link between learning and life.

The Internet facilitates collaborative learning

You will soon discover that one of the most efficient ways for your students to use and explore the resources available on the Internet is through small-group, project-centered activities. The simple fact is that because the Internet is so big and offers so many resources, teamwork makes a huge positive difference in the quality of the outcome of any Internet search.

Send four groups of students to separate Internet connections to search for information about any subject; they'll all come back with different information, from different sources, written with different biases, for different audiences, and with differing levels of credibility. Bring those four groups back together and ask them one question to get the collaboration going: "What is the best (or most useful) information and why?"

Of course, there's that "excited learners are contagious" thing that we educators all understand. Put one student on the Net and watch how many others flock around. Imagine the possibilities!

The Internet offers opportunities for telementoring

Everyone out there has looked to a friend or colleague for information at one time or another. The Internet offers incredible opportunities to meet and learn from people around the globe on just about any topic you can imagine. *Telementoring*, literally helping or receiving help via telecommunications links, is the way most of us learned to use the Internet back in the days before the *. . . For Teachers* books hit the shelves, of course. Electronic mail, newsgroups, and Internet chat all provide ways to interact with your peers, learning all the while. You will find that the Internet is useful both for teaching and for learning (and even for some curbside psychiatry when the going gets rough).

The Internet is all about communicating

Editing a Supreme Court decision and posting it to the Internet takes about eight hours. Finding it takes about eight seconds. The Internet represents a communication opportunity that will probably have a profound impact on everything from politics to potato farming. Posting a message on the Internet and getting replies from Russia is cool. (No pun intended.) Logging on to the Internet and chatting live with anthropologists exploring Mayan ruins is an amazing experience. Students telecommunicating with their peers, *no matter where in the world they live,* is about as exciting a prospect as I can imagine.

The Internet can cater to different learners in different ways

Like a good library, the Internet has print, sound, photograph, and video resources. The kind of information students choose to access and the way that they choose to access it is often as revealing about the students' capabilities as the quality of the information they collect. The Internet offers opportunities to browse or to target information with excruciating precision. You'll find that everyone, from the reluctant learner to the bookworm, can find something of interest on the Net. Helping them explore their interests and channel their efforts toward furthering their educational goals is up to us teachers, of course. With sufficient goals and direction, virtually every student can experience success.

The Internet is a culturally, racially, physically, sexually blind medium

It is truly a strange feeling when you first meet someone with whom you've telecommunicated for a long period of time. In the early years of Macintosh technology, I had occasion to sign on to America Online (actually, it's predecessor, called Q-Link) and ask for help. A clear and accurate response came almost immediately from someone who had seen my posting on the network. Over the next year, I came to rely on "Person X" to help me with problems that ranged from installing new network wiring to resurrecting hard drives that had crashed and burned.

At an educational conference two years later, while wandering the aisles looking for free demo disks and cheesy mousepads for my classroom, I stumbled upon a bright young lady playing a MIDI keyboard, connected to her Macintosh, in front of a crowd buzzing with excitement. After her stunning performance, I walked up to congratulate her. On her name tag was written her AOL screen name (the name by which everyone on the network knew her). I was floored. I had been corresponding with a young lady who was ten years my junior — what's more, she was an accomplished performance artist. I suddenly felt the need to give her a hug, or write her a check, or *something*. Now she's writing musical scores for movies, and I'm writing books — go figure!

Through this experience, and many others since, I realized that communication through the Internet was *blind*. Suddenly race, religion, appearance, speech — all the things we may use to form opinions about the people that we meet — become invisible. Communication through the Internet is *pure* communication.

The downside is that, because much of communication is nonverbal — for example, observing facial features, silly grins and all — you can lose something in the translation. But that makes the challenge even sweeter.

Exploring the Internet can rekindle a teacher's interest in learning

As educators, we pride ourselves in valuing education. We spend our lives helping others to learn *how* to learn. Unfortunately, there seems to be precious little time to learn things that will help *us* teach or live better. Unlike other new initiatives in education, I've seen exposure to the possibilities of telecommunications and technology motivate even the most reluctant teacher-learners to learn more and try different things in their classrooms. The excitement brought about by an infusion of so many resources is hard to resist. (See Figure 3-2.)

Other teachers are learning about the Internet because they don't want to drown. These teachers feel, perhaps with justification, that if they *don't* learn about the Internet and other technologies, the tidal wave of change will wash them out of a job. Of course, you've taken the time to buy this book, so you'll be smugly surfing on top of that wave, doing the "queen's wave" to all the "little people" treading water below.

We have an obligation to society

Okay. It's soapbox time. (Just for a minute!) I'm scared *not* to tell folks about the Internet. We are all used to dealing with students from radically different backgrounds: some from families that have two cars and four computers — some that are lucky to get three meals. I'm afraid that the ever-present socio-economic gap will be further widened into two distinct groups: those that know, can use, and have access to technology, and those who don't. It is already apparent that investors can use the information they gain over the Net to make more informed decisions that result in increased wealth. People with e-mail addresses seem to communicate with more people more often. What about all the people that don't have access to telecommunications technology? Will they be left behind?

Figure 3-2:
The Web
may be just
the thing to
rekindle a
teacher's
interest in
learning.

It's like science fiction. Will we face a future society of the information-rich vs. the information-poor? I may be overreacting, but I think that it is educators that will help prevent that not-so-wonderful scenario from becoming a reality. We've got to help *all* students appreciate the value of knowledge and information. Knowledge gained from the Internet is certainly no exception. Moreover, we've got to fight to make sure that anyone and everyone can get access to the Internet if they have the desire. In the not-too-distant future, not having an e-mail address may be like not having a mailing address. I can go on forever about this topic, but I think that you get the point. Let's spread the word about the good, the bad, and the ugly of the Internet to all of our students — it will probably help them lead better lives in the future.

End of sermon.

That's the big eight! You can surely think of more as you think about the role the Internet may play in your classroom. In the next section, I'll tease your brain cells with a bit of prose about what your and your students can do with Internet access.

Some really cool Net statistics

Pick up most magazines and you'll see a sprinkling of Internet statistics throughout. Funny thing, though, is that none of the stats seem to match. One source lists 23 million Net surfers; another lists fewer than 2 million. Who's right? After scouring the Net and the most reliable sources, I've put together this list of stats for your reading pleasure. Use these when you present your "how to get the Net in my school" plans to your administration or school board.

✔ From July 1994 to July 1995, the number of registered *host computers* (computers accessing or providing content on the Net) grew from 3.2 million to 6.6 million. By the year 2000, more than 120 million machines will be connected. (Internet Society http://www.isoc.org; Mark Lottor, http://www.nw.com/zone.host-count-history/)

✔ The *education domain* (sites that end with the .edu extension) is second only to the growth of the commercial (.com) sites on the Internet. In July of 1994, there were 856,243 sites; by July 1995, the number had grown to an amazing 1.4 million sites. (Internet Society)

✔ The number of World Wide Web servers on the Net grew from 130 in June of 1993 (less than a year after the introduction of the Web as a form of Internet access) to more than 40,000 by the end of 1995. (Internet Info, http://www.webcom.com/~walsh/)

✔ The average Internet users who buy products through the Internet are "young, predominately male, and well educated" with a median age of 32. (Rochester Institute of Technology)

✔ The average Web user in the US is 36. Half are married. Fifteen percent (15%) are female. Average income of all users is $55,000. Most have college degrees. About 20% access the Web through an online service like e-World, Prodigy, or America Online. (Georgia Tech, http://www.cc.gatech.edu/gvu/user_surveys/)

✔ More than 3,000 schools have created and posted their own WWW sites on the Internet. (Yahoo! http://www.yahoo.com/education/)

For additional resources, check InterNIC (http://www.internic.net) and Matrix Information and Directory Service (MIDS) at http://www1.mids.org/ or do a "Yahoo!" search for "statistics " and "internet."

Beyond the Web: What Can I Do with the Internet?

The Internet is not the total answer to all the challenges facing an educator today. The Internet will not:

- ✔ Watch your class while you hit the lounge for a well-deserved Valium break
- ✔ Cause the school cafeteria to stop serving mystery meat
- ✔ Make your students' scores on standardized tests jump dramatically

I only mention standardized tests because that seems to be the way that many measure the success of a new tool in education. Carefully orchestrated use of the Net can help students develop critical-thinking skills and skills in the location and evaluation of knowledge, but it is unlikely that use of the Net will help them with the answer to number three on the ITBS (you know, that wonderful standardized test that consumes #2 pencils and too many brain cells). But then again . . . who knows?

The key to using the Net effectively with students is to set your expectations reasonably and use the tool when appropriate. How do you decide when it is appropriate to use the Internet instead of, say, a workbook? Knowing what the Internet can provide will help.

Here's a sampling of what the Internet has to offer you and your students:

- ✔ **Global electronic mail:** Send a note to anyone else with a Net address, anywhere, anytime. Suddenly, you have the ability to build linkages between people everywhere without regard to those things that blind us from the appreciation of knowledge. Such things as race, color, creed, gender, and physical disabilities all disappear when you board the information superhighway.

  A teacher in my school district used electronic mail to correspond with a teacher in Alaska who gave a play-by-play description of the Iditarod. Every day the teacher in my district checked to see what condition the dogs were in, who the front-runner was, and what interesting anecdotes were available about the challenges faced by the windblown racers. She then passed the information on to her students, who wrote articles for an "Iditarod Update," made maps of the trip, charted weather conditions, and calculated windchill temperatures. Is this project interdisciplinary or what?

✔ **Knowledge navigation:** Zip around the world via the Internet to locate documents, pictures, sounds, and even digitized movies to keep your knowledge, skills, and curriculum up to date. Glance over at your bookshelf, tug on the textbook that says, "Some day man will go to the moon," and think about how useful having instantaneous information for use in the classroom can be. Got a unit on weather coming up? Use Internet resources to pop over to NASA (`http://www.nasa.gov/`) to access ready-made classroom activities, surf to the Library of Congress (`http://www.loc.gov/`) or your local library and build a bibliography, and then head for the Jet Propulsion Lab (`http://www.jpl.nasa.gov/`) for digitized satellite photos.

✔ **File exchange:** Send and retrieve files containing documents, pictures, movies, sounds, and programs. Need the latest version of virus protection software? Jump onto the Net, hop to the vendor's file server, and copy the program: `http://www.yahoo.com/Business_and_Economy/Companies/Computers/Software/Virus_Protection/`

✔ **Discussion groups:** Engage in a discussion with other Internet users about any topic you can think of. A media specialist using a discussion group (also called a *newsgroup*) began a discussion about selecting software for a circulation system. Four weeks later, he went before the board of education with testimonials and facts from 23 school systems from around the country about the system he had selected. His board of education bought it — lock, stock, and barcode.

✔ **Live conferencing:** Talk "live" to other Internet users. Get into a debate about outcome-based education, or Bloom's *Taxonomy*, or whether to have Coca-Cola or Pepsi in the faculty lounge machines.

There's much, much more. By its very nature, the Internet is a *dynamic* medium. It changes just about every nanosecond as people add or delete information. The body of knowledge on the Internet is growing exponentially. Between the time that I wrote this page and the time that you read it, there will have been *thousands* of new Internet resources added.

Whether it's the rich resources or the chance to collaborate globally that attracts you and your students to the Internet, the potential benefits (both tangible and intangible) can be substantial. Once linked into the Net, the emphasis in your classroom will shift quickly toward fostering the quest for new knowledge and helping students interpret, navigate, evaluate, and apply the knowledge they gain. The Web is good for students, good for teachers, and, yes, good for education. Web and learn!

Surfing, mining, browsing — we need a new metaphor!

In one of those rare quiet moments driving to a meeting, I got a great chance to talk to a fellow Net user about the semantics of the Net. Words are important. How you say things really does have an effect on how people react. So, what does the word *surf* really mean?

My friend suggested that surfing is a term that indicates pointing yourself in one direction and ending up somewhere you don't expect. It suggests a lack of control over where the user ends up. Perhaps. She prefers to use the term *mining*. She said that mining means that you know what you're looking for, you go find it, and along the way you find lots of other good and bad stuff. Not a bad metaphor, I think.

How about *browsing*? Is this an aimless activity? Maybe. Is doing an activity "aimlessly" *all* bad? Maybe not. One the ways I've found some of the best resources is by browsing from site to site. When I see a great site, I add it to my browser's address storage list (called a *bookmark list*) and move on. Later, when I need a specific resource (I guess I'm mining then), I call upon those things that I found while I was browsing.

Okay. I think I've figured it out. When you first sit down at your computer, you're likely wearing your *surfer* clothes. You point yourself toward a search page or a known point and use it as a jumping-off point for what comes next. You don't really know what's next, but you're pretty glad that you're there.

Next, you *browse* a bit, searching the items you found when you entered your search terms on the search page. You may stumble now and then and find places that you wish you weren't or places that you want to remember for later. Soon you begin to focus on the task at hand — time for the *miner's* hat.

As you *mine*, you're looking for specific information and choosing links and jumps in a very organized and purposeful way. So . . . maybe the sequence is surf, browse, mine . . . or maybe not. <grin>

I think that we have a much richer word to describe what we're doing. When we access the Net we're not surfing, mining, or browsing. What we're doing is *tapping*. Not the shuffle-ball-change thing, not the beer thing, the *other* tapping. *Tapping* infers that we're making a connection, or opening an outlet for information. The key words here — connection and outlet for information — make me think more about what we're really doing. The word doesn't have a value judgment — it doesn't suggest that what we're doing is a bad, good, or even fun thing. It's value-neutral, unlike *surf*. We're *connecting* with others and using our computers and lots of phone lines as an *outlet for information* that we'll use to make decisions, solve problems, or just file away for later use. Maybe it's a stretch, maybe not. Next time you jump on the Internet — see what resources you can *tap*.

Chapter 4
One Link in the Internet Chain

- -

- -

he Web is only one link in a chain of information resources and tools that stretches (literally) around the globe. The Web is different from other Internet resources in that it actually provides "one-stop shopping." Through the Web, you can send e-mail, download files, read newsgroups, subscribe to mailing lists (*LISTSERVS*), and even chat live with other Internet users.

Unlocking the Internet

Ready for a field trip? In the following sections I'll drive you around the Internet, stopping to talk about each resource that is reachable through the Web. Of course, I can't resist a bit of commentary here and there. Hope everyone has their permission slips, because here we go!

Cyberletters, anyone?

Chances are good that your first use of the Internet was (or will be) sending *electronic mail (e-mail)*. The Internet provides the bridge that carries e-mail between computers all over the world. Users on America Online (AOL), for example, can send e-mail to users on e-World (or any other service) with the click of a mouse.

Web browsers are not great mailing systems. In fact, most Web browsers allow you only to *send* e-mail, not to receive it. To *get* e-mail, you have to log on to an online service or dial-up your Internet provider and launch an e-mail program such as *Eudora*.

E-mail messages are routed based on Internet addresses. E-mail addresses are assigned by your Internet provider and have three parts: a *username*, a series of letters and/or numbers that forms your unique identity as an Internet citizen; a *domain name* that bears the name of the one (or more) computer(s) to which the account belongs; and a *top-domain name* that describes the type of location from which the message is sent. An @ sign separates the username from the domain name and top-domain name.

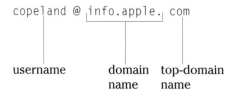

Your username (the letters and numbers to the left of the @ symbol) is assigned to you by your Internet provider. Depending on the size of your organization, sometimes these usernames can get really lengthy. You may, for example, see a username such as this:

```
mickey%mickey.mouse@disney.com
```

Some usernames are strictly numeric, such as this CompuServe address:

```
72344.1234@compuserve.com
```

The first letters and/or numbers in the domain name (to the right of the @ symbol) describe the name of your Internet mail server.

An America Online (AOL) address, for example, may look like this:

```
e.idle@aol.com
```

If you are on e-World, your address may be the following:

```
grail@eworld.com
```

The `grail` is the user's ID, and `eworld.com` is the name of the online service.

A Prodigy address may look like this:

```
VWXY123@prodigy.com
```

If you're connected through a university or commercial information provider, your address could be this:

```
monty.p@university.edu
```

or

```
j.kleese@shrubbery.python.com
```

The last few letters, referred to as the top-domain or zone name, are separated from the Internet computer's name by a period and help you determine what kind of organization sent the mail — business, government, education, and so on — and (in some cases) the country of origin. In the following address, .edu (the top-domain name) indicates that the mail originated from an educational site, such as a college or university:

```
bart.simpson@mit.edu
```

A tough critic

Most Web browsers allow you to send simple e-mail messages, such as the address of a favorite Web site, for example; but unlike *Netscape Navigator* Version 2.0, most Web browsers do not allow you to retrieve e-mail messages sent from other users. Sending mail is as easy as selecting a menu item. (See Figure 4-1 for an example of an e-mail message.) To retrieve your mail while using most Web browsers, however, you have to exit your browser and launch a mail-reading program such as *Eudora*. For more information about how to use e-mail and *Eudora* in your classroom, check out *The Internet For Teachers* (IDG Books Worldwide, Inc.).

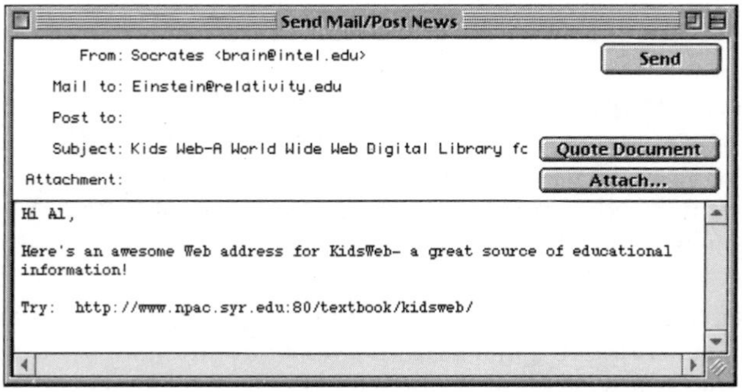

Figure 4-1:
The e-mail
send screen
from the
Netscape
Web
browser.

```
┌─────────────── Send Mail/Post News ────────────────┐
│    From: Socrates <brain@intel.edu>      [ Send ]  │
│  Mail to: Einstein@relativity.edu                   │
│  Post to:                                           │
│  Subject: Kids Web-A World Wide Web Digital Library fc [Quote Document] │
│ Attachment:                              [ Attach... ] │
│ Hi Al,                                              │
│                                                     │
│ Here's an awesome Web address for KidsWeb- a great source of educational │
│ information!                                        │
│                                                     │
│ Try:  http://www.npac.syr.edu:80/textbook/kidsweb/  │
└─────────────────────────────────────────────────────┘
```

For educators, electronic mail can be a terrific classroom tool. From simple pen-pal exchanges to more challenging writing exchanges, e-mail can breathe new excitement into lessons focusing on all types of writing. Opportunities for peer evaluation and critique abound. I recently e-mailed a copy of a column I write for an educational publication to a teacher in Queens, NY who passed it to a 15-year-old high school student for review. What I received in reply were eight terse (but correct) content "suggestions" and two ideas that I'll use for my next article. When I wrote back to the student to thank him, he replied, "That'll be $50.00." Sigh.

Mailing Lists

A mailing list is, in many ways, like a magazine subscription. It enables you to select a topic of interest and read the thoughts and ideas of folks from around the world. What's the thing that makes mailing lists really cool? *You* can add *your own* thoughts! Your ideas can be electronically published to thousands of unsuspecting Internet users at the touch of a button. Ooooo . . . a scary and exciting thought, no?

Because you can send e-mail through most Web browsers, subscribing to a LISTSERV is easy to do. However, because your e-mail cannot be retrieved through your Web browser, you have to log on to your service provider and get your incoming mail there.

Serving Up a LISTSERV

Mailing lists (also known as *maillists*) are special kinds of electronic mail addresses that automatically forward topic-specific discussions to your e-mail doorstep — just as a magazine subscription does. In fact, as the next section explains, to receive mail from a list, you must first subscribe to it.

Mailing lists enable you and your students to talk with more than one person at a time. In essence, you're joining an online discussion. Mailing lists are sometimes referred to as *discussion groups* because they focus on specific topics, such as elementary education or touring castles in Great Britain. You can also hear mailing lists referred to as *LISTSERVS*.

So . . . if you find a subject that you like (for example, media or distance learning), you can subscribe to a maillist and read what other subscribers have to say. One warning, however: subscribing to too many mailing lists may jam your mailbox with lots of messages you and your students may never have time to read. Choose judiciously.

Rodents to the Rescue?

Gopher is a program that runs on Internet servers and helps you and your students navigate through the terabytes of information that are now available on the Internet.

To access the Gopher program, you log on to an online service, such as America Online, or dial in through your Internet service provider and launch a Gopher front-end program such as *TurboGopher* (Macintosh) or *HGopher* (Windows).

Choose Gopher when you are searching for information about a broad topic or when you just want to "surf the Net" until some topic catches your eye. Gopher makes navigating many types of Internet resources, such as text files, pictures, and downloadable programs, as easy as a click of your computer's mouse.

Most Web browsers allow you to sign on to Gopher servers just as you would sign on to a Web page. Although the Gopher screen holds primarily text and folder icons, navigation is easy.

What is Gopher?

Gopher is the name of a database and communications system that runs on Internet-connected computers that are called *Gopher servers*. Gopher will burrow as deeply as you like to help you and your students find the information that you're searching for. Gopher is really a *browsing* tool more than anything else. Not all the information you may browse in Gopherspace is text — with the proper extensions to your *Gopher*-getting software, you also can browse pictures, sounds, movies (video), and computer programs.

Figure 4-2 shows an example of the first screen I see when I log in to the Gopher server at the U.S. Department of Education using the *Netscape* Web browser. The folders are clickable and provide a gateway to other Internet resources.

The really cool thing about a Gopher session is that the directories shown in your Gopher window may each come from a different server. As you click effortlessly from level to level, you're actually zooming from server to server, and the action is practically transparent to the user. You simply "go fer it," and it's there!

What good stuff can I find with Gopher?

In addition to holding hundreds of text files, many Gopher servers include ways to access other Internet information. Here are some of the tricks that Gopher can do:

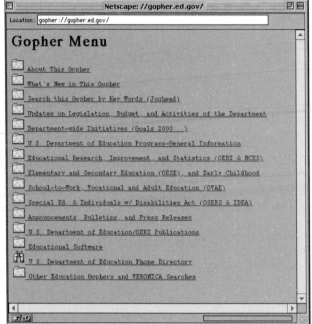

Figure 4-2:
The Gopher
server at the
U.S.
Department
of
Education.

✔ Browse and download files from popular FTP sites

✔ Serve as a gateway to the *Archie* file archive database

✔ Access *WAIS (Wide Area Information Servers)* — distributed-database systems

✔ Provide direct links to several types of electronic phone books

✔ Conduct full-text searches on many of the documents archived on local servers and on remote databases

✔ Access preconfigured telnet sessions for connecting to popular electronic library catalogs and information servers across the Internet

✔ Provide links to every other Gopher server in the world (*and* to all the unrestricted services that they offer)

Accessing Gopherspace

To browse Gopherspace, most people use front-end (or *client*) software such as *TurboGopher* (Macintosh) or *HGopher* (Windows) and log on to a Gopher server. These programs present the information contained on Gopher servers as a series of folders, not unlike the icon view on the desktop of your Macintosh or Windows machine. These folders, categorized according to topic, contain more menus, files, and resource information.

Get Down with FTP

FTP is a method used to send and receive files on the Internet. Say you just bought a brand new bells-and-whistles laser printer for your school's computer lab, and you suddenly realize that you don't have the *driver* (printer control file) to run this great new printer. You could get on the telephone between classes and beg the vendor to mail you one, knowing that you'd get it via "snail mail" three days later — or you could jump onto the Net and fire up your FTP program.

Web browsers make FTP almost effortless. After signing on to an FTP server, a double-click of the mouse downloads the file to your computer's hard disk or floppy. Creating hypertext links (buttons) that allow you to download files from within Web pages is also possible when you are signed on to an FTP server.

Files for almost nothin'

FTP is an acronym for *File Transfer Protocol*. FTP is technically a *protocol* (set of rules) for data transfer. FTP allows files (programs, pictures, sounds, movies, and so on) to be exchanged between different kinds of computers, without regard to how the computers are connected or what operating system they are running. Through FTP, you can transfer files from a host computer to a floppy disk or to a hard disk drive.

To understand what people mean when they talk about FTP, you've got to get out your parts-of-speech manual. You use FTP, the noun, when you refer to the actual File Transfer Protocol, as in, "that file is available via FTP from Microsoft." When you describe the process of sending or receiving files on the Internet, you use ftp as a verb, as in, "ftp that file from Harvard's server."

The Internet allows access to zillions of files. Whether your students are searching for a picture of the Statue of Liberty, a movie showing a proper golf swing, or a sound file of JFK's Inaugural Speech, you can probably find it through FTP.

FTP is sometimes referred to as *anonymous FTP* because the host computers don't require the user to have an account to log in and access information. Anonymous FTP sites allow anyone to enter publicly-accessible directories, so that you and your students can (anonymously and legally!) sneak in and access the files.

What can I do with FTP?

Using FTP is a little like going to a flea market. You can find nearly anything there that you can imagine, but not all of the merchandise is high-quality stuff. As you browse the Internet, you and your students will develop lists of favorite FTP sites and the resources found there. Luckily, there are plenty of files to browse.

TECHNO TERMS

Squeezing files

Some programs and files, especially pictures, take quite a while to download. But downloading could be worse. Most files are squeezed (*compressed*) by using data-compression software before storage on the host computer. The good news is that downloading a compressed file takes less time. The bad news — and it's really not that bad — is that you have to *decompress* the file before you can view it, run it, or read it.

Most of the files on the Internet look a little different from the files on your hard drive. Files on the Internet have lots of extra letters attached. Some of the letters indicate the file type, and some cue the user about how the file was *compressed* (packed) before sending.

Here's an example:

```
tiger.bin.hqx
```

In this example, the .bin indicates that the file named "tiger" is a *binary* file (in this case, a picture), which is readable with most graphics programs and some word processors. The extension (suffix) .hqx shows that the file is in BinHex format. *BinHex* is a special cross-platform format that allows files to be accessed by almost any computer, regardless of the hardware or software installed.

You may also see the extension .bin is short for *binary*. This format is most common for pictures. Binary format must be converted before your computer can read it. Programs such as *BinHex* or *uulite* (available from gopher.soils.umn.edu) make this conversion easy.

Most Macintosh files are compressed by using a program called *Stuffit*. When the files are compressed, the author (or the program) appends the letters .sit to the end of the filename to let

you know what kind of compression was used. Here's an example of a file that was compressed by using *Stuffit*:

```
roadrunner.gif.sit
```

After downloading the file, Macintosh users can unpack it by using a program such as *Stuffit Expander,* which is freeware on the *Internet For Teachers* disc, or the commercial, fully-featured program *Stuffit Deluxe*. DOS users can use *PKUNZIP,* and Windows users can use *WinZip*. (Use *Chameleon* or another FTP program to download *WinZip* from ftp.halcyon.com. The file is in the win3/util directory and is called winzip55.exe.)

Literally hundreds of compression formats are out there. Here are the extensions (suffixes) for a few of them:

✔ .zip (a DOS file created by *PKZIP*)

✔ .shar (UNIX, shell archive)

✔ .arj (another DOS-compression scheme; created by ARJ)

✔ .z (a file compressed by UNIX)

✔ .tar (another UNIX-compression routine)

✔ .sit (a Macintosh file created by *Stuffit*)

✔ .shk (Apple II format; created by an Apple II program called *Shrinkit,* available from Andy Nicholas, shrinkit@moravian.edu)

✔ .sea (an .sit file that is self-extracting)

Sometimes folks get really crafty and use more than one compression scheme on a file. In general, *Stuffit* and *WinZip* can handle those, though.

Watch that computer virus!

Unlike the files you download from an online service, files from the Internet have probably not been screened for computer viruses. That means you have to screen them yourself. Stop what you're doing right now and do two things:

✔ Establish a school policy on screening downloaded files for viruses.

✔ Visit an online service, search the Net, or go to a local computer store and purchase a virus-protection-and-screening program.

(Some great freeware, shareware, and commercial virus-protection programs are out there.)

If you work in a school, you've probably already had to deal with virus-infected computers. Dealing with such a situation is not fun. Now you have to worry about files coming into the school from *all over the planet* instead of just all over your community. Never fear, though: the virus-scanning programs work very well. Just be proactive.

Hundreds of systems that are connected to the Internet have file libraries, also called *archives*, that are open to the public. Much of what's in these libraries is free or low-cost computer software for all types of personal computers.

Here are a few samples of what you can download by using FTP:

✔ A QuickTime movie of JFK's Inaugural Address

✔ The sound of a dog barking

✔ A program that strips unnecessary carriage returns from a text document

Figure 4-3 shows an example of resources available via FTP from the U.S. Department of Education.

Are Internet programs really free?

Well, some are; some aren't. You can sort the files on the Net into three categories: public domain software, freeware, and shareware.

✔ *Public domain* programs and files carry no copyright. There are no limits on their redistribution, modification, or sale.

✔ *Freeware* programs and files are free for you to use and give away, but not to sell or modify. The author retains the copyright.

✔ *Shareware* programs and files allow you to road test programs for a short evaluation period and then either pay the author a small fee or erase the program from your computer. The author retains all copyrights; and although you can give shareware programs to your friends, all shareware information must accompany the program, and your friends have to pay the author, too.

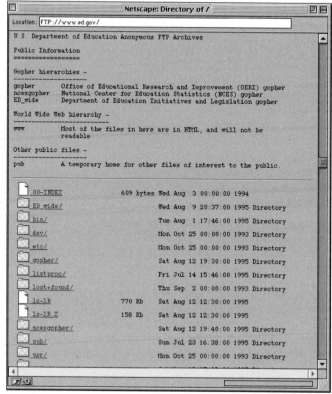

Figure 4-3:
The U.S.
Department
of Education
FTP server
offers many
resources
for
educators.

Using USENET

A newsgroup is a way to freely share information among Internet users. *Newsgroups,* also referred to as *USENET newsgroups,* are like public access bulletin boards. Users float by and electronically tack messages into special message areas organized by topic. While users are in the message areas, they can read the hundreds of messages posted by other users.

As with unmoderated mailing lists, nobody picks through the posted messages. The contents are often off-topic, risqué, and disorganized. Unlike mailing lists, the messages you read on newsgroups are sent to community mailboxes (whose home is on some huge hard drive on a server, called a *newsserver,* somewhere on the planet) where everyone can access them. Newsservers are chock-full of messages and responses to those messages. Mailboxes are organized by topic and offer a running dialog about a wide variety of subjects.

Most Web browsers have an option that allows you to subscribe to, and view, newsgroup news. Simply visit the Preferences menu and tell your browser the name of the newsgroup server you'd like to use, and you're well on your way.

USENET anonymous

Every day, USENET users pump upwards of 40 million characters into the Internet — roughly equivalent to half of the information in a large encyclopedia. You'll find that, if you're not careful, you'll spend countless hours reading newsgroups and posting messages such as, "....Single white male seeking female with a doctorate...."

Controlling OPCs

Telnet allows you to log in to computers from a remote site and appear, to the host computer, as if you're issuing commands from right down the hall. In other words, logged-in telnet users are able to *control* other people's computers (OPCs).

Although your students are not likely to launch any bombers, they can control other people's computers in more productive ways to, for example, find a book in the public library or register for classes at the local college.

So, telnet is all about using OPCs. By the way, if your students see the computer message:

```
Would you like to play a game?
```

from a mainframe buried deep in a Colorado hillside, have them answer *no* and save the military a lot of grief.

Web browsers are able to launch secondary (or *helper)* programs that help read certain kinds of files or access certain kinds of Internet resources. When you click on a hypertext link from a Web page that calls for telnet access, a *helper application* called *NCSA telnet* (or the equivalent) is automatically launched. When you've finished your telnet session, you are returned to your Web browser.

What is telnet?

Telnet is a remote login protocol that enables you and your students to network by telephone. By running a telnet program on your computer after you are logged into the Internet, you can have your Macintosh or PC simulate a *dumb terminal* (typically, a hard-drive-less computer directly connected to a host computer) and take advantage of information resources at the host site.

You type commands on your keyboard, and telnet relays those commands from your computer terminal to your local Internet service provider. Then *telnet* relays those same commands from your local Internet provider to the remote computer that you have accessed. If you have a fast Internet connection, using telnet is just like *being there*.

Because telnet is like being there, the performance of the computer system for those people who *are* there will be affected by your access. The bottom line, then, is that you should telnet only when:

- ✔ You've been given your own username and password to gain access to a specific computer for a specific task (such as registering for a college course)
- ✔ You need resources that you can't retrieve in any other way

What can I do with telnet?

Gaining access to other people's computer systems can "net" some very productive results. Among other things, you can do the following:

- ✔ Access huge databases to do research
- ✔ Use resources in libraries around the world
- ✔ Register for classes
- ✔ Fill out forms to request information and supplies
- ✔ Gain easy entry into the world of Gophers and the World Wide Web

Figure 4-4 shows what a telnet session looks like using the *NCSA telnet* helper application from within a Web browser.

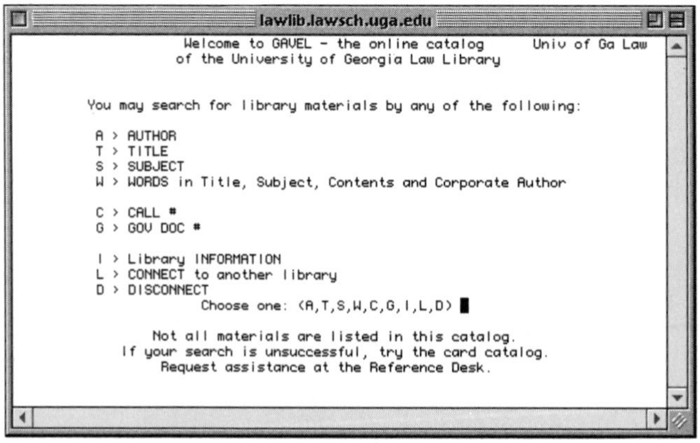

Figure 4-4:
Welcome to
GAVEL via
telnet.
GAVEL
provides
legal
resources to
University of
Georgia
students.

```
▭                     lawlib.lawsch.uga.edu                          ▣▤
                    Welcome to GAVEL - the online catalog      Univ of Ga Law  ▲
                       of the University of Georgia Law Library

         You may search for library materials by any of the following:

         A > AUTHOR
         T > TITLE
         S > SUBJECT
         W > WORDS in Title, Subject, Contents and Corporate Author

         C > CALL #
         G > GOV DOC #

         I > Library INFORMATION
         L > CONNECT to another library
         D > DISCONNECT
                       Choose one: (A,T,S,W,C,G,I,L,D) █

                  Not all materials are listed in this catalog.
               If your search is unsuccessful, try the card catalog.
                      Request assistance at the Reference Desk.
                                                                             ▼
◀                                                                       ▶  ▨
```

You'll hear the word *telnet* used both as a noun, as in, "I will use telnet to access the database," or as a verb, as in, "Please telnet to our server to register your software." Regardless of the part of speech, telnet can be a powerful tool in your Internet toolbox.

Internet Live!

Internet Relay Chat (IRC) is the Internet's answer to a fire drill. Imagine hundreds of people, many of them bored college students with idle time in a computer lab, chatting live across the wires on any topic that you can imagine.

IRC offers real-time conferencing that's similar to conference chats on online services. IRC is not very pretty, but it can be very useful as a collaborative tool.

Just as Web browsers call upon a program called *NCSA telnet* to access other computers, Web browsers require an accessory program, called a *helper application*, to allow you to interact with other Net users in real-time. You can easily configure your Web browser to call upon helper programs such as *IRC4Win* or *ircle* to make chatting easy.

IRC: Chatter at 14.4

As shown in Figure 4-5, *IRC* is a program that enables you to hold live online conversations with people around the world. The whole setup kind of reminds me of a global CB-radio network that you access via computer. This network is a free-for-all place where people speak their minds to whoever will listen. The network is organized into *channels* that are based on topics.

Figure 4-5:
By using the Net or an online service, you can participate in *real-time* (live) chats.

```
On IRC via server jello.qabc.uq.oz.au :University of Queensland, Australia
idle for 130 seconds
Topic is: #Education :Yippee!
#Education :Bard Boppo Pug Demi Gradu Gavel TFool MacS Acne Fred
Teacher Kidz Banshee Scotter @Master
Mode is +tn

*** Candice [Trustee@iquest.net] has joined #Education

Boppo changed the mode on #Education to "+o Boppo"

<Bard> What kind of multimedia do you use in your school?
<Pug> Mostly CD-ROM and some videodisc.
<Scotter> HyperStudio is great for videodisc stuff.
<TFool> really, Scotter?  Is it easy?
*** Signoff: Gavel
*** Signoff: Kidz
<Pug> It's so easy my third graders are making multimedia so much I had
to buy a 1 GB hard drive!
```

Basically, after you log on to the Internet and join a chat (channel), you type something on your computer, and all the other people tuned into your channel can see it instantly. At any one time, hundreds of channels are buzzing with chatter. You can either join one of the active channels or create your own channel.

After you learn how chats operate, you can make your chats public, private, or by invitation only; and you can even assign yourself a nickname.

If you and your students want to study humanity, *IRC* is a great way to begin. IRC is raw, uncensored, mile-a-minute dialog, and spelling doesn't count! As with any free-form medium, you are likely to see things that will curl your hair. I recommend that you use *IRC* very cautiously with your students, and use it only with a specific purpose in mind. The best use of *IRC* may be to begin your own chat and invite other classes from across the country to participate. Use newsgroup or mailing list postings to invite other classes to join you.

The Right Tool for the Right Lesson

The only tools you really need to surf the Internet are a computer, modem, Internet provider, and a full-featured Web browser. With most Web browsers, such as *Netscape* and *Mosaic,* you and your students can tap into all the Internet resources, such as FTP, newsgroups, mailing lists, telnet, and live chat. Unfortunately, when you use any all-in-one tool, you often lose specific features that are available in one-task, stand-alone programs. Sending and receiving Internet e-mail, for example, is much easier if you use the new features included in *Netscape Navigator* Version 2.0, or a stand-alone e-mail program such as *Eudora.*

Here's a list of the basic programs that you and your students can use to jump onto the Net and explore resources if your Web browser doesn't measure up. Guess what? These programs are *free* (or are very inexpensive shareware)! Each of these applications can be plucked off the Net at the following addresses:

```
ftp://archive.umich.edu
ftp://ftp.cica.indiana.edu
ftp://ftp.ncsa.uiuc.edu
```

Tools	Macintosh	Windows
Electronic mail	Eudora	Eudora
FTP (file transfer)	Fetch	WS_FTP
Gopher (database search)	TurboGopher	HGopher
USENET newsgroups	NewsWatcher	Trumpet News
World Wide Web (WWW)	Netscape	Netscape
telnet	NCSA Telnet	Trumpet Telnet
Live chat	ircle (or Homer)	IRC4Win

For step-by-step instructions on how to use all of the tools mentioned above, rush out to the bookstore and grab a copy of *The Internet For Teachers* (IDG Books Worldwide, Inc.). You'll be the school Net-guru in no time!

Chapter 5

Before You Surf

- -

In This Chapter

▶ Shopping for a surfboard

▶ Choosing a connection

▶ Hunting for an Internet provider

▶ Configuring your Internet workstation

▶ Checking your checklist

- -

Chances are good that your teacher-education program dealt with student management, educational psychology, dealing with special needs students, and textbook evaluation. Chances are better that you received absolutely no instruction in the use of computers or, more specifically, telecommunications. Luckily, that situation is changing. Colleges and universities everywhere are spending more and more time helping educators understand and become comfortable with computers. Most educators, however, haven't gotten up to speed on the particulars of selecting an Internet connection. In the next few sections, I hold forth my opinions on connecting your school to the Internet. If you've already got an Internet connection, skip to the pre-surf checklist at the end of the chapter.

Shopping for a Surfboard

Do you know how hard it is to find a store that sells surfboards in Atlanta, Georgia? I'd imagine it's akin to looking for a Coke machine in a desert. After much investigation, I finally found, hidden away in a tiny Atlanta suburb, a hole-in-the-wall store run by a real, live, transplanted Hawaiian surfer. After 20 minutes on the phone, I came to two conclusions:

✔ Buy a surfboard for how it surfs, not how it looks

✔ Buy the best surfboard that you can get, or you'll be looking for another one soon

Because I'm beating the surf-the-Net metaphor to death (okay; it's an excuse for me to learn more about my secret desire to become a surf bum on a California beach), I'll tell you that when you are choosing your Internet connection, you should follow the same two rules. With a little rewording, here they are:

- ✔ Buy an Internet connection because of how efficiently it operates, not because it's inexpensive
- ✔ Your Internet connection can never have enough speed

In other words, buy the best (and the fastest) Internet connection that you can afford, and you won't be sobbing at the Surf Shack for a newer and better model of connection when you and your students become power surfers.

Types of Connections

As with any other choice, you need to know the facts before you make a decision about the best way for your school to access the Internet. Doing some research can keep you from getting caught in the bog of administrative bureaucracy.

The two ways to get connected to the Internet are by a *direct connection* or by a *dial-up connection*. These connection methods vary widely in cost, ease of access, and the amount of support needed to maintain the connection.

Before you read on, I've provided a table at the end of this chapter that gets right to the heart of the matter. If you have only a minute before your technology committee meeting, read the table. Otherwise, read on for some hints (and hazards) that can help with your choice of connection to the Internet.

Direct or not?

In a *direct connection,* your computer or your local area network (*LAN*) is connected to the Internet all the time. To achieve a direct connection, your computer or LAN is connected to a magical box called a *router,* which carries a signal that has been translated from your computer's language into the official language of the Internet, *TCP/IP* (which stands for *Transmission Control Protocol/Internet Protocol* — just the term to throw around to impress your friends). The router is then connected via special high-speed telephone lines to the nearest *Internet gateway,* usually a university or research institution.

Why choose a direct connection?

A direct connection has many benefits. Because you're always connected, the Internet becomes just another resource on your network. A direct connection is also very fast, so that you don't have to wait for files to transfer, and your e-mail zips along faster than you can lick a stamp.

Another benefit is that a direct connection supports multiple users at the same time. This multiple-user business means that you and several other users in your school can gain access to the Internet over the same single high-speed line. Because you control the network, you also can easily control which Internet resources are available to users. This feature is especially nice for restricting certain newsgroups or limiting those inevitable naughty-file transfers.

What's the bad news? Cost. Direct Internet connections cost big bucks in the short term but may save you money in the long run. You have to buy the router (which can cost several thousand dollars) and get the thing installed (more money). But the biggest cost is the installation and maintenance of the high-speed lines. These lines are priced according to the speed of the connection. A 56 Kbps (fast) connection costs much less than an ISDN, T-1, or T-3 connection (very fast). These phone lines can range from $200 to $1,000 per month to maintain.

Over the long haul, however, a direct connection may be the most cost-effective route for most schools. Not having bunches of phone lines saves some money. You're also not paying a service provider a monthly fee for each Internet account as you do with most dial-up accounts.

Don't forget to consider a potentially large hidden cost of a direct connection — support. With other types of connections, the Internet provider is responsible for troubleshooting the system. With a direct connection, you need a Net-savvy person to maintain the gateway, assign and maintain user accounts, and troubleshoot. Luckily, the technology is moving toward easier-to-manage and more trouble-free connections.

Take a good, hard look at this type of connection if you're looking at ten or more connections from your school or at some type of county-wide or district-wide networks. Think about what you need both now and in the future.

With a direct connection, by the way, you can request your own domain name. The *domain name* is the part after the @ symbol in an Internet address, and it tells the receiver of your message where your computer is located. If you hail from Lawrenceville Middle School, for example, your address could be:

`yourname@yourschool.edu.`

The `edu` identifies the address as one for an educational institution. (For more information about domain names and addresses, see Chapter 2.)

Establishing a direct connection

Here are the general steps to take if your school decides to establish a direct connection to the Internet:

1. **Determine your school's needs.**

   How many concurrent users do you want to be able to support, and how fast do these connections need to be?

2. **Contact the operator of the nearest Internet gateway host.**

   Call a local university's computer center.

3. **Plan and design your Internet connection.**

   Get help from the university or from another school that has been through this. Don't forget to think about how you'll handle the maintenance and support of equipment and Internet accounts.

4. **Apply for an IP address.**

   You need to fill out lots of forms; find out how from your university contact.

5. **Have an experienced person install the hardware and phone lines.**

   Companies such as Apple Computer now offer Internet server bundles that are very easy to assemble. (The company claims you can be up and running within minutes.) Nevertheless, you can never have enough gurus around for the tough parts.

6. **Set up your Internet gateway accounts, do some general housekeeping, and set up an acceptable use policy (see Part III of this book).**

A direct connection to the Internet makes sense if you have a good size startup budget (including money for monthly lease fees), want the fastest available connection, and need to support many simultaneous users. That's it — surf's up!

Dial it up

The second type of connection is a *dial-up connection*. In a dial-up connection, you use your computer to dial another computer or server where your account is established. That *host computer* is directly connected to the Internet. This setup is kind of a direct-connect, once-removed. Chances are good that, because of cost or politics, your first Internet connection will be a dial-up connection.

Dial-up connections can be made through a local bulletin board service (*BBS*), an Internet service provider (*ISP*), or a commercial online service (*COS*). (I just made that last acronym up because these acronyms are everywhere!)

A dial-up connection is great because it has a very low initial cost. You can use all the dandy graphical interface tools that directly-connected users do, too. Dial-up connections are also very handy for home users and for users who are just occasional surfers.

The downside is that because a dial-up connection uses *POTS* (plain old telephone service), it's slower than a direct connection. You can still whiz along at 14,400 or 28,800 baud though, and that's plenty fast for most of us (well, for now it is!).

Another problem that you occasionally run into with a dial-up service is a busy signal. Depending on the time of day, these busy signals can get mighty frustrating. You know the drill — 40 students sitting on the floor impatiently waiting for you to dial into the Net for a demonstration. You get a busy signal. Luckily, most service providers limit the number of subscribers based on a ratio of subscribers to phone lines. Check this ratio when you choose an ISP.

Because you are dialing into another computer, you may not have as much access control as you would in a direct-connection scenario. Some ISPs and BBSs, and most of the online services, offer some kind of parental control options. These options allow you some control over access to downloaded files, chat rooms, and other such places where the craftiest among our students will undoubtedly surf their way to trouble.

Need another *pro* to balance the *cons* above? With a dial-up connection, you can rely on someone else (the service provider) to troubleshoot when things go wrong. Because you're not maintaining your own Internet server or gateway, those nightmares fall to someone else. Mighty convenient if you don't have time to teach six periods, grade papers, and manage a network node.

SLIP or PPP

Yep. Another couple of acronyms. These are pretty simple ones, though, so I spare you most of the techie-talk and get right to the point.

If you're dialing into the Internet through an Internet service provider, you'll most likely be offered a choice of what *type* of dial-up account you want. Remember, choice is good if you're an informed decision maker. You can request a couple of kinds of accounts: *SLIP* stands for Serial Line Internet Protocol (*CSLIP,* compressed SLIP, is its close cousin), and *PPP* is Point-to-Point Protocol.

A SLIP account or a PPP account is the next best thing to a direct connection. You can use all the software tools, such as World Wide Web (WWW) browsers and e-mail packages, very easily. SLIP and PPP accounts also enable you to immediately store transferred files on your local hard drive. Other connections, such as those usually provided through a university dial-up account, first store files on the host computer — requiring an extra step to move them to your home or school computer.

SLIP and PPP accounts cost less, too. You can get one of these accounts for about $35 per month with unlimited time online. A bargain! Remember, though, that you need one phone line for every account.

 If you have a Macintosh, you should choose a PPP account if you have a choice. Although the Mac runs both SLIP and PPP, PPP is a newer type of account that's generally more dependable and works best if you're using the WWW, which sends lots of graphics in short bursts.

 If you have a PC that is running Windows, you may want to consider a SLIP connection. You can run a dandy program called *WinSock (Windows Sockets),* a standard way for Windows programs to work with SLIP. *WinSock* applications, such as *Trumpet* and *Chameleon,* are great for Net-surfing.

What about an online service?

Commercial online services such as America Online, CompuServe, e-World, and Prodigy offer dial-up options that are also attractive to schools. Not only do you get Internet access through a single, easy-to-use interface, but many other resources are available through the service itself. If you're a casual user or want a great way to learn to Net-surf, try a commercial online service. Commercial online services offer software that is easier to install and, in general, easier to use than some other Internet software programs.

Another plus is the number of educational activities and resources that are available through the online services. America Online offers tons of online projects, ready-made for teachers, in its online Electronic Schoolhouse. The service also makes contacting other educators very easy. The "raw" Internet isn't so friendly.

 What's the downside of a commercial online service? Here's that money thing again. Online services most often charge a flat monthly fee, and then the meter runs by the hour. If your students get lost in the Web or stuck in a Gopher hole, the meter could ring higher than the national debt. Luckily, a couple of the online providers enable users to prepay for blocks of time each month. After the limit is reached, the service shuts you out until the next month. Easy cost control.

As with the dial-up service, you may also get a busy signal from time to time. America Online runs more than 1,000,000 sessions a day. Not even Alexander Graham Bell could have prepared for that. Remember, too, that you need one phone line for each connection unless your online service provides for direct TCP/IP connection.

Accessing the Internet via a university network or a BBS

If you use a telecommunications program to dial into a BBS or a university computer for Internet access, you may have what's generally referred to as a *shell account.* When you dial in, you get only a computer letter (like a DOS prompt) or a symbol prompt such as % or >. You can do almost anything other Net users can do, but the environment is strictly a text environment, and you have to deal with *UNIX,* a computer language that only a serious computer programmer could love. Luckily, most universities are moving quickly to offer PPP and SLIP access soon.

This kind of dial-up access enables you to do FTP (file transfer), telnet, and search for documents with WAIS. By using a host-based program called *Lynx,* you can get a text front-end to the graphically stunning World Wide Web. Lynx displays only the text items and links on Web pages in seriously boring monospace format. (Using *Lynx* is kind of like going to a movie blindfolded. You get access to some information, but you miss all the online maps, diagrams, logos, and pictures.) Of course, *Lynx* is better than nothing!

In some cases, while using a BBS or a university computer, files that you download get sent to your host computer and not directly to your own hard drive or floppy. When this type of file transfer happens, you need to go through the extra step of transferring the file from the host computer to your own computer at the end of your session. The process is a bit confusing, but it works. (All Internet traffic used to work this way.)

Sometimes, local BBSs or university nets offer users a limited tier of Internet services, like e-mail, Gopher, and telnet. This kind of account (sometimes referred to as a *shell account*) is the one that's the least expensive (often free) and most restricted. But, if the price is right. . . .

Establishing a dial-up connection

Here are the general steps to take if your school decides to establish a dial-up connection to the Internet:

1. **Determine the needs of your school.**

   How many concurrent users do you want and how fast do these connections need to be?

2. **Install phone lines (one per dial-up connection needed).**

3. **Buy a modem and a computer (any computer and the fastest modem you can afford).**

4. **Get an Internet service provider, online service, or the number for an Internet-ready BBS.**

   These providers can give you the details, such as the number you should dial and your account name.

5. **Build a collection of freeware, shareware, and commercial Internet tools (for SLIP or PPP accounts) or request front-end software from a commercial online service.**

   (Note that many of these online service startup kits come with a bit of free time for you to use in evaluating the service.)

6. **Do some general housekeeping and set up an acceptable use policy (see Part III).**

7. **Dial — and you're in!**

Decisions, Decisions

To sum up all the stuff for you, Table 5-1 compares dial-up accounts to direct accounts:

Table 5-1	Dial-up vs. Direct Internet Accounts	
Factors	*Dial-Up Connection*	*Direct (Dedicated) Connection*
Capacity	Limited to number of telephone lines	Unlimited
Short-term cost	Low	High
Long-term cost	High	Lower (the more users, the more savings)
Access control	Information provider allows limited control	You determine what resources users use
Speed	2400 to 28,800 baud	Faster than a speeding bullet
Line type	POTS (plain old telephone service)	T-1, T-3, ISDN, ATM
General recommendations	Great for single user (you) and limited school use until you can afford a direct connection)	Great for school-wide connection to the Internet

Locating an IP (Internet Provider)

After you decide what route to take to connect to the Net, you need to contact an information provider. If you've decided to use an online service, all that's left for you to do is to make a phone call to the online service's toll-free number.

If you're dialing up a local BBS, you need a computer, a modem, a communications program, and the BBS's phone number. Many free or inexpensive communications or terminal programs are available. A *terminal program*, such as *Z-modem* or *CrossTalk*, is a program that allows your computer to shift the burden of number crunching to a remote computer and act as a "dumb terminal." Contact a local user group or dial in to a BBS to find such a terminal program.

There are basically three ways to find an information provider:

- ✔ Let your fingers do the walking (check your local *Yellow Pages* under "Telecommunications").

- ✔ Check magazines and other popular press for advertisements. (*MacWorld, PCWorld,* and *Internet World* are all great sources for Internet provider listings.)

- ✔ Call someone who's already connected.

TIP

Ten questions to ask your IP (Internet Provider)

Ready to interview a prospective Internet provider? Here are ten questions to ask to find out if the IP meets your needs.

1. How many toll-free telephone lines do you control? (The more, the better.)

2. How many users currently use your service? (Check for a low ratio of users to lines.)

3. What kinds of accounts do you offer? (SLIP, PPP, or other.)

4. What does establishing an account cost? (Hopefully free for educators.)

5. How much time do I get for my monthly fee? (Unlimited is nice.)

6. How many and what kind of newsgroups do you carry? (Read: "Do you block certain Net resources?")

7. Can I spin my own Web (page)?

8. How is your customer support? (When you call them, do you get an answering machine or a live person?)

9. Do you have any special deals for educators or schools? (Free is good.)

10. What kinds of front-end, tool, and installation software do you supply? (Again, the more, the better.)

Can My (Insert Computer Name Here) Surf the Net?

Now that you've got an Internet provider, it's time to determine which system in your school you can use to make the link. Chances are that you probably won't have to purchase much new equipment. For example, you probably already have a computer and a modem. Most surfing tools are available free for educators on the Net. That situation just leaves you needing a phone line (groan) and an Internet account. Take a look at each section that follows to see how to build the vehicle for your first trip on the information superhighway.

All those chips and no place to go

In March of 1995, there were more than 2.6 million computers connected to the Internet. They range from Amigas to Apples, IBMs to Compaqs, Sun workstations to dumb terminals, mainframes to minis. Some of these machines (usually, but not always, big ones) are service providers (*hosts or servers*), and some are regular desktop computers (*clients*) that extract information from the host computers.

The great news is that you can use just about any computer to connect to the Internet. The only caveat is that you have to have enough memory (RAM) to unpack large files or to process and view pictures that you download.

If you're using a Macintosh or Windows machine, I would suggest 8MB (*megabytes*) of RAM, although 4MB will do in a pinch. (*RAM memory* is the electronic holding area, which only exists when your computer is turned on, where your programs and documents live while you're working on them.) Additional RAM enables you to work more quickly and efficiently as you process the information that you've retrieved from the Net.

If you're in the process of choosing a computer and want an awesome resource, check out *Macs For Teachers* (IDG Books Worldwide, Inc.) by my good IDG buddy and teacher-friend Michelle Robinette. The book is fact filled, and you'll laugh your way to becoming *the* computer guru in your school.

Your gateway to the Net

Perhaps the most important choice you can make is which Internet provider to use. The provider supplies your gateway to the Internet and your very own Internet e-mail address. (More and more people are putting their e-mail addresses on their business cards. You're a professional — you should have a business card, too. Get your business card printed and ask the printer to put your e-mail address on it.)

How you access the Internet determines, in large part, what resources you may have access to as well as whether you'll operate from a graphical user interface (GUI) or suffer from command-prompt disease.

You need to ask some essential questions before you select a provider. For those questions, see the sidebar "Ten questions to ask your IP (Internet Provider)" in this chapter.

Get with the program

The software that you need for Internet access depends on how you're connected. If you get connected via an online service, all the software that you need comes on the disk that you'll get in the mail with your subscription kit. Users of university networks or UNIX shell accounts can use off-the-shelf telecommunication packages such as *Microphone* (Macintosh) or *CrossTalk* (DOS/Windows) to access host-based programs.

If you connect via an Internet service provider, most providers send you a disk that's preconfigured with all the necessary software, when you subscribe. Simply install the programs on your computer, and you're on your way! If your information provider doesn't send you preconfigured software, you're still in luck. Search through the paperwork, or get on the phone to your provider, and get the answers to the questions in the "Internet Web-surfer's geek-speak checklist" that follows. After these questions are answered, zip to your *MacTCP* control panel (if you're on a Macintosh), or your *WinSock* config program (if you're using a PC running *Windows*), and enter the information from the chart in the blanks provided.

A modem is a modem is a modem?

A *modem* is the hardware device that translates the electronic signal from your computer into a form that's transmittable over a telephone line. (Modem stands for *modulator-demodulator*, in case anyone asks in the teachers' lounge.)

Modems generally come with two cables: one connects to the *serial* or *com port* on your computer; the other (a standard telephone cable) connects to your telephone wall jack.

Internet Web-surfer's Geek-speak checklist

Get the following information from your service provider so that you'll have all the information you need to set up your software for Internet access. Examples of the information are shown in parentheses. (If your software comes preconfigured, you can skip all of this.)

1. Your Internet provider address: (such as: 123.456.78.90) _____

2. Your username (login name): (flintstone) _____

3. Your password: (letters and/or numbers) _____

4. Your destination (or *gateway*) address: (256.256.1.1) _____

5. Your broadcast address: (123.123.255.255) _____

6. Your domain name: (bedrock.com) _____

7. Your e-mail address: (flintstone@bedrock.com) _____

8. Dial-up phone number(s): _____

9. Mailserver name (or POP server or SMTP server): (bedrock.com) _____

10. News host server name (or nntp server): (nntp.bedrock.com) _____

11. Domain name server: (234.345.123.0) _____

12. Subnet mask: (255.255.0.0) _____

13. Account type: (SLIP, CSLIP, PPP, shell) _____

14. Port settings: (baud rate, com/serial port #) _____

15. Domain suffix: (bedrock.com) _____

16. Ph server (not every service has one): (bedrock.com) _____

You only have to make two decisions when you purchase a modem:

✔ Do you want an internal or an external modem?

✔ How fast do you want to travel the information superhighway?

When you think about internal and external modems, think about the future. Your choice may depend on whether you're a nomad or a settled soul. If you're likely to purchase a new computer within the next year or two or may need to use the modem somewhere other than with your computer, consider an external modem. If you're using a laptop or a computer that'll be in a place where desktop space is limited, an internal modem will do.

The one neat thing about external modems is that the only real difference in modems for Macs and PCs is the cable that runs from the computer to the modem, and you can change that. So purchasing an external modem ensures that you'll be able to switch platforms should the "gotta buy a new computer bug" hit you anytime soon.

Since the whole point of owning a modem is to move *data* back and forth through the telephone lines, the faster you can move that data, the better. When shopping for a modem, always get the fastest modem that you can afford. Modem speeds are expressed as *baud rate*, with numbers such as 2400, 9600, 14.4 (14,400), or 28.8 (28,800) *bps* (bits per second).

The industry standard now is 14.4 (14,400 bps), but that standard is already creeping up to the next level. If you're buying now, don't settle for less than a 14.4 modem.

Make sure that the modem is Hayes compatible. The folks at Hayes pretty much invented the modem as we know it today and established a standard for how modems talk to one another. Most every modem you purchase today bears a "Hayes-compatible" label.

You knew there was a catch!

Teachers have chalk. Teachers have textbooks. Teachers do not have telephones. Even as we approach the year 2000, teachers are one of the few professionals without easy access to a basic communication tool — the telephone. Some lucky people work in schools (built by forward-thinking school districts) that have a telephone in every room. Hooray for them!

If there is any catch in getting hooked up to the Internet, that catch is in getting easy access to the phone line. There are basically two reasons for this problem:

- ✔ Phones cost money to install
- ✔ Phones cost money to maintain

(It's that money thing again.)

Luckily, there are ways to save money and still get your phone line. Here's how.

Your school probably has two kinds of phone lines: integrated and dedicated. Most schools that are large enough to have more than a couple of lines have signed contracts with telephone companies to install *integrated* custom phone systems that give you everything from intercoms to voice mail. Although this kind of system has some great features, it may present a problem for telecommunications.

The problem with integrated systems is that, along with your phone call, your telephone handset sends signals through an electronic switch box before your call exits the building into the real world. Because you're dialing out with a modem rather than with an especially configured handset, sometimes the modem has difficulty getting a dial tone. (If you have to dial 8 or 9 to get an outside line, you may have an integrated phone system.) Unless your phone system is configured specifically for modem communications, dead air is all you'll hear when your modem attempts to connect. The answer is to either have the phone company make an adjustment for one or more lines or get a dedicated phone line.

A *dedicated* phone line is a standard phone line like the one in your home. (The phone company calls it *POTS* for *plain old telephone service* — really!) It goes straight from any telephone to a junction box that transmits the signal, unchanged, to the lines outside your building. In general, if you can plug a telephone from home into a jack and it works, a modem will work there, too. Dedicated phone lines are the best bet for schools, especially because you don't have to share the line with 28 other teachers who are trying to call to let Johnny's parents know how well he's doing in school.

Your Internet phone line needs to be convenient if you're going to integrate it into the classroom. You need to locate it in the media center or, in the best case, in your classroom.

One way to save money on phone lines is to install *extension* lines. One dedicated line to the media center can be split and run to classrooms. The downside? Only one user can dial out at a time. Someone will always be waiting.

Here's a tip for avoiding the "I'm on the phone" problem. Visit your local electronics store and pick up a phone-line-in-use light for each extension. They're under $20 and well worth the money.

If it turns out that you want to investigate Internet connections at faster-than-dial-up speeds, you have several options. Your school can pay for the installation of a super-fast line (sometimes known as a *leased line* because you pay a premium to lease the line from the phone company) called a *T-1, ISDN,* or *T-3 line,* or an almost-as-fast *56 Kbps line,* if you have the money. You'll need a T-1 or T-3 line if you want to become *your own* Internet service provider (that is, have a *direct*, 24-hour, hard-wired connection to the Net).

Surfer's Tips: Passwords

Whether you're using an online service, a university network, or an Internet service provider, you should *never*, repeat, *never* give your password to anyone else. Your password can be just as valuable (and as potentially dangerous) as your PIN number is for your automatic bank teller machine.

Here are a few tips for protecting your password:

 Change your password regularly: The majority of students will respect your right to keep your password private. However, some students will make it their life's quest to discover your password. Foil them by changing it regularly. And please, *don't* write it down under the blotter on your desk or on the corner of your grade book. Students are sure to look there. If you have a really rotten memory, just write the password down and stick it in your wallet or purse. But, just to be safe, split the password between two tiny pieces of paper.

 Use a combination of alphabetic and numeric characters: You'll be tempted to use the principal's name or the initials of the school as a password — don't. That's the first thing someone trying to gain unauthorized access to your account will try. Make up a password that combines letters and numbers that have some meaning to you but not to others. Try the number of years you've been a teacher and the initials of your two favorite uncles' names, for example 16WATHJT.

 Look over your shoulder before typing your password: Just as teachers have eyes in the backs of their heads, students have razor-sharp vision when it comes to getting their teacher's password. Most programs show your password as •••••••• when you enter it so that it's protected from prying eyes; but remember that students can see your fingers on the keyboard, too.

 Resist the temptation to use an autologin program: *Autologin* settings in your software enable you to access the Internet with a simple mouse click, *without* having to remember the password. With autologin, you pre-enter your password and save it to disk. This method is very handy when you're in a hurry, but it's also a cinch for others to use when they want unauthorized access to your account. I'd say use autologin *only* if you or members of your family are the only users of your computer *and* there's never a time when unauthorized users are anywhere around your computer. (In other words, if the computer is in your home or in some other very controlled environment.)

Now, I know this must seem like overkill, but I've seen what happened when a student got hold of a commercial online account and used more than 100 hours in a week. A word to the wise. . . .

Final Pre-Surf Checklist

You've got your Net connection, liberated (er, borrowed) a computer from somewhere in the school, and finagled a phone line. You've also thought about how you'll use the Net and wracked your brain for a password scheme you can live with. You're ready to surf.

One final tip from my new-found Atlanta surf buddy — "noodle before you kaboodle" — loosely translated — "think before you surf." Check out Part IV of this book for management tips, acceptable use policies, and staff development ideas. As with any educational endeavor, preplanning pays.

Part II
Riding Your Web Surfboard

Principal Johnson discovers cut-rate Web access powered by Ms. Carter's after school detentions.

In this part . . .

*B*efore you can *hang-28.8* (that's 28,800 bits per second, in modem language), you'll need to collect a few tools and learn some basic skills in using a Web browser. This part guides you step by step as you learn to use a popular Web browser, called *Netscape*, to do everything from hyperlinking to other Web sites to ftping your favorite file. (I know. Lots of nerd-speak. Don't worry. You'll understand it in no time!) I also take a look into the Cyber-crystal ball and give you my predictions about where the Web might be in the future. (*Future,* in the Internet world, means "after today" — things are moving quickly!)

Chapter 6

Web On-Ramps

In This Chapter

▶ Accessing the Net

▶ Browser bonanza

▶ The right choice

*G*rab your propeller-beanie from the shelf, because you're almost ready to jump onto the World Wide Web. After you've determined how you'll connect to the Web via the Internet, your last and final task is to choose a Web browser. *Web browsers* (called *clients* by the techno-literate) are the programs that you run on your computer to access the World Wide Web. Browsers are available for nearly every flavor of computer on the planet and are either built into an online service (such as the Web browser in AOL) or are stand-alone programs (such as *Netscape* or *Mosaic*). Whether you're using a Macintosh, a PC running Windows, or a terminal on a UNIX network, you're in luck — Web browsers are everywhere!

Accessing the Net

As with just about anything technological, there's more than one way to skin the Net. Here are three basic ways to access the World Wide Web:

✔ Through a commercial online service such as America Online, e-World, CompuServe, and the like (using a built-in browser)

✔ Through a commercial Internet service provider (using a browser)

✔ Through a LAN/college/university account (through a local area network, using a browser)

Your choice depends on what Internet resources you already have available and what tools (such as browsers) you'd like to use. Browsers are differentiated by their ability to display graphics, their features (such as support for FTP, e-mail, and telnet), and their support for enhanced scripting languages such as HTML 2.0 (scripting languages are used by Web authors to create Web pages).

In the next sections, I give you a glimpse of the pros and cons of each type of Web access; then I give the techno-weenie beanie propeller a big spin and launch into a discussion of which type of browser is best for you and your students' needs.

Surfing via online services

Commercial online services generally provide the easiest method of connecting to the Web. All the tools (programs) that you need are built into the software you get when you subscribe to a commercial online service. Whether you're dialing into America Online (AOL), CompuServe, e-World, or MSN (Microsoft Network), accessing most Internet resources (including the Web) is a matter of simply clicking an icon.

On America Online, for example, you and your students begin your cyber-journey by visiting the Internet Connection area (Keyword: **Internet** — or choose Internet Connection from AOL's main menu). From there you have point-and-click access to almost all Internet resources, including the World Wide Web. Figure 6-1 shows AOL's Internet Connection menu.

Figure 6-1:
AOL's
Internet
Connection
menu
features
easy access
to the Web.

Clicking the World Wide Web icon launches the Web browser, which is built into the Windows version of AOL and is a stand-alone "helper" application on the Macintosh. After the browser (Figure 6-2) appears, access to it is as easy as entering a URL (Internet address). By the way, the Web 66 site shown in Figure 6-2 is one of the best sites on the Net for locating other schools with Web pages.

You can also find easy access to the Web on CompuServe, e-World, Prodigy, and many other online services and BBSs (Bulletin Board Services). So what's the downside of accessing the Web through an online service? Price.

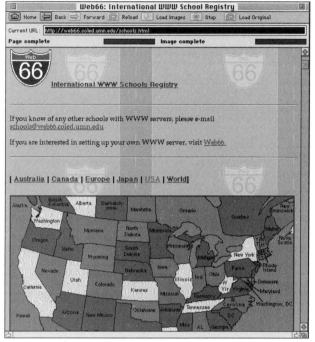

Figure 6-2:
AOL's Web
browser has
most of the
features of
other
commercial
Web
browsers.

Unlike commercial Internet providers that typically offer a monthly fee for unlimited access to the Internet, commercial online services are like taxi cabs — the meter runs all the time that you're riding on the info superhighway. Before you totally discount online services as your on-ramp, however, remember that these services offer many *value-added* services that may make the purchase worthwhile for teachers. America Online, for example, complements full Internet access with the following:

- Live online chats dealing with topics of interest to educators
- Thousands of downloadable files that are guaranteed virus-free
- Resources that allow you easily to find and collaborate with other schools and educators around the world
- Full text of many education-related periodicals
- And lots more

Accessing the Internet through an online service is an ideal way to "get to know the Net" before you launch a search for a stand-alone commercial Internet provider.

Web acce$$ via online $erviçe$

What will it cost for your school to access the Net through an online service? The table below was constructed based on sample school usage. Each school used the Net, primarily through supervised access in the media center or computer lab. The average monthly cost is based on an average for a school that uses the service almost daily, but plans well and minimizes "browsing time." (Figures below indicate a school that uses about 25 hours of access time per month.) Other commercial service resources, such as forums and online chats, add to time spent online, but those resources are certainly worthwhile and may steer your school toward considering using online services such as America Online, e-World, or CompuServe.

Service	Monthly Fee	Hrs. Included	Cost/Add'l. Hr.	Avg. Monthly Cost
America Online	$9.95	5	$2.95	$60
CompuServe*	$9.95	5	$2.95	$60
Delphi	$10.00	4	$4.00	$180
e-World	$8.95	4	$2.95	$60
Genie	$9.95	5	$3.00	$100
Prodigy	$9.95	5	$2.95	$70

You can reach the online services at the phone numbers and addresses below:

Service	Phone	Web Address
America Online	800-827-6364	http://www.blue.aol.com
CompuServe*	800-524-3388	http://www.compuserve.com
Delphi	800-695-4005	http://www.delphi.com
e-World	800-775-4556	http://www.eworld.com
Genie	800-638-9636	http://www.genie.com
Prodigy	800-776-3449	http://www.prodigy.com

*CompuServe rates may be lower if you use their Super Value Plans. Also note that, with CompuServe, a PPP connection comes with your monthly fee. All CompuServe dial-in network numbers are PPP capable.

Internet service providers

Just about every city features at least one Internet Service Provider (ISP). An *ISP* is a company that sells Internet access through a dial-up connection that does not go through a commercial online service. Unlike an online service, when you dial into the Internet through an ISP, you use software tools like Web browsers, e-mail programs, and Gopher programs to retrieve information on the Internet.

Accessing the Net via an ISP provides schools with the following three benefits:

- ✔ Accessing this way is less expensive (unlimited time vs. a "meter" always running)
- ✔ Choosing the tools that you use is your own decision (you choose the browser, the newsreader, and the like)
- ✔ Customizing your connection is easier (that is, screening out unwanted content is easier, if you have the right software)

The downside? Because you're using lots of different programs to do lots of different things, the learning curve can be greater than when using an online service. In addition, setup is usually more of a pain; although most ISPs now offer turnkey disks that make this setup process much more simple than such a setup process once was.

What's the answer if you wish to have all the benefits of a direct connection but none of the cost? Become your own Internet node. The next section (Online via university network or LAN) tells you what's in store for your school if you choose that route.

If you're crafty, you can get an ISP to donate an account to your school. If not, you can plan for $10 to $35 per month for unlimited use of the Internet via any computer at your school.

Online via university network or LAN

If you attend a college or university, there's a very good chance that you can access the Internet via the servers in the computer center of that institution. Most times, such access is *free* for students, too! These accounts typically allow you to dial-in from your school to the university's computer system and jump to the Internet from there. Contact your campus computer center for information about establishing an account and accessing the Net.

Another option for connecting to the Web is to create your own Internet node. Chapter 5 (and others) give you what you need to know to begin that process, but here are the benefits:

- ✔ Lower long-term cost (high up-front cost)
- ✔ Maximum control of data entering and leaving your school/district
- ✔ Flexibility in growing and expanding Internet access

Using your own node or one provided by a university gets you all the benefits of using an Internet service provider with less cost in the long run. Up-front costs (for example, setting up your server, obtaining high-speed phone lines, and paying someone to maintain the whole shebang) can be steep. On the other hand, the cost to connect additional users can be very small and "unlimited time" becomes a standard instead of a dream.

Choosing a Web Browser

I had the distinct privilege of observing a home economics class a few years ago. The topic was "shopping wisely" for fruits and vegetables. For fifty minutes, I watched students poke, prod, stick, and smell every kind of melon, bean, apple, and watermelon you can imagine. I learned that you thump melons to check for air pockets (deeper toned thumps are better), and you squeeze onions to check for the density of the vegetable tissue (they should not be squishy). A tasty experience!

Gone are the days when I would dash into a supermarket and grab the first apple off the shelf. Now that I know what a *good* apple feels and smells like, I can't settle for less than Grade A. Basically, knowing a bit about Web browsers really helps when it comes to selecting one that'll be useful for you and your students. Like the vegetables, some Web browsers are really rotten, and some are so wonderful that you're glad that you bought them.

There's a cornucopia of Web browsers on the market today. The biggest differences among them are found in the following areas:

- ✔ Support for advanced graphics such as colored backgrounds, special forms, and formatted tables
- ✔ Speed (some browsers are faster than others)
- ✔ Cost (some are freeware and others are shareware; still others are commercial products)
- ✔ Platform support (support for the Mac O/S, Windows 3.x, Windows 95, OS/2, and so on)
- ✔ Support for enhanced (advanced) scripting languages (such as HTML 2.0 or greater)

Looking through Netcom Windows?

If you're using a computer running Windows, you've got several great options for accessing the Net. One option, a dandy integrated software application called *NetCruiser*, has an easy-to-use interface. With *NetCruiser*, you can browse the Web, access Gopher, connect to other computers via telnet, copy files from remote computers to your home computer with FTP, read newsgroups, and tap all the functions of e-mail. It's really a great way to introduce students, and reluctant teachers, to the Net! *NetCruiser* only works when you access the Internet through Netcom (a country-wide Internet service provider).

Browser specifics

In general, most Web browsers present images (pictures) when you log in to a Web site on the Internet. However, a recent expansion of the programming language called HTML opens the possibility of embellishing your Web page with fancy backgrounds, multi-column tables, and interactive forms. Not all Web browsers, however, support the new codes (HTML 2.0 and, soon, HTML 3.0).

Because of the way that Web browsers are written, some are a bit faster than others. Given the same connection (most schools connect at 14.4 or 28.8 bps), two browsers may work at different speeds. If you're lucky enough to access the Net via high-speed T-1, T-3, or ISDN lines, just about any browser will *fly*.

Educators can obtain just about any Web browser free if they intend to use it in their classrooms or for educational purposes. Thanks to the generosity of companies like Netscape (maker of the top-of-the-line Web browser) and others, you can download updates right from the Net and use them in your classroom free. If you're not an educator, you can obtain the same browsers for a modest shareware fee or purchase off-the-shelf browsers at your local computer store.

Browsing the Browsers

Netscape's Navigator is currently the foremost of all Web browsers; but others, such as *Mosaic, MacWeb, and WinWeb* run a close second. Several online services such as AOL, Prodigy, and the new Microsoft Network, have integrated Web browsers.

Because most Web browsers are programs that run on your desktop computer, you must be careful to choose a browser that's compatible with your operating system. Table 6-1 gives you a rundown of the most popular browsers and the platforms they support. Watch for the "teacher recommended" asterisk that indicates those that I recommend for use by students and teachers.

Table 6-1		Web Browsers			
Browser	**Company**	**Source**	**Mac**	**Win**	**UNIX**
AIR Mosaic Express	Spry	`http://www.spry.com/`		X	
Arena	W3O	`http://www.w3.org/`	X	X	X
Cello	Cornell Law Sch.	`http://www.law.cornell.edu/`		X	
Charlotte	BC Systems Corp.	`gopher://p370.bcsc.go.bc.ca/`		X	
Chimera	UNLV	`http://www.unlv.edu/`			X
Emacs W3	William Perry	`http://www.cs.indiana.edu/`		X	
*Enhanced Mosaic	Spyglass	`http://www.spyglass.com/`	X	X	X
GWHIS	Quadralay	`http://www.quadralay.com/`	X	X	X
HotJava	Sun Microsystems	`http://java.sun.com/`	X	X	X
InternetWorks	Booklink/AOL	`http://www.booklink.com/`	X	X	
Line Mode Browser	CERN	`http://www.w3.org/`			X
Lynx (text only)†	Univ. of Kansas	`http://kuhttp.cc.ukans.edu/`	X	X	X
NCSA Mosaic	NCSA U. of Ill.	`http://www.ncsa.uiuc.edu/`	X	X	X
*MacWeb	EINet	`http://www.einet.net/`	X		
NetCruiser	NetCom	`http://www.netcom.com/`	X	X	
*Netscape Navigator	Netscape Comm.	`http://www.netscape.com/`	X	X	X
Secure NCSA Mosaic	EIT, RSA, & NCSA	`http://www.commerce.net/`	X	X	X
SlipKnot	Peter Brooks	`http://www.interport.net/`		X	
WebSurfer	NetManage	`http://www.netmanage.com/`		X	
WinWeb	EINet	`http://www.einet.net/`		X	

† *Lynx* is accessed via any computer connected to a server running *Lynx*.

The last criterion for choosing a browser should be a consideration for what type of scripting languages are supported. As you discover in Part III of this book ("Weaving Your Own Web Page"), Web browsers interpret a scripting language called *HTML* (HyperText Markup Language). There are several different "generations" of HTML code around. The most recent generation allows users to see and script fancy backgrounds, stunning tables and charts, and "on-demand" application ("applet") downloads. Figure 6-3 shows an example of the cool WWW TV home page (http://www.tvtrecords.com/tvbytes) as displayed using the most recent version of *Netscape Navigator*.

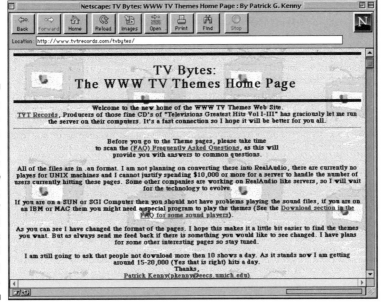

Figure 6-3: Cutting-edge browsers, such as *Netscape Navigator*, offer really cool backgrounds and stunning tables.

Some of the older browsers don't support the newer HTML command sets. Those browsers written for multiple platforms, and those that are regularly revised, usually do support the most recent innovations in Web scripting. *Netscape Navigator* is the browser that seems to be setting the standard for revisions that keep up with the newest HTML code. That's why I think that, if you don't use an online service, *Netscape Navigator* is the way for your school to go (and I tell you how to get it *free* in Chapter 7).

The Right Choice

Ultimately, the choice of browser may come down to what your Internet provider has to offer. If you purchase bundled software, such as Apple's Internet Connection Kit, or the *Chameleon* suite of software for PCs running Windows, you're likely to get a better bargain. Remember, too, that many Web browsers are available free to educators on the Net. Whatever browser you choose, know that you can always change your browser as your needs change.

Regardless of how you and your students access the World Wide Web and what tools you choose, you're likely to see great jumps in the number of features and the speed of network connections available. Chances are, the browser that your students are using now will be thought of as prehistoric by the time they graduate from high school, even if their graduation is only a year away!

In the future, Web browsers will continue to offer new and more exciting features. As you'll see in Chapter 10, cutting-edge technology, such as virtual reality, is already creeping into the next generation of Web browsers

What's an educator to do? Take a tip from the Nike folks and "just do it!" The knowledge and skills that you and your students build as you learn to use the Net are a skill set that's transportable well into the future. The only thing constant about technology is that it changes.

Getting wired: Internet or caffeine?

Next time you're traveling, pop into one of the cafes below and grab a muffin, a hot cup of coffee, and a smidgen of Internet access. C'mon, you can't resist. These "wired cafes" offer a spot where you can relax and Web-surf to your heart's content — for a small fee, of course!

San Francisco, CA: Brain Wash (Folsom St.), Club Zero (Valencia St.), Laundry Cafe (Green St.), Icon Byte Bar & Grill (my personal favorite; 9th and Folsom)

Matthews, NC: The On-Ramp (Matthews St.)

Ashland, OR: Paper Moon Espresso Cafe (North First St.)

Cambridge, MA: Cybersmith (Harvard Square)

Nashville, TN: Bean Central (West End Avenue)

Portland, OR: The Habit (SE 21st Avenue)

Berkeley, CA: Coffee Source (Telegraph Avenue), Cafe Milano (Bancroft Way)

. . . and there are many more! To find a Net-cafe in your hemisphere, check out the alt.cybercafes newsgroup or let your fingers do the walking.

One day, you're likely to wake up and find that your teachers' lounge is the newest cybercafe. Well . . . we can all dream, can't we?

Chapter 7

Let's Go Web Surfing!

*I*n the prehistoric telecommunications era (1970-1980), going online was a major production. You had to know baud rate, stop bits, parity, checksum, logon codes, modem strings (that looked like something from that college statistics class that you skipped at least once), and much more. Thank goodness that telecommunication in general (and the Net, specifically) is easier today than ever. You need know *none* of the above terms to get started on your Internet journey.

This section guides you on a quick journey through the Web using a browser called *Netscape Navigator,* one of the best browsers on the market. More than 70 percent of the people using the Web use *Netscape Navigator* on their computers.

Internet 101: Netscape Navigator

Netscape Navigator is a program that enables users to browse the World Wide Web. The program is actually the offspring of another browser called *Mosaic,* a freeware program that paved the way for *Netscape's* enhanced capabilities. *Netscape* provides users of Macintosh and PCs running *Windows* with a fast, easy-to-use interface that makes zipping around the Web easy. *Netscape Navigator* is feature-rich, provides access to WWW, Gopher, and FTP resources, and — here's the best news — some versions are *free* for educators!

Get Your Copy!

First things first. It's time to grab *your* free copy of *Netscape Navigator*. The good news is . . . it's free to educators and can be downloaded from Netscape's home page: http://www.netscape.com

The most recent version of *America Online* along with its browser (both Macintosh and Windows versions) is on the CD.

To use the program, you need Internet access (via an Internet service provider) and a Macintosh or PC running Windows. Here are the easy installation instructions:

1. **Obtain a copy of *Netscape Navigator* from your Internet service provider or download it like I just described.**

2. **Double-click the *Netscape Navigator* icon to start the program.**

   You need about 3MB of free space on your hard drive for the program.

That's it! Now a recent version of *Netscape Navigator* is safe and sound on your hard drive, and you're ready to begin to do some Web surfing! For updates of your software, you can visit *Netscape's* Web page at:

http://www.netscape.com/

The Netscape Interface

When you launch the *Netscape Navigator* Web browser by clicking the *Netscape Navigator* icon, you are presented with a screen containing eight major components:

- ✔ A menu bar
- ✔ A toolbar
- ✔ A title bar
- ✔ Directory buttons
- ✔ A status bar
- ✔ A viewing area
- ✔ Scroll bars
- ✔ A URL bar

Figure 7-1 can help you match the components with their location on your computer screen. By the way, Figure 7-1 shows the Weather Underground page from the University of Michigan (http://groundhog.sprl.umich.edu).

Title bar   Toolbar   Directory buttons   URL bar

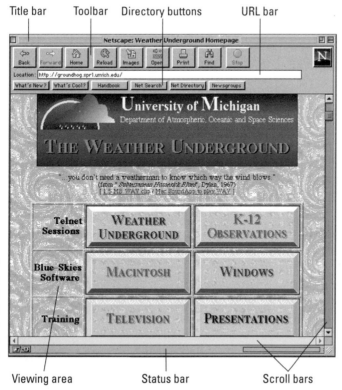

Viewing area   Status bar   Scroll bars

Form follows function

Here's a brief summary of each of the components that make up *Netscape's* main window and the functions of each component. If you'd like to get started right away (those of you who still rip the wrapping off holiday gifts faster than someone can say "Wait!"), skip to the next section and come back and read this section later.

The *title bar* shows you the name of the current Web page that you're viewing.

The *menu bar* has lots of pull-down menus. Many of the commands in these menus are replicated on *Netscape's* toolbar.

Netscape's toolbar contains many useful buttons. Figure 7-2 gives you an up-close look at the toolbar. Basically, the toolbar gives you easy access to commonly used features. To use the tools, simply click the buttons.

Figure 7-2: An up-close look at *Netscape's* toolbar.

TECHNO TERMS

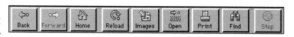

Meet URL

URL (pronounced *earl*) stands for *Uniform Resource Locator.* A URL lists the exact location (address) of virtually any Internet resource, such as a file, hypertext page, or newsgroup.

URLs look like this:

Resource	*Example*
a WWW page	`http://www.info.apple.com/education/`
a picture file	`ftp://fabercollege.edu/graphics/otter.gif.sit`
a newsgroup	`news:alt.binaries.great.fraternity.pkt`
a Gopher site	`gopher://gopher.tc.umn.com`
a telnet session	`telnet://teachable.tech.com`

URLs are made up of a *resource type* (Web, newsgroup, FTP, and so on) followed by a colon and two forward slashes, the Net address of the resource, and (sometimes) the pathway that locates the files among all the subdirectories on the destination server.

```
http://www.info.apple.com/education/
```

Resource (WWW) — `http:` ; Net address — `www.info.apple.com` ; Subdirectory — `education/`

What do you *do* with these URLs? Type them into the "Open" box in your Web browser (or other Internet tools) press Return (Enter), and you're on your way!

Here's a rundown of the buttons on the toolbar:

Tool/Button	Function
Back	Returns to the previous Web page or document.
Forward	Moves forward to the next Web page or document. (If you're on the last item in your Recent list, the command will be grayed out.)
Home	Returns you to the first page that you see when you launch *Netscape*.
Reload	Reloads current Web page or document. (Use this when your screen looks strange or if images [pictures] don't load correctly the first time.)
Images	Loads pictures into your Web page if your "autoload images" preference is set to off.
Open	Enters a new URL (Internet pathway).
Print	Prints the current document.
Find	Finds text in the current document or current page.
Stop	Cancels incoming graphics or text information. (Useful if you're impatient and don't want to wait for long image transfers.)

An area called the *URL bar*, just below the toolbar, shows the full Web address of the site to which you've surfed.

The *directory buttons* whisk you away to *Netscape Navigator* resources such as the popular "What's Net" (new Web pages) and several Web search resources.

You find that all the text and images (graphics) reveal themselves in the largest area on your screen, the *Page/Document Area*. This is where the good stuff comes in.

On the bottom of the screen is a *status bar*. The status bar shows you where you're headed and whether the document is *encrypted* (electronically coded before transmission). If you're at a site that's protected by encryption, an unbroken key shows up if the file you're reading is encrypted for security; most sites aren't protected. The status bar also gives you information about how large a Web page is and how long it will take for the images and text to download to your computer.

Scroll bars help you move up and down (or, in some cases, side to side) on Web pages that are larger than the viewing area of your screen.

You can hide the directory buttons and other items to give you more screen real estate by choosing Options⇨Show directory buttons.

Connecting to the Web via Netscape Navigator

You've retrieved your copy of *Netscape Navigator* via FTP (using *Fetch, AOL's FTP*, or another program), and now you're ready to fire up the program and get surfing! *Netscape* is a leader in browser interfaces for a very good reason — it's very easy to use and very powerful. Using the program is as simple as starting the program and entering a URL (an Internet address). Here's how:

1. **Connect to the Internet by choosing MacPPP, MacSLIP, or InterSLIP from your control panel menu and then double-click the *Netscape* icon to launch the program.**

   You can also double-click the *Netscape Navigator* icon, and your computer will automatically access the proper resources and make your Net connection as it launches *Navigator*. Figure 7-3 shows *Netscape's* home page.

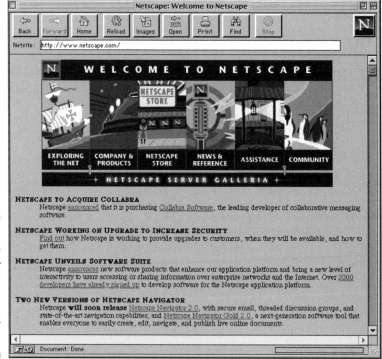

Figure 7-3:
Netscape Navigator automatically logs you onto *Netscape's* home page.

As you move your mouse over some of the words and pictures on the home page (they're blue or purple if you have a color monitor), the mouse pointer turns into a pointing hand. Clicking on these words or pictures takes you to another Web page. Clicking the word Netscape Navigator 2.0, for example, zips you to a server somewhere on the planet that has the most recent version of *Navigator* software.

2. **To browse the WWW, either click one of the hypertext (blue) items on the screen or choose File⇨ Open Location (⌘+O) at the top of the screen and enter a URL.**

   Want a cool place to start? Try BobAWorld. The BobAWorld page is one of the oldest, and best, general education (and other stuff) sites on the Internet.

   Click the Open button or press ⌘+O (or choose File⇨Open Location) and type this URL (address):

   ```
   http://gagme.wwa.com/~boba/kidsi.html
   ```

   When you click OK, you are whisked away to the BobAWorld site. Easy, huh?

   Figure 7-4 shows what you see when your browser reaches BobAWorld.

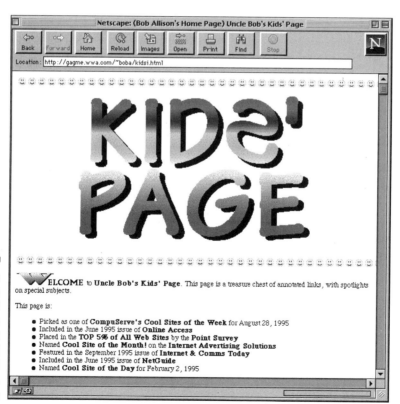

Figure 7-4:
The BobAWorld home page is a great source of educational links.

Use the button bar to activate commands such as <u>B</u>ack (⌘+[) to return to the last WWW site, <u>H</u>ome to return to *Navigator's* home page, and <u>S</u>top (⌘+.) to cancel your request and try another WWW site.

Don't get excited if you encounter a `404 not found` **error** or a `Connection refused by host` error. These messages just mean that the WWW site is busy, has moved, or that your URL wasn't typed correctly.

Occasionally, your browser will fail to load pictures correctly and will display a "broken icon" graphic. Click the <u>R</u>eload button (⌘+R) at the top of the screen, and *Navigator* refreshes the graphics on your screen.

3. **When you finish surfing, exit *Netscape Navigator* by choosing** <u>File</u>⇨<u>Q</u>uit (⌘+Q).

Remember that you've only quit the browser and have *not* quit the Net itself. You must return to your PPP, SLIP, or *WinSock* tools to terminate your connection.

Use <u>File</u>⇨<u>S</u>ave (⌘+S) to save the contents of a Web page on your disk for later viewing.

The Web provides several pages that are either lists of other sites or that contain a searchable database of Web addresses. Try one or more of the jumping-off points given in the list below. Use the <u>O</u>pen button (⌘+L) to reveal a window where you can type in any URL. Here are a few jumping-off points you and your students may enjoy. From these, you can get virtually anywhere on the World Wide Web.

```
http://www.yahoo.com

http://www.netsurf.com/nsd/index.html

http://kuhttp.cc.ukans.edu/cwis/organizations/kucia/
uroulette/uroulette.html
```

Navigating the tangled Web

Finding things hidden in the Web can be as tough as finding a free moment to make a phone call during the school day. Hundreds of thousands of Web pages are out there, with more pages being added every day, so it's tough for any one place to have a full listing of what's on the Net.

What's more, URLs come and go and change their structure regularly. This means that some links that you come across, or have collected yourself, may evaporate at a moment's notice.

FAQ and other TLAs

When you learn to surf the Internet, you and your students are learning a new language with lots of new jargon and, of course, lots of acronyms. Many of the acronyms dealing with technology tend to have three letters, so we affectionately call them *TLAs* (three-letter acronyms). One very useful TLA that you'll find all over the net is FAQ. *FAQ* stands for *frequently asked question,* and an FAQ is a document containing answers to all the questions swirling around in your brain right now. Most sites have FAQs, especially those sites dealing with newsgroups or FTP (file transfer) sites.

One cardinal rule for students and teachers. If you spot an FAQ file, read it. You'll save everyone lots of grief. FAQs often contain information that can save you embarrassment, ridicule, time, and money. I know. All you folks out there who are now staring at all the software and hardware manuals on your shelf (those manuals that are *still hermetically sealed in their original shrink-wrap*) are going to chuckle. Just wait, though; eventually someone will throw the "Didn't you read the FAQ?" message at you. This message is similar to RTM (read the manual — expletive deleted).

A great activity for students is to send them on a hunt for TLAs and have them make an Internet dictionary. Here are a few to get them started:

FAQ	TCP	LAN	FTP
BBS	DNS	URL	AOL
GIF	RFC	IRC	MUD

And for extra credit: NII.

The search is on!

After you've dialed into the Net and you've launched your Web browser, you can visit specific sites, called *search engines*, that feature fill-in-the-blank forms that allow keyword searches of Web sites and content. One of the best Web search engines is called WebCrawler. Like other search engines, WebCrawler is merely an especially written Web page that is designed to take a user-entered query and find all the sites on the Net that match the query's criteria. The WebCrawler's URL is:

```
http://www.webcrawler.com/
```

WebCrawler searches for documents whose title *or* content matches your keyword.

Using the WebCrawler is easy; simply enter the search term and click the Search button. (See Figure 7-5.)

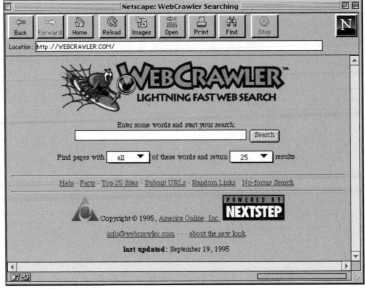

Figure 7-5:
WebCrawler offers a simple one-line interface and a very comprehensive search engine.

Another terrific Web search page that you and your students will want to visit is called the *World Wide Web Worm (WWWW)*. The Worm's URL is:

```
http://www.cs.colorado.edu/home/mcbryan/WWWW.html
```

Mr. Worm is not quite as efficient as WebCrawler, but Mr. Worm still works very well.

And here are a few more especially constructed Web pages that link to search engines that will chug away until they find what you and your students are looking for:

```
http://www.openmarket.com/info/internet-index/
http://nearnet.gnn.com/wic/newrescat.toc.html
http://www.yahoo.com/
```

Trouble on the Highway

When you have a room full of wide-eyed fifth-graders at 2:30 p.m. on a Friday afternoon — that's when things will fail. (This situation is the educator's corollary of Murphy's Law.) The kinds of errors you see, and how you handle them, depend mostly on your Web browser software. *Netscape Navigator*, and the other "big guys," give you lots of feedback when problems arise; other Web browsers sometimes leave you hanging.

Following is a short list of the most common problems that you and your students might encounter and what you can do about them:

Problem/Message	Remedy
"The server may be down or unreachable"	It's busy (so wait) or it's off-line for maintenance (so wait some more).
"404 not found"	Check your URL; the cause is usually a typo or a link that's moved or evaporated.
"The server does not have a DNS entry"	Check your URL, another typing mistake.
"Broken pictures" (a fragmented icon that represents where a picture should be)	Reload the image or Web page.

Sometimes your browser just freezes and doesn't seem to be doing anything at all. Most of the time, you can press ⌘+. (that is, press the ⌘ key and the period key) or Ctrl+. (that is, the Ctrl key and the period key) to stop the execution of a browser command. With most browsers, you can check the bottom of the active window for a message that tells you what request the browser has made. The big chill sometimes happens when the messages read as follows:

- ✔ Looking up a host (The farther away the host, the longer it's likely to take to find it.)

- ✔ Contacting host (Your browser is awaiting access; sometimes the requested server is too busy.)

- ✔ Host contacted. Waiting for reply. (The host computer knows you're there, but you're in a queue awaiting access.)

- ✔ Transferring data (Moving the text or images from the host to your computer; this stage can take a *long* time if the Web page features large graphics or lots of text.)

How to Get Fewer Gray Hairs

Here are some points to ponder that can save you loads of time (and a few gray hairs):

- ✔ If images are coming in too slowly, deselect Options⇨Auto Load Images. This action gives you a text-only interface. After you've reached a page that you'd like to examine more closely, click the Reload button (⌘+R) to see the Web page's graphics.

✔ If at first you don't succeed . . . sometimes the third time's the charm. WWW pages can be very busy.

✔ Remember that you can copy, print, or save the text and graphics that are displayed on any WWW page.

✔ *Bookmark files* (files that allow you to keep a running list of your favorite WWW sites — read more about these in Chapter 8) can quickly fill up with lots of dead-end links. Determine a policy and/or organizational method for storing your Web bookmarks and share the policy with your students.

You've seen that surfing the Web is really not much more than pointing and clicking on words and pictures. It's easy — no kidding! I've had great success with surfers from my neighbor's first-grader to my friend's grandmother. My dad spent several hours pointing and clicking his way to an expanded stock portfolio. Once your students understand the metaphor of a point-and-click "hot linked" environment, you can shift their focus to the more important task of evaluating the Net's wealth of information and toward developing strategies for capturing and using the information that they've found. In the next chapter, I get you started on the road to organizing your soon-to-be humongous list of Web sites.

Navigate with *CyberFinder*

CyberFinder (a program for Macs that I've included on the CD) provides a fast and easy way to navigate the Internet. *CyberFinder* is really a control panel that lets you use a menu to create bookmarks pointing to your favorite spots on the Internet. All you need to do is double-click a *CyberFinder* bookmark; *CyberFinder* then launches the appropriate application and takes you where you want to go. With *CyberFinder* you can even use a special *hot key* to jump to Net sites from within any application! And be sure to take advantage of *CyberFinder* as a bookmark manager, too.

Chapter 8

Hotlists and Bookmarks

. . . .

In This Chapter

▶ Building your hotlists

▶ Getting organized

▶ Surfing cool links courtesy of WWWFT

. . . .

*I*t's confession time. I am a supreme pack rat. Recently, I moved from one house to another and faced the daunting task of rediscovering all the old wonders in my closets, basement, attic, and garage. I realized that things had gotten out of hand when I discovered boxes of purple ditto masters (don't you just *love* those!) and a set of class rolls from my first teaching assignment more than 15 years ago. I've kept all this stuff because I'm afraid that someday I may need it.

If you're not careful, you'll become a Net pack rat, randomly printing thousands of copies of Web pages on your printer for future reference. Not only is this practice not good for our unsuspecting tree friends, but it compounds an already overwhelming paperwork load that we educators deal with. Luckily, most Web browsers offer tools called *bookmarks* that will help you store and organize the addresses (URLs) of your (and your students') favorite places.

Saving Your Hotlists/Bookmarks

You've gone Net-surfing and discovered a great resource for your students. Sooner or later, you'll have the need to return to the site for information, and you'd like to make that return as easy as possible. With Web browsers, you've got four choices:

✔ Print the page

✔ Save the Web page image to disk

✔ Copy down the URL (complete with slashes, dashes, and periods)

✔ Save the site as a bookmark

Folks, this one should be a no-brainer. Save the trees, valuable disk space, and carpal tunnel syndrome by choosing the fourth option — make a bookmark.

Saving the cool stuff

Your first time on the Web, you're likely to go bananas, surfing from page to page and marveling at all the great information and cool graphics you see. Forgetting where you've been is very easy. Luckily, *Netscape* and other browsers have an easy way to remember where you've been. It's called a *bookmark*. I'm going to use *Netscape Navigator* for my demos (so see Chapter 7 if you want to find out how to get this software!).

Setting a bookmark is easy:

1. **Surf to the Web page that you want to save.**

2. **Choose Bookmark▷Add Bookmark (⌘-D).**

Your favorite URLs are added to the list that appears in your Bookmark menu on your menu bar in the order that you enter them. Your bookmark list waits there patiently until needed. Using bookmarks, you can "resurf" a Web page, Gopher address, or FTP site by choosing that location directly from the Bookmark menu. Figure 8-1 shows what my Bookmark menu looks like. You guessed it: my Bookmark menu is just as packed as my basement and attic (but my Bookmark menu is much more organized)!

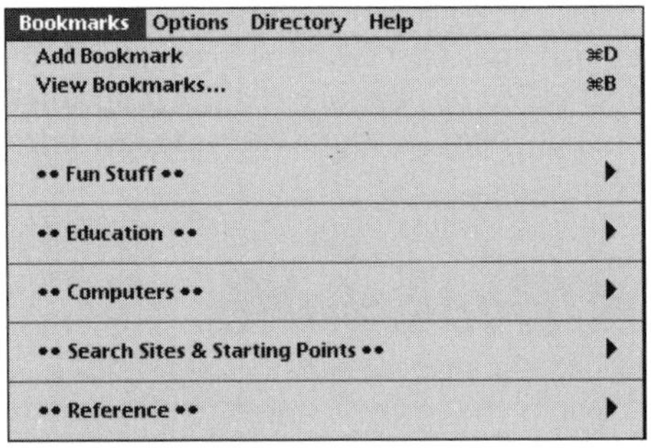

Figure 8-1:
Use
Bookmarks
to create
instant links
to your
favorite
Web pages.

Bookmarks	Options	Directory	Help	
Add Bookmark				⌘D
View Bookmarks...				⌘B
•• Fun Stuff ••				▶
•• Education ••				▶
•• Computers ••				▶
•• Search Sites & Starting Points ••				▶
•• Reference ••				▶

Organizing bookmarks

You can add, delete, and reorganize your bookmarks by choosing Bookmark▷View Bookmarks (⌘-B). Figure 8-2 shows the View Bookmarks dialog box. Using the commands on this screen, you can organize your bookmarks by topic, add spacers (called *separators* or *dividers*), and even export your bookmark list to your favorite word processor for inclusion in school newsletters and student assignments.

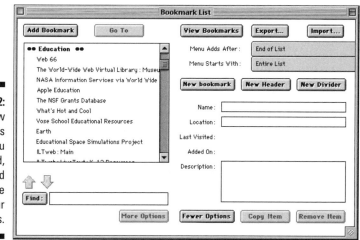

Figure 8-2:
View
Bookmarks
allows you
to add,
delete, and
organize
your
bookmarks.

Before you can say "Sloppy Joe," you'll have a hundred or so WWW sites in your bookmark files. Before you know it, your bookmark files will be information chaos. Think about how you'll organize your bookmarks before you save too many of them. Doing so will save you lots of time later!

Creating and Organizing Hotlists

If you take a look at *The World Wide Web For Teachers CD-ROM* that is included with this book, you'll see that I've provided a bunch of documents called hotlist pages. *A hotlist page* is a specially created Web page that features a collection of links to Internet resources that appear in Web-page format. The disc contains hotlists for every Web address in this book. (You're most welcome!) Here's how I created these hotlist files.

1. **I surfed the Net and found some of my favorite pages.**

2. **I cut and pasted each URL (Net address) into my word processor.**

   (You could also use your Macintosh or Windows Notepad.) I could have written each address down, but I'm much too lazy for that!

3. **I added HTML codes to the links and formatted the page by using my word processor and some HTML codes that you'll learn about later in this book.**

   (I could also have used *Adobe PageMill, WebWeaver,* or some other Web-creator program.)

4. **I saved the file of links to a disk in my Macintosh with a filename ending in *.htm* (so that PCs running Windows 3.11 or earlier, machines that**

read only three-character extensions, could read the file). You can find
the file called `main.htm` on *The World Wide Web For Teachers CD-ROM*
in the *edweb* folder.

After I went through these fairly simple steps, I realized that I could make things
even easier. Because *Navigator* allows you to *export* (copy data from within one
program for use in another program) easily, I could streamline the process by
merely adding my favorite pages to my bookmarks and exporting the bookmarks to be read by my word processor.

To create your own hotlist pages (the easy way), do the following:

1. **Launch the Web browser by double-clicking the *Netscape Navigator*
   icon.**

2. **Choose B̲ookmarks⇨V̲iew Bookmarks (⌘-B).**

   The Bookmark List window appears.

3. **Click the Export button.**

   Navigator will convert the data into standard (ASCII) text and ready them
   for saving on your disk drive.

4. **Save the exported file to your hard disk or a floppy by naming the file
   and selecting a destination in the Save dialog box.**

5. **Open the file with your favorite word-processor program (or a Web-page-
   creator program like *PageMill* or *WebWeaver*) and edit the URLs, drop-
   ping all the ones you don't want to keep or share and adding more URLs,
   if necessary.**

6. **After you've edited the URLs, save the file as a *text* file using the format**
   `filename.htm` **(DOS, Windows, Windows 95) or** `filename.html`
   (Macintosh).

To use your newly created hotlists, choose F̲ile⇨O̲pen (⌘-O), and the file opens
just like other Web pages on the Net. The list displayed provides a sort of
customized table of contents of links that can be accessed with a simple mouse
click. Figure 8-3 shows you an example of what this exported and renamed file
might look like.

These "customized local Web pages" (hotlists) are very handy for offering
topically organized menu pages for students. You might, for example, want to
export and edit a hotlist to create a specialized list of bookmarks for your media
center or a hotlist specifically targeted toward investigations in science.

You can also use Export to save your hotlists to floppy disks to share with other
teachers. Sending those exported files over the Internet is also easy. Make it a
point to ask your teacher-friends around the Net to share their hotlists, and
you'll soon have useful links a-plenty!

Figure 8-3:
Export your
bookmarks
and then
save them
as HTML
files to
create quick
and easy
menus.

Hotlists on the Disc

Hotlists are a great way to catalog the hundreds of Web addresses you're bound to collect. Throughout the Web, you and your students will surf to hundreds of home pages that feature links to thousands of Internet resources. Keeping your own hotlists is a great way to organize strategically in support of your curriculum.

On your copy of *The World Wide Web For Teachers CD-ROM* are some hotlists that I've put together for you. To use these hotlists, simply launch your Web browser (such as the AOL browser) and use File⇨Open (⌘-O) to see them. After the links are loaded, they are "live." Every Web link mentioned in this text was placed, by my wonderful hotlink-making elves, on one of the customized hotlist pages found on the disc.

Imagine the Possibilities!

Now that you know how to create your own bookmarks, you can use this strategy to build a library of URLs organized by subject area, grade level, topic, or whatever you can dream up. Choose a topic that your students will be studying in about two weeks and build a customized bookmark file containing URLs that will be useful in expanding or enhancing the study of the topic. Try handing off the bookmark file to your students for their use as a starting point in their journey on the Web. You'll quickly see that a little bit of bookmarking can save hours of aimless surfing. Here are a few more ideas for using bookmarks to support or enrich your curriculum:

✔ As an alternative to a book report

✔ As a customized presentation tool for presenting information for a report

✔ As a "use these links only" tool to discourage access to content that may be inappropriate for your classroom

✔ As a tool to help younger Net-surfers navigate

✔ As a template for an Internet staff-development session

✔ As a template for a scavenger hunt (you supply the headings and subject areas; they supply the links)

✔ As a portal to your own WWW yearbook (You'll learn later that you can actually have your students create their own Web pages and then link them all together.) (**Note:** Lots of server space is required for this!)

Pain in the bookmarks?

You and your students will quickly discover that the task of organizing hundreds (or thousands) of bookmarks is a major one. What the world really needs is bookmark organization software that adds order to this chaos in a way that's user-friendly and flexible enough for each teacher's needs.

The Netscape Communications folks, the same good folks who brought you the *Netscape* browser are thinking ahead. Their bookmark organizational product, called *SmartMarks* (at press time, only available for PCs running Windows), is a step in the right direction. The program allows users to organize their favorite Web sites into a flexible hierarchy of folders (subdirectories) and has smart agents that keep tabs on your links and help you to keep the links current. In addition, *SmartMarks* users can choose to receive "digital coupons" for goods and services offered through Web sites around the world. Look for even more enhancements of bookmark organizational software, including versions for your Macintosh, in the near future.

For more information on *SmartMarks*, visit Netscape's home page at http://www.netscape.com.

Chapter 9

The Advanced Class

● ●

In This Chapter

▶ Going Gophering

▶ Finding newsgroups with your browser

▶ Mailing with the browser

▶ Discovering other Net resources

● ●

*W*hen I was around 13 years old, my grandfather gave me my first Swiss Army knife. He explained that the knife would do just about everything from opening cans to whittling sticks. No self-respecting kid should be without one. (I later retired the knife after I cut myself slicing burned marshmallows on a Scout trip.)

Today's Web browser is the modern-day electronic equivalent of a Swiss Army knife. The modern Web browser does just about everything related to the Internet, and all those Web-surfing tools are built into one amazing program.

In the next few sections, I give you a glimpse into how the Swiss Army knife works to locate documents, transfer files, send e-mail, and connect to remote computers. All these processes might sound complicated, but they're not. Just a mouse-click in the right place, and you and your students are in business!

Gopher Your Browser

There are rodents hiding in your browser. Don't panic, though. These rodents aren't in violation of your school's "no hairy creatures in the classroom" rule. *Gopher* is the name given to one type of Internet resource that provides you with hierarchical menus of documents and directories. You and your students can search Gopher servers worldwide by using your browser.

To access Gopherspace, surf to a site that has Gopher items in the menu (see Figure 9-1) and click the Gopher links. (Remember, Mac users, you'll find a stand-alone Gopher search tool called *TurboGopher* on the CD.) Gopher links are usually shown as hierarchical files and folders (subdirectories). To navigate, simply position your mouse on the directory of choice and double-click. Each double-click will take you deeper into the Gopher server's files. The ultimate goal of a Gopher search is usually a text document (but your goal can also be graphics, sounds, or movie files) that can be copied and pasted into your favorite word processor or saved to your disk drive.

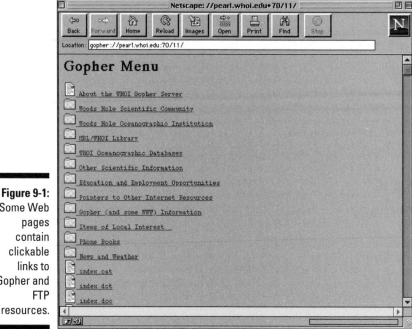

Figure 9-1:
Some Web pages contain clickable links to Gopher and FTP resources.

FTP and Me

Gopher's relative, FTP (File Transfer Protocol), allows you to transfer actual files (programs, graphics, sounds, movies, and so on) from remote computers (*hosts*) to your computer with the click of a mouse. To access FTP, simply double-click the FTP links you see on many Web pages. FTP files display much like Gopher files but feature icons that look like little disks or have filenames that suggest a program instead of a text file. (See Figure 9-2.) Double-clicking begins the file transfer process, and the progress of the transfer is shown on your browser's status bar (located at the bottom of the screen).

After the file is saved on your hard drive, you can use the program as if you'd loaded it yourself from an installer disk. One word to the wise, however: files on the Net are *not* generally certified as "virus-free." It's up to you to set an example for your students by using a virus-screening program, such as *Virex* or *Norton Anti-Virus,* on all files downloaded from the Net. (Find out more about viruses and virus protection in *The Internet For Teachers,* IDG Books Worldwide, Inc.)

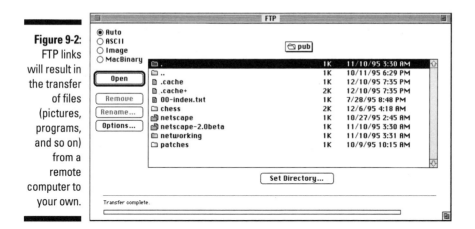

Figure 9-2:
FTP links will result in the transfer of files (pictures, programs, and so on) from a remote computer to your own.

Newsgroups and Browsers

Netscape's Navigator browser contains a fully-featured newsreader that'll have you and your students scanning the information on the Net in no time. Most other browsers have really weak newsreader capabilities — yet another reason to go with *Netscape!* (Remember, you can also use AOL to access newsgroups or search the Net for stand-alone newsreader programs.)

Reading newsgroups begins with telling *Netscape Navigator* where to get your news. Choose Options⇨Preferences and select Mail and News from the dialog box near the top of the window. Enter the domain name of your Internet provider's newsserver in the box marked "News (NNTP) Server." Your domain newsserver probably has a name similar to news.edunet.edu. (If you haven't gotten your copy of *Netscape Navigator*, see Chapter 7.)

To read a newsgroup, either choose Directory⇨Go To Newsgroups and *subscribe to* (request information from) newsgroups that you'd like to read or type in the URL of a known newsgroup. Newsgroups' URLs typically look like this:

```
news:comp.PowerMac.statistics
```

After you've subscribed to a newsgroup, use *Netscape's* browser to read the articles contained in the newsgroup by simply double-clicking the newsgroup's name. Figure 9-3 shows what a popular education newsgroup's window may look like.

Please, Mr. Postman

One of the things that Web browsers don't do well is handle e-mail. This situation probably developed because so many terrific mail programs are out there already; and all the bells and whistles associated with those existing

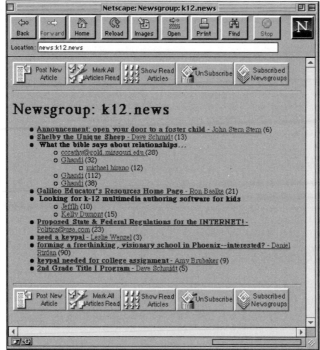

Figure 9-3:
The K-12
elementary
newsgroup
features lots
of ideas and
information
related to
elementary
education.

programs would just make the Web browser so fat that it wouldn't fit in your school's Macintosh or Intel-based computers with only 2MB of memory. (You are going to buy more memory, aren't you?) Luckily, both browsers and computers are coming with more memory these days.

If you are using *Netscape Navigator* (see Chapter 7 for details), make sure to visit *Netscape's* Options⇨Preferences area and set up your mail address and other important information.

The mail functions in *Netscape* are primarily designed to make it easy for you to share your favorite URLs (Net resource addresses) with your friends. For example, you surf to a great resource for artwork, such as San Francisco's Exploratorium (http://www.exploratorium.edu) and want to send the URL to a friend. Simply choose File⇨Mail Document, fill in the form (the URL will already copy itself into your mail message), and click the Send button. Zip — there goes your message across the Net. Pretty soon your mailbox will fill with dozens of these URLs from your Web-surfing friends all over the world. (That's how most of the URLs in this book were found!) Figure 9-4 shows what *Netscape's* Mail Document window looks like. Look closely at the URL in the window; this URL is the address of a great education resource!

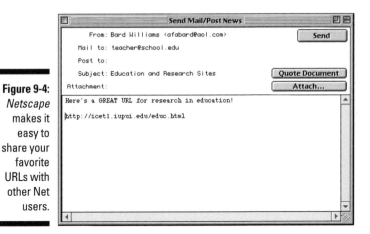

Figure 9-4:
Netscape
makes it
easy to
share your
favorite
URLs with
other Net
users.

The current version of *Netscape Navigator* is not designed to receive mail, so you still have to seek out *Eudora*, or your favorite mail program, to read all those URL messages that folks keep sending you. Future versions will feature full mail access.

Other Net Resources

Currently, most Web browsers don't support live chat on the Internet. To chat live, you have to log on to an online service or use one of several *Internet Relay Chat (IRC)* programs, such as *Homer* or *ircle*, available at Internet sites everywhere.

Other Net resources like *Finger* (a way to locate other Net users) and *telnet* (a way to log on to other's computers as a remote terminal) are either not supported or are poorly supported by Web browsers. To use these resources, it's generally better to use another Internet program like *Finger* or *NCSA telnet*, available at sites around the Net. (One good source for programs such as these is `ftp://ftp.ncsa.uiuc.edu` in the `/pub` directory.)

For lots more information on obtaining other Net tools, including WAIS, telnet, *Finger*, and *IRC*, grab a copy of *The Internet For Teachers* (IDG Books Worldwide, Inc.) at your bookstore.

As you can see, you'll find that your Web browser may be the only software tool that you and your students need in order to get the most out of the Internet. As browsers become more sophisticated, so will what can be accomplished with them. Your homework for tonight — find a Web page that offers files available for download (FTP) and transfer a file to your computer. (Don't forget to check for viruses!)

Chapter 10

Web to the Future

*E*ver taken time to ponder what life will be like in the classroom of tomorrow? Will you look out at a classroom of precious second graders (all wearing multicolored virtual-reality helmets hooked together by infrared signals) and wonder what country/planet/data bank they're exploring today? (They're smiling about something!) The World Wide Web and the Internet could be the vehicle that'll make this possible.

A quick glance at the video-game market might tell us what's in store for education. Game manufacturers are creating faster, more user-friendly hardware and more visually stimulating software; and experimentation has already begun with alternate input and output devices. Will the uniform of tomorrow's schools be "Net-ready" clothing — complete with motion sensors, network interfaces, and (of course) the obligatory brand-name logo. Will future students purchase cyberjeans made by Apple Computer?

Kick back and let your imagination wander as you browse through the following pages that explore some of the innovations related to the Net and the Web that are available today. Then go hug a good book.

Total Web Integration

There is already much discussion about whether Internet resources can replace textbooks. Of course, "they" said that about audiotapes, videodiscs, and computers, too, and it didn't happen — yet. The next generation of textbooks will probably feature Internet addresses in the sidebars of student and teacher texts, along with carefully constructed cyberjourney activities that offer up-to-the-second information, via the Internet, about the curriculum concept or skill being explored.

Content delivery via the Web has already begun. Companies like the forward-thinking American Cybercasting (http://www.americast.com/K12), CNN (http://www.cnn.com), and others have already begun to develop specific objective-linked activities that students can explore while online. These activities are designed, for the most part, to complement and supplement, not replace, more traditional classroom activities.

The advantages of curriculum delivery via telecommunications are obvious. Information can be presented in a just-in-time fashion, and Web pages can be easily customized for schools, classrooms, and even individual learners. The major disadvantage is still that we are far from the point where every student has easy access to Internet resources. Access is the one issue that could really slow the timeline for information exploration by students.

Web 3-D

Never underestimate the creativity of fellow humans. I'll be willing to wager that, at some time in your life, you could be seen donning a pair of paper 3-D glasses; you know, those silly one-eye red, one-eye green things. Let me guess: you were probably viewing some really cheesy sci-fi or horror movie (the ones with the ghoul reaching out and tapping you on the head with a ten-foot sword), looking at a comic book, or maybe you were experiencing a multimedia extravaganza at some Disney theme park. Viewing two-dimensional things in three dimensions is neat, but those glasses made folks look silly (and sometimes the effects weren't very stunning at all). Enter VRML.

VRML stands for Virtual Reality Modeling Language, a new standard on the Web that will let you to create an environment that users can explore, via the Internet, in three dimensions. Soon Net-surfers will be able to walk down the halls of the Louvre, turning to look at any picture or sculpture they desire, or take a tour of the solar system with planets whizzing past them. Because no nerdy bicolor glasses are used, the 3-D effect is, well, limited to the two dimensions of your screen. The overall effect is kind of like peering into a 3-D window (all you *Doom* or *Marathon* players out there know exactly what I'm talking about). Luckily, the speed with which the information is transmitted doesn't allow flying bullets — yet.

The VRML language was created by Mark Pesce (http://hyperreal.com/~mpesce/) who later ended up in a partnership with Tony Parisi (a browser-wiz) and the "Father of the Web," Tim Berners-Lee (who created the original HTML). This team of cyberrangers is currently busy working on ways to make VRML available to more computer users.

If you and your students are ready for 3-D, in-your-face, Web action, try surfing to Silicon Graphics (the developer of the *WebSpace* 3-D VRML browser) at `http://www.sgi.com/Products/WebFORCE/WebSpace` (see Figure 10-1). A competing product, called *WorldView,* is under development at `ftp://tcc.net.org` or `http://www.intervista.com/worldview.html`. By the time that you read this, both *WebSpace* and *WorldView* should be available for Windows 3.1, Macintosh, UNIX, and Windows NT machines.

Figure 10-1:
A new 3-D Web tool, called *WebSpace*, allows users to explore a new dimension in information access.

Way Ahead Stuff

Nobody can really predict what'll happen with technology. The creativity of the human mind seems unlimited (Yes, someday that roustabout in your third period class will own a $2 billion company!), and outside forces, such as government initiatives and special interest groups, may alter the path of the use and implementation of technology in society (and schools) with the stroke of a pen. This section gives you a little teaser about a few initiatives that are right around the corner. These initiatives deal with technologies that may have a profound impact on the way that you teach and learn.

Don't wear the harvest gold bathrobe!

Current software and hardware allow you to do much more than just *type* to your friends. With technology like *CU-SEE-ME*, you can actually see (in close-to-real time) the person to whom you're connected. The message? Don't wear the harvest gold bathrobe (you know, the one that's been your friend since 1972) while you're surfing! (I'm going to use a movie star's picture that I've cut out of the latest magazine. It'll be much more pleasing.)

The hardware for live Internet videoconferencing requires a camera (such as the really cool looking "eyeball camera" QuickCam by Connectix), a computer, special software (some of which is available free on the Net — the most common is *CU-SEE-ME*), and a high-speed connection (such as an ISDN or T-1 line).

Of course, Internet videoconferencing technology isn't perfect. Unless your connection is a very high-speed line, the images make everyone look like a modern-day Max Headroom. As the technology improves, however, your students should be able to converse live with authors, engineers, politicians, and anyone else who can click a mouse.

Talk shows online

Audio can also be transmitted on the Internet. Plenty of sites currently offer sound files, digitized by their creators, that can be *downloaded* (copied) to your computer for your listening pleasure. Recent advances in file compression make the downloading of those files much less painful than it once was.

Live audio (including *telephony* — using your computer as a telephone) is also coming to the Net. While Ma Bell shouldn't get too nervous, it looks as if real-time audio quality will continue to improve, and people will be turning to their computer screens for less-expensive conversations.

Hot java in the teachers' lounge?

Next time you grab a quick cup of java in the teachers' lounge, you may be surfing the Net. One of the hottest Web browsers that promises 3-D interactive access was recently birthed at Sun Microsystems. Dubbed *Hot Java,* this browser reads the Java language, which can instruct objects (such as graphics or text) to jump, rotate, wiggle, and make lots of other strange movements. Java-ready browsers, such as Netscape's upcoming version of *Navigator,* will search for the Java code when you enter a Web site and then download the Java code to your computer before springing screen objects to life. The upside is that the images that you see on your browser can now be animated. The downside is that the language is fairly complex. More job security for Webmasters and (again, on the downside) the code is large, meaning potentially long download times. Whether the download time for the *Hot Java* graphics will be short enough to hold the attention of hormonally challenged middle schoolers remains to be seen.

Everybody's on the Net

If the number of people with Internet access continues to grow at the current rate, everybody on the planet will be online within ten years. Will you and your students be some of the first? (Nudge, nudge.)

In Part III of this book, I take you on a step-by-step journey to create your own WWW page. Nowadays, almost everyone is a personal Web publisher. (Those who aren't, want to be!) The ten-year-old down the street is just as likely to have her own Web presence as a Fortune 500 company is. All of the major online services (AOL, CompuServe, e-World, Microsoft Network, and Prodigy) are making personal Web publishing easier with built-in graphical tools that allow subscribers to create their own simple Web pages.

TECHNO TERMS

Elvis lives! (On the Net)

Remember being amazed when wristwatches began to store telephone numbers and VCRs (through VCR+) began to program themselves? Get ready to be amazed — again. The creative folks at the Voyager Company (`http://www.voyagerco.com`) now have a way for your Internet connection to talk to your computer's CD-ROM drive.

Imagine that your students are surfing the Net, looking for information about pop music, and they stumble upon a Web page from *Spin* magazine (a popular music publication). Scrolling down through the lists of clickable Internet links, they see Elvis. (Now you know where he's *really* been all these years.) One click and their screen flashes to lots of great information about The King, and a flashing button on the screen reads "Don't Be Cruel" (an admonition perfect for students). Your students click the button, and suddenly the room is instantly filled with the sounds of The King himself — in stereo. Amazing, huh?

The King's croonings come from a CD (one that you've sneaked into the CD-ROM drive of your computer beforehand) that was activated by a Web browser helper application called *CDLink*. The folks at Voyager believe that the possibilities of *CDLink* are wonderful. Now Web sites can interact with multimedia CD-ROMs to bring life to the two-dimensional Web. Educators can author Web pages that serve as a front end for a myriad of multimedia CD-ROM-based data. So now you know: Elvis is alive and well — on the Internet.

Famous Last Words

Will the Internet ever replace the textbook? Probably not in our lifetime. I do believe that telecommunications skills (information management, search and retrieval strategies, and the evaluation of data sources) will become as essential as the three Rs. In view of the latest evolution of Internet-access tools, I'd say that it's a safe bet that you'll see the integration of Internet and other telecommunications methods spread like wildfire (and you'll find that this information access will become less expensive, less time-consuming, less difficult, and more fun!).

Part III
Creating Your Own Web Page

The 5th Wave   By Rich Tennant

In this part . . .

Read this part when you're ready to make the move from information consumer to information producer. I help you whip up a dandy Web page for yourself, or for your school, in a cyber-flash. You'll also find tips on designing Web pages and find out what to do when you're ready to publish your fabulous Web creation to the Internet.

Chapter 11

Anatomy of a Web Site

· ·

In This Chapter

▶ Dissecting the Web

▶ Going hier

▶ Thinking about content

· ·

*W*alk around your school and look at the keyboards attached to the computers on people's desks. If the home-row keys are dark and look dirty, you've just found out a very important thing about the user: He or she reads a newspaper. Newspapers would be much better if their ink didn't magically jump from the paper onto your computer keyboards. When I get to school (before the rooster crows), I like to take a second to catch up on education and technology news from the local paper. Next, I move to answer the zillions of e-mail messages that spontaneously generate in my mailbox between 11 p.m. the previous evening and rooster time. Oops. More newsprint ink on the keyboard. Sigh. Wait. There *is* a point to this story, I promise!

If you glance at the front page of your daily newspaper, you see that it consists of the name of the paper (the masthead), various "hot" stories with headlines of different sizes, and lots of references to what's inside.

A Web site is just like its distant cousin, the newspaper. The first page (screens in Web space are called *pages*) that you see when you enter a Web site gives you information about the location of the server (school name, company name, and the like — a virtual masthead) and just enough information to tickle your fancy ("teasers"); it then points you to other pages (*links*). This chapter leads you though a brief look at the components that make up a Web site. Be sure to wash your hands before using your keyboard!

Dissecting a Web Site

A Web *site* is basically all the text, graphics, sounds, hypertext links, and other resources that make up your presence on the World Wide Web. A Web site is made up of three basic components:

- ✔ A home page (the topmost page in your site)
- ✔ Local and remotely stored pages linked to your home page
- ✔ Supporting content (documents, images, and sounds)

In the following sections, I'll hold a "faculty meeting" to brief you on how these components work together. Reading these pages can give you a great idea of how Web pages are structured, and these pages also give you several options for creating your own Web site.

Going home

A *home page* is the first page that users see when they enter your Web site. Because it sets the tone for the organization and content in your site, careful planning of your home page is important. First impressions, after all, *are* important.

Figure 11-1 shows an example of a home page created by yours truly. Visit the real-time version at `http://www.mindspring.com/~bardw/bard.html`.

Home pages usually contain a *header* (like a newspaper's masthead) that gives the name or affiliation of the creator. These electronic mastheads can be as simple as text, as in the home page of Maynard High School in Massachusetts (`http://www.ultranet.com/~maynard/mhs.html`) shown in Figure 11-2.

Or home pages can be as complex as a graphic containing "hot" areas where users can click and be whisked away to other pages. Figure 11-3 shows a home page from the Los Angeles Unified School District (`http://lausd.k12.ca.us/`) — one of the better examples of district-level Web pages to pop up on the Web. The *images* (that's Netspeak for picture) at the top of the page are "live" — clicking different parts of the images takes you to other pages or other Web sites.

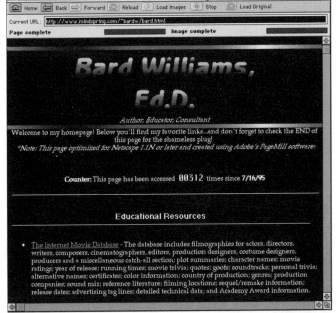

Figure 11-1:
A home page is the topmost page in a Web site.

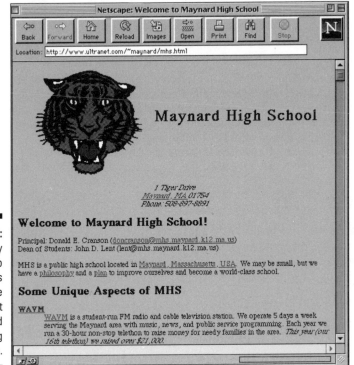

Figure 11-2:
Many school Web pages feature simple text headers and roaring mascots.

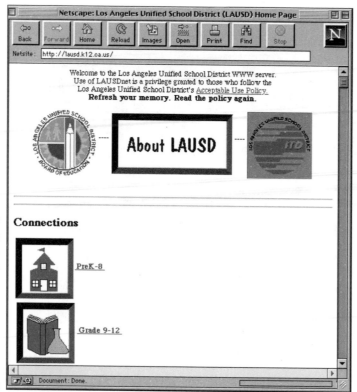

Figure 11-3:
Some Web
pages
contain
clickable
graphics
that sweep
you away to
new places
to explore.

Don't be too intimidated by fancy graphics and artwork, though. Your school or district can begin with a much simpler page and work its way up. Note that *students* are very often the perfect Webmasters at education sites. First, the students are much more comfortable with the technology (in general); and second, they'll never turn down a challenge (especially when you explain that your Web page can be seen by millions of people).

Links-R-Us

Most of the time, a home page contains text that, when clicked with a mouse, performs one of several magical tricks. In Netspeak, we refer to clickable text (sometimes graphics are clickable, too) as *links* or, more correctly, *hypertext links*. Clicking on a text or graphic link might do one of the following:

- ✔ Transport you to other Web pages at the same site
- ✔ Zip you along to other Web pages at different sites

🖙 Jump your cursor to another place on the same page

🖙 Cause a file to be downloaded (copied) from the Web site to your computer

🖙 Link you to another Internet resource such as mail, FTP, newsgroups, or Gopher sites

The ability to create your own links easily gives you and your students the power to create everything from a simple list of "favorite sites" to a complex mini-Web of interconnected pages.

Are You Linear, Hierarchical, or Web Crazy?

Sorry for the personal question. What I'm asking is if you'd like to design a Web site that is *linear*, one that is arranged in a more complex *hierarchy*, or one that has the highly complex *Web* arrangement. The design style you choose is based largely upon what type of content you intend to deliver and your expertise in designing Web pages.

Going straight

The easiest Web page organization is to "go straight," that is, create a linear design. Linear designs are like books. You begin with the title page (your home page), and links take you from your home page to page 2, from page 2 to page 3, from page 3 to page 4, and so on.

Figure 11-4:
Linear Web sites are designed like books — access is sequential.

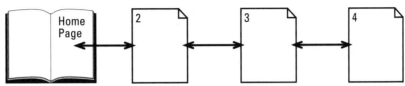

Linear design is perfect if you are presenting a series of steps or tracking a process from start to finish. Linear organization makes sense when you're presenting a series of documents. Its simple design keeps users from clicking into never-never land. Good linear organization offers clickable buttons that allow users to select "next page," "previous page," or "back to home page" options.

Getting hier

Hierarchical structures are the most common Web-site designs. This design type looks kinda like your family tree. In hierarchical design, the home page serves as a contents page that branches to other pages that, in turn, branch to still other pages. Unlike linear design, hierarchical design provides more than one path that a user may take.

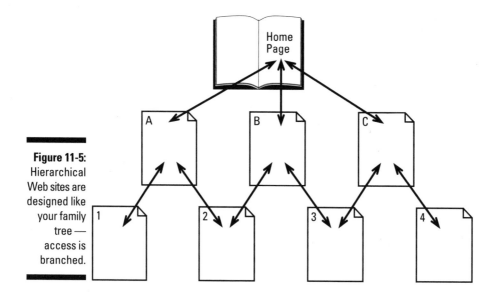

Figure 11-5: Hierarchical Web sites are designed like your family tree — access is branched.

The spider's choice

The most daring type of Web design allows users to jump (branch) from any point in a Web site to any other point in that site with the click of a mouse. With Web structure, your home page can take people to lots of different places; but no matter where each link takes them, they find multiple links to other pages, including back to your home page.

It's easy for educators to imagine the complexity of this design if we think of that *food web* that we drew in fifth grade; you know, the one where you start with the "bears," and students eventually connect virtually every living thing on the planet with their bear's food chain.

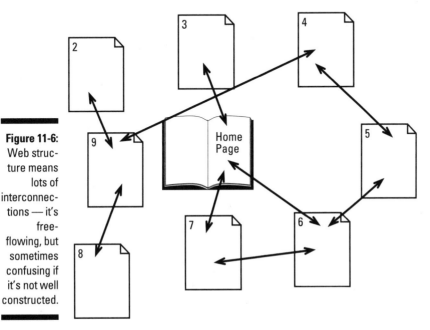

Figure 11-6:
Web struc-
ture means
lots of
interconnec-
tions — it's
free-
flowing, but
sometimes
confusing if
it's not well
constructed.

TIP

The Web itself, of course, is designed like the food web. If you choose to build very complex Web structures, giving your viewers lots of visual cues as to where they are and what they're seeing is a great idea. Using standard pointers such as "forward," "back," and "return to home page" on every page helps to keep folks from wandering endlessly in Cyberspace. For more information on Web design, check Chapter 13.

Form Follows Function

No matter how snazzy your Web site's design, if nothing is important, interesting, or particularly useful on your Web page, you're just "computing in the wind." It's a good idea to begin your discussion with what content you intend to offer to fellow Internet surfers.

Content on your Web page can take one of many forms. Here are some things that you might consider placing on your Web page:

- ✔ Documents (about your school, community, education in general; student writing, public-domain reference resources, and the like)
- ✔ Images (pictures of your school, community, students, mascot, football team — whatever — a WWW Yearbook!)
- ✔ Sounds ("Bueller? Anyone? Anyone?" — for the Ferris Bueller fans!)
- ✔ Downloadable movies (a visit with the principal?)
- ✔ Links to other interesting or useful sites (chosen by students and teachers)

In the next chapter, you can read about some helpful tips for weaving a Web page that everyone will be proud of.

Chapter 12

Planning Your School Web Site

● ●

In This Chapter

▶ Going for the goal

▶ Flowing charts

▶ Mining tools

● ●

*T*he time has come to move up the Internet food chain and become a Web producer instead of a Web consumer. Ready or not, the first steps follow.

If you're like most educators, you want to create a Web page for one of the following reasons:

✔ You can't find what you really need on everyone else's Web page, so you want to make your own

✔ You can't wait to see your school's name on its own billboard on the information superhighway

✔ Your administration said "make a Web page"

✔ You're steamed because more than 3,000 schools have already created Web pages, and you hate being behind

✔ Because it's there

 Before you can go further, pull together a committee of your peers and figure out *why* you want to create a Web page. Fact is, creating something useful takes a bit of time, and creating a Web home page requires that you find a place (an Internet provider) willing to host your new creation. All this means an investment of time and a bit of money, resources that are mighty scarce around most schools. Planning is critical to ensure time well spent in building a product that meets your goals. So what do you do first? Set goals, of course!

Set Your Goals

Creating a Web presence is not unlike deciding upon a slogan for a marketing campaign. Your Web page is your school's electronic greeting card and annual report, all rolled into one neat package. Obviously, you want your Web page to be the most friendly and most attractive home page that it can possibly be. Don't forget, though, that it is the *content* that makes your page something more than just another pretty electronic face.

Choosing content

Deciding the type of content that you would like to share really depends on three factors:

- The goals for the Web page
- Copyright-free resources that your school can collect and share
- What resources your school values

Your school's Web page can be designed to share information about your school and community, provide access to databases of text, graphics, movies and/or sound, provide a handy jumping off point to links that you and your students have collected, or any combination of all of the above!

If your school's goal in creating a Web page is to share new information, you should think about what *kinds* of new information you can access, or generate, that would be of interest to others. Be sure to think in terms of local *and* global information, because lots of people *not* from your hometown will be flocking to see your new Web page. While local items such as school calendars, local sports scores, and important phone numbers are helpful resources for your immediate community, you might consider posting student writing, newsletters, custom-built documents containing new information, or other resources for those of us who will be "virtual visitors" in your school.

The copyright monster

Beware of the copyright monster. You may be tempted to take advantage of the gigabytes of information that your school has on CD-ROM and/or floppy, but beware. Copyright laws most certainly extend to protect information that you've paid for from being shared free over the Internet. Be sure to check carefully with a vendor if you try to offer some commercial or shareware product through your site. Be careful with any art that you might use on your Web page, too.

Some starving artist likely worked hard to create those snazzy logos or nifty lines, and that artist deserves compensation (or at least a request for permission to use the artwork) before you release your page to the public. Large libraries of public-domain artwork for use on Web pages are available at most Web development sites. One of the largest collections can be found at `http://www.netscape.com/`, the home of *Netscape Navigator,* the quintessential Web browser. Check out Chapter 7 to see how you can get a free copy of *Netscape Navigator.*

Does anyone care?

The third thing to think about as you plan your Web site is what information your school values. That is, what information is important for both your local community and your external audiences, whether those audiences consist of global visitors or School Board members, local politicians, local businesses, or students dialing in from home. Remember: Your Web page is your calling card. First impressions are important. Make your Web page content-rich and visually magnetic — an easier task if you plan well.

Charting the Flow

Because Web sites can consist of lots of pages and resources linked together, it is important to plan where the links are and how they'll be connected before implementing your Web plan. Here's a great opportunity to use a flowchart or outline and show your students just how useful these tools are! Work with your students to create your outline by featuring major headings and subheadings and indicating whether pictures or other resources are present.

Next, get out the crayons or colored pencils. Have students create a *storyboard*, a sketch of the layout of the appearance of your home page and each of the sub-pages in your site. Use one sheet of paper per page; then tack the pages up on your classroom bulletin board and use yarn to connect the pages and show the links. This method is a handy way to create your Web site and move things around *before* you begin to write your pages.

Choosing a Tool

The last step in planning your Web page is to determine what tool you and your students will use to create your Web page. Your answer depends largely on your available time and resources.

Surf before you create!

Before you create your own Web page, be sure to allow plenty of time to browse other sites. Here are a few Web addresses that can serve as jumping off points to help you find your way to the thousands of schools (and other sites) that are on the World Wide Web:

`http://www.webcrawler.com/`	*enter "school" or "k-12" as a search term
`http://www.yahoo.com/education/`	*the Mother of All Link Catalogs
`http://web66.coled.umn.edu/`	*more school Web sites than you can imagine
`http://k12.cnidr.org:80/ janice_k12/k12menu.html`	*extremely well-connected Web site featuring the latest in Web research

Each of the above sites offers hundreds of links to school and district home pages for your surfing pleasure. Need an assignment for your students? Create a Web Site Evaluation Form and challenge your students to focus on the best-of-the-best.

There are basically three tools you can use to create a Web page:

- ✔ WYSIWYG editors — what you see is what you get
- ✔ Stand-alone "easy-paste" editors — paste HTML tags into text with the click of a mouse
- ✔ Word processors (with appropriate export utilities) — use your word processor to write code and then export it

Whether you're using a Macintosh or a PC running Windows, you can use any of the above tools. With students, I've found that the specific type of tool really doesn't matter, as long as you stick to one creation tool. All three methods are easy to learn, and you'll quickly be focusing on the content instead of the process as you instruct your students.

In the following sections, I share some suggestions (and reviews) of Web-creation tools. All these tools are available via FTP on the Internet. Some are shareware and carry fees, some are commercial, and some are freeware.

WYSIWYG editors

With WYSIWYG editors, you'll be able to get a good idea of what your Web page will look like without launching a Web browser or posting your page to the Net. WYSIWYG editors are great for learning how to use HTML. Although there are several WYSIWYG editors on the Net, two programs really stand out as "A students" in the world of WYSIWYG. One is called *PageMill* (by Adobe). *PageMill* is a quick-and-easy Web page layout and design program. A demo version of *PageMill* can be found on your *World Wide Web For Teachers CD-ROM*. The second, called *HTML Pro,* is a great tool for the high-end HTML programmer. Check these out at the following location:

```
http://www.ts.umu.se:80/~r2d2/shareware/htmlpro_htlp.html
```

HTML Pro displays two editable windows: a *source window* that shows the HTML code that you're entering and a *preview window* that shows a preview of what your page will look like. *HTML Pro* (shown on Figure 12-1) is an excellent tool for those just getting started with Web-page creation.

Cut-and-paste editors

Easy-paste editors allow users to easily insert *HTML tags* (commands), often by choosing them from a menu or a floating palette. One such editor is *Web Weaver*. Information about Web Weaver is available at the following spot:

```
http://www.potsdam.edu/Web.Weaver/About.html
```

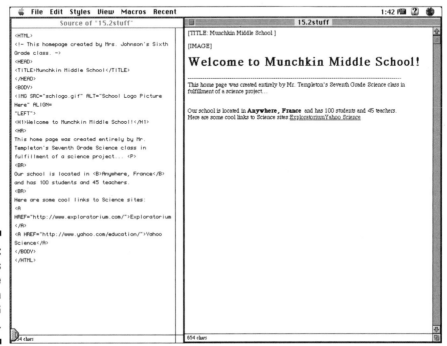

Figure 12-1:
HTML Pro is an example of a WYSIWYG editor.

This powerful application, written by Robert C. Best, offers an easy way to remember HTML tags. Simply highlight the text that you'd like to format and choose the proper tag from a floating menu. This application is included FREE on *The World Wide Web For Teachers CD-ROM*. Currently, *Web Weaver* runs on only Macintosh computers.

A second cut-and-paste editor is *HoTMetaL Pro*. Check the following site for the latest on this application:

```
http://www.sq.com/hmpro.html
```

HoTMetaL Pro is a feature-packed HTML editor that's available for Macintosh, PCs running Windows, and XWindow environments. Although *HoTMetaL Pro* has features such as a spelling checker and thesaurus, it is a memory hog and a bit tougher to learn than most other cut-and-paste editors are. Tags appear as graphics, however, making it less likely that you and your students will confuse tags with your text.

Word processor export utilities

A word processor is likely to be the tool that you use most on your computer. Word processors are also the tools most often available in schools. Lots of the vendors who make word processors have begun to incorporate Web-specific tools into their programs to make the job of creating a Web page easier. Most word processors and desktop publishing programs are more powerful than stand-alone Web-creation tools, but are less able to handle graphics and links. Most of the tools below are available for both Macintosh and those computers running Windows. Here are a few add-on tools that you can use with your word processor:

Claris XTND

ClarisWorks 4.0	Built-in
Web-It	`http://www.umich.edu/~demonner` `/Primer_main/primer_main.html`

PageMaker

WebSucker	`http://www.iii.net/users/mcohen/` `websucker.html`
Dave	`http://www.bucknell.edu/bucknellian` `/dave/`

Microsoft Word

ANT HTML	`http://www.w3.org/hypertext/WWW/Tools/Ant.html`
rtftohtml	`ftp://ftp.cray.com/src/WWWstuff/RTF/rtftohtml_overview.html` (Other tools are also available at this site.)
TIA	The Internet Assistant for Word for Windows (included on the CD).

Quark Xpress

BeyondPress	`http://www.astrobyte.com`

In general, content should be organized from simple to complex. Test your Web designs with a variety of users, with regard to age, computer expertise, and familiarity with the Net. Watch when and where they click, take good notes, and ask questions like, "What could I have done to make navigation easier?" Their answers will improve your Web page, and, most probably, prevent you from having any sort of social life until the Web page is revised.

Chapter 13

Elements of (Web) Style

. . . .

In This Chapter

▶ Webbing with style

▶ Touring the Web: best of the best

. . . .

*A*s you and your students create customized Web pages, think *style*. Style is the element that keeps the reader interested. Adhering to a style helps you write clearly and concisely. When you and your students face the challenge of creating your own Web page, you've got a terrific opportunity to reinforce good writing habits. Go ahead and dig out your copy of Strunk and White's *The Elements of Style* or grab a fantastic book called *If You Want to Write* by Brenda Euland. These books will help you remind students how to write understandably and concisely for a wide audience — and the Internet is the widest audience you can imagine. Web pages are *not* dissertations — have fun with this!

Cut to the Chase

As you create your Web pages, remember how people use the Internet. Typically, they hop around from place to place while glancing to see what's interesting or useful. They *browse*. As a Web-author, it's your responsibility to show browsers what's on your pages in as concise a manner as possible, so that when they zip to your site, they can see quickly what's in store for them. The top of your Web page should give the reader an idea of the content, a reference point (name of your school/location), and a brief picture of your site.

Here are a couple of tips you can use to make even the boldest browser smile:

- ✔ Use bullets for lists (student names, school activities, and the like) whenever you can. Bullets are terrific for browsers (the human kind) and are easy to create with browsers (the software kind).

- ✔ Put the important stuff first. People who design television commercials will tell you that they seek to capture your attention in the first five seconds. If they miss, you'll likely hit the channel button or dash off for a quick snack. Web pages should grab a reader's attention with important content (and with a bit of flash on the side).

Proofread

Imagine for a moment that your school decided to advertise by billboard. Think one step further: think of the implications of having a spelling error on the billboard. What would that say about your school (directly or indirectly)? What would the thousands who see it think?

Your Web page is the Mother of All Billboards. There is the potential for *millions* to view it. The caveat here is, no matter how hurried you are to publish your Web page, always proofread your documents before you release them. In fact, have *someone else* (students, parents, or both) read the documents and check for errors.

If your computer has text-to-speech capability, have your computer read the document to you. You'll undoubtedly find that a useful way to catch errors, and (given that no computer has truly mastered speech) the experience should be entertaining as well. I have to admit that I tried having my Macintosh read back a couple of chapters from this book. I found myself talking like the "Fred" voice for two days.

All emphasis is no emphasis

Remember when you created your first Macintosh or Windows document? Most beginning users have the philosophy that if you *have* 20 fonts in your computer, you should *use* each and every one of them on every document. And how about that boldface and outline style — it looks so cool you should use it everywhere, right?

Nope. Resist the urge to use any type of emphasis (**boldface**, *italics*, <u>special formatting</u>), or you'll ultimately lose the effect.

KISS

As in most writing, the KISS rule applies. Keeping it simple means that, in addition to being careful of how you use emphasis in your text, you don't overuse graphic elements or images (pictures). Remember that some users will view your Web page using very slow connections, so no matter how great it would look to have a color photo of each and every student in your class on your home page, don't do it. Having too many images places the viewer into "download limbo," and most viewers won't wait — they'll surf on to another site. Also remember that some users can't view images at all, so you should make sure to use the ALT (alternative image) tag for those using *Lynx* or some other text browser so that those "graphically challenged" folks will see words that describe what they are missing.

Bottom line? Say what you want to say as concisely as possible. When it comes to words on your home page, less is more.

Use the rule

As with anything you read, white space helps. HTML (the language that you'll use to create your Web pages) allows you easily to insert horizontal lines to separate graphics or text elements. Horizontal lines have lots of uses on Web pages, including:

- ✔ Spacing your text for readability
- ✔ Dividing categories or topics (useful when organizing hypertext links)
- ✔ Separating parts of your Web page (head, body, tail, and so forth)

Like other graphical elements, use rule lines with care. Too many lines distract the reader. If you want to get fancy, use an image of a rule (a colored or textured line graphic) instead of HTML's built-in rule line.

Ground yourself

Everyone likes compliments. Just as I try to write positive comments on student papers when students do exemplary work, I also make it a point to drop a note to the Webmaster whenever I encounter a really useful or graphically stunning Web page. Most good Web designers list their e-mail or snail-mail (sorry, postal service!) address on the bottom of their home page. The hypertext language (HTML) also has a command called *mailto* (see Chapter 14) that lets you dash off a note with the click of a mouse.

Although a return e-mail address is a good feature on your home page, letting the reader know where your school is geographically located is also important. The person accessing your Web page is just as likely to be from Australia as they are from Akron. An important piece of information for your school's home page should be text or a graphic that tells where your school is and a bit about it. **Remember:** Your home page is like an advertisement of good will to other global cybersurfers — road signs help on the information superhighway!

Pages with pizzazz

Your classroom is no doubt personalized. From your favorite posters (thank goodness for book clubs and computer shows!) to that burlap on the bulletin board, your classroom reflects your style. A Web page is no different. A great Web page reflects the style and personality of its creator or the school, business, or other entity that it represents. As you surf the Net and visit other Web sites, think about the personality each page conveys.

A visit to Ben DeLong's home page (`http://www-unix.oit.umass.edu:80/~bdelong/`) as shown in Figure 13-1, for example, shows an intelligent student with a playful personality. A glance at the home page for a commercial enterprise like Microsoft (`http://www.microsoft.com/`) presents a businesslike approach. Think about what's most appropriate for your Web page and create it. No matter how wacky your ideas, try them out. Just be sure that the medium doesn't overwhelm the message (that is, that your content isn't overshadowed by the flash of your page).

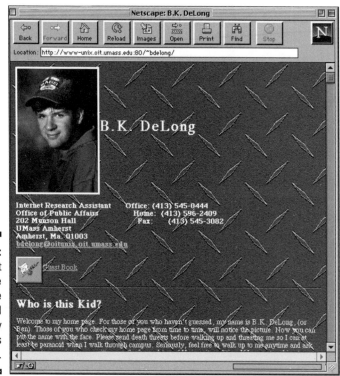

Figure 13-1:
A great Web page reflects the style and personality of its creator.

Strunk gets Webbed

You can't talk about style without mentioning the Father of All Style Manuals. That's right, Strunk, of *Elements of Style* fame, is on the Web at `http://www.columbia.edu/~svl2/strunk/`. You and your students can access all the tips and techniques without having to search for the dog-eared copy of the Strunk and White style manual in your school media center. The Web page was created according to HTML 3.0 standards (that's Cyberspeak for a new set of hypertext language commands readable by cutting-edge Web browsers such as recent versions of *Netscape*) and offers great examples of the enhanced formatting available with the newer HTML 3.0 command set (that's Cyberspeak for "it looks way cool").

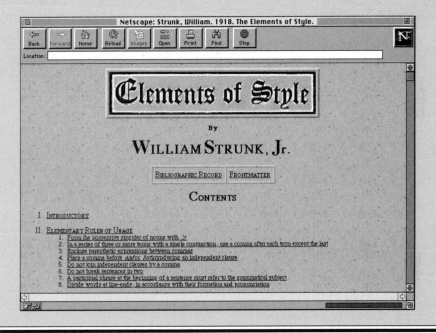

Go modular

As you think about the content that you'll provide via the Web, think about how the average user will access your page. Try to keep the pages' topic/content focused and make each page one complete thought or idea. Pages should stand alone, if at all possible. The key to modularity in Web page design is storyboarding. Check out Chapter 12 for more on designing modular Web pages.

Visual overkill

Be aware that lots of folks will view your Web pages; most folks will not have much time to spare, and many will have slow connections. How can you help? Use images only when necessary to support content. Your students' first impulse will be to scan everything in sight and splash those graphics across your Web page. Although this is certainly visually stunning, the only thing a person seeking access to your Web page will notice is how stunningly long it takes for all those graphics to load. Testing your Web page with a "slow" connection (9600 or 14.4) is a good idea (just to discover about how long Web surfers from average schools might have to wait to see your handiwork).

Link it

Most schools on the Web feature a list of their favorite Web sites. Instead of just listing the *URL* (Internet address), it's good practice to make the text representing those Web sites into *hypertext links*. Links allow users to zip away to other Web pages and Net resources with the click of a mouse.

Basically, there are five types of links that you'll find on a Web page:

- Links to other Web pages
- Links to documents
- Links to Web pages on the local Web server
- Explanatory links (definitions, footnotes, and the like)
- E-mail links (allow you to send e-mail from within your Web browser program)

If you choose to use lots of links on your Web pages, be sure to organize them by topic or category for easy reference. Changing your links on a monthly (or more frequent) basis will ensure that users keep coming back for more.

Style on the Net

Here's a quick listing of a few commercial and educational Web pages that are among those that get my award for "style" in publishing. The Thurgood Marshall High School's Web page (`http://nisus.sfusd.k12.ca.us/ schwww/sch853/tma_page.htm`) shown in Figure 13-2 is a good example. What distinguishes such pages are the use of common elements (such as toolbars), stunning graphics, open, readable designs, and, of course, lots of *useful* content.

Figure 13-2:
Here's a
Web page
from
Thurgood
Marshall
HS, CA —
they'd get
an *A* for
style in Web
publishing.

Award winning styles

Site	URL
The Coca-Cola Company	`http://www.cocacola.com/`
Town School for Boys	`http://www.town.pvt.k12.ca.us/`
Netscape Communications	`http://www.netscape.com/`
Cupertino Union School District	`http://www.cupertino.k12.ca.us/`

Site	URL
Apple Computer, Inc.	`http://www.info.apple.com/education`
Estonia (an international delight!)	`http://www.edu.ee/`

Here's a chance for a great learning activity! Given the criteria suggested above, have your students create a "style manual" to be used later in the creation of your own home page. Their style manual should address such things as:

✔ Style do's and don'ts

✔ Conventions for the type and amount of content you might include

✔ Ideas for common elements (elements that appear on each Web page and unify your documents)

Need some design assistance? Rush down and kidnap your yearbook editor or advisor. Most of the elements of style used in designing your Web page are similar to those that yearbook staffs have been wrestling with for years.

Chapter 14

Weaving Your Web Page

1 take my job as your Internet coach very seriously. That's why I've taken great pains to make sure that, unlike most books, this one is written *above* the readability of most off the shelf computer books, but with less technical language. This chapter is written for those of you ready to take the next step in building: understanding the HTML language that is used to create pages for the World Wide Web. Before you slam the book closed and say to yourself, "I'm not ready for this 'advanced' stuff yet," let me assure you that this stuff is *simple, easy-to-learn,* and *worth knowing,* especially for educators like you. Really.

Web pages are created using a simple scripting language called HTML. *HTML* (HyperText Markup Language, an FLA — Four Letter Acronym) is much easier than programming in languages like BASIC and Pascal because most commands are "plain English," and the structure is pretty forgiving. HTML was derived from *SGML* (Standardized General Markup Language — eek, another FLA!) as a way for developers to quickly create Web pages that can be accessed by a variety of different computers.

Building Blocks

Getting the hang of HTML is very simple. The scripts are written using a standard word processor (see, told you it was easy!), or a special HTML-creator program like *Web Weaver* (included on *The World Wide Web For Teachers CD-ROM* in the back of this book!), and saved as standard ASCII text files. All this techno-babble means that creating a Web page is a little like creating a standard text document, with some special commands scattered in for flavor.

HTML code is written according to general conventions that are very easy to follow. Before I talk more about HTML, however, here's a sample of what the code looks like on your word processor or HTML-creator program

```
<HTML>
<HEAD>
<TITLE>Munchkin Middle School</TITLE>
</HEAD>
<BODY
<H1>Welcome to Munchkin Middle School!</H1>
This home page was created entirely by Mr. Templeton's Sev-
enth Grade Science class in fulfilment of a
science project... <P>
<BR>
Our school is located in Anywhere, France and has 100 stu-
dents and 45 teachers.
</BODY>
</HTML>
```

Is this easy, or what? As you can see, it's just a bunch of text that is preceded and succeeded by special commands that are sandwiched inside open and closed angle signs (also known as "less than" and "greater than" signs).

Open and shut

Web-browser software reads these commands and transmits them into formatting commands to give you the nifty Web page appearance you see when you're surfing. With a very few commands, you can make a really terrific Web page. In this chapter, we'll walk together, step-by-step, through the HTML commands. Then, in Chapter 15, you'll add hypertext links, fancy formatting, and graphics!

Take a detailed look at the sample Web page you've already seen. With a quick glance, you might learn one of the most important rules of HTML code creation — if you open it, close it. That is, while some HTML tags (such as the <HR> tag to be described soon) stand alone, most exist in pairs. The beginning tag is called the *open* tag; the end tag is the *close* tag. *Open and close tags* tell the Web browser when to start and stop following a particular formatting instruction.

Every HTML document should begin with the tag <HTML> and end with </HTML>. These tags tell the Web browser that the information contained within is written in HTML code The slash (/) always precedes the close tag.

```
<HTML> (Here's an open tag)
<!- This homepage created by Mrs. Johnson's Sixth Grade
          class. ->
<HEAD>
<TITLE>Munchkin Middle School</TITLE>
</HEAD>
<BODY>
<H1>Welcome to Munchkin Middle School!</H1>
<HR>
This home page was created entirely by Mr. Templeton's
Seventh Grade Science class in fulfillment of a science
project... <P>
<BR>
Our school is located in Anywhere, France and has 100
students and 45 teachers.
</BODY>
</HTML> (Here's a close tag)
```

Playing Tag

Okay. The secret's finally out. A Web page is really nothing more than lots of text (also graphics and sound), formatted with lots of HTML codes (called *tags*), that are set apart from standard text using an open angle bracket (<) and close angle bracket (>). These tags are read by Web browsers on the fly and are interpreted to reveal your page.

Figure 14-1 shows what the very same text looks like using the *Netscape Navigator* browser. To view the file, I simply used the Open command from the File menu in *Netscape*.

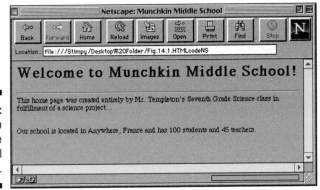

Figure 14-1:
Munchkin
Middle
School
online.

Step by (Web) step

The following are the basic steps in creating any Web page:

✔ Plan your content.

✔ Type your content into a word processor or Web-page-creation program.

✔ Highlight text and insert formatting (HTML) tags, links, and graphics (or other multimedia).

✔ View your Web page off-line with your Web browser.

✔ Use FTP to transmit your file to your Internet provider's computer.

✔ Test your Web page by logging onto the Net, launching your Web browser, and entering your home page's URL. (For more information on URL's see Chapter 7.)

✔ Visit your Web page frequently to keep content fresh and to update or add to your links.

In the remainder of this chapter, I take you through the step-by-step analysis of our sample Web page. As you read, think of how easy it'll be to create a Web page for your classroom or school. By the time you finish, you'll be able to zip along on your own to create some really cool Web pages.

The easiest way to create HTML documents is to begin with a template or with source code that you've copied (with permission) from another site. For the purposes of a quick startup, just use some of the templates on *The World Wide Web For Teachers CD-ROM.*

Locate the templates in the tutorial folder on the CD-ROM. Use your word processor or Web-creation tool to open the file called temp1.htm. (Macintosh users will note that I've had to shorten the filenames for the DOS/WIN folks — sorry!)

After you've launched the word processor and loaded the template, your screen should contain the HTML script shown in Figure 14-2.

First Things First

The first thing that you'll notice is that you've just opened a "generic" text file that doesn't (yet) contain any special commands. One key to good Web page design is to get your text (*content*) entered first and then go back and fiddle with the HTML code (*commands*) to get the text to look good.

```
<HTML>
<HEAD>
    <TITLE>Munchkin Middle School</TITLE>
</HEAD>
<BODY>
Welcome to Munchkin Middle School!
<HR>This home page was created entirely by Mr. Templeton's
Seventh Grade
Science class in fulfillment of a science project... <BR>
<BR>
Our school is located in Anywhere, France and has 100
students and 45 teachers.<BR>
</BODY>
</HTML>
```

Figure 14-2:
Your screen
should look
like this with
your
Temp1.htm
template
open.

The first step to take is to customize the template for your school. We're going to "cheat" and just replace the content in the file to match your needs. Next, we'll insert some HTML tags and some other fancy stuff.

"Schoolifying" Your Web Page

Let's begin with some simple find and replace tasks. Scroll down through the document and replace the words "Munchkin Middle School" with the name of your school and change the "located in," student, and teacher information in the paragraph below.

```
Munchkin Middle School
Welcome to Munchkin Middle School!
This home page was created entirely by Mr. Templeton's
Seventh Grade Science class in fulfillment of a science
project...
Our school is located in Anywhere, France, and has 100
students and 45 teachers.
```

Easy, huh? Right now, all you've got is standard text. Now it's time to add the HTML tags (commands) to format your document for your Web browser.

Tag, You're It

Now go through and add the following HTML tags that will make your Web page properly display on the WWW. Remember that almost all tags have both an opening and a closing tag. Check your finished product with the script that follows.

```
<HTML>
<!- Created by Nita Alison, Dataflex. ->
<HEAD>
<TITLE>Munchkin Middle School</TITLE>
</HEAD>
<BODY>
<H1>Welcome to Munchkin Middle School!</H1>
<HR>
This home page was created entirely by Mr. Templeton's Seventh
Grade Science class in fulfillment of a science project... <P>
<BR>
Our school is located in <B>Anywhere, France</B>, and has 100
students and 45 teachers.
</BODY>
</HTML>
```

Go to the Head of the Class

When we taught our students to write a letter, we carefully explained to them that the beginning of the letter contained information called a *heading*, the main text of the letter was called the *body*, and the ending a *salutation*. HTML code structure follows the same model. To help you keep things straight, HTML files are commonly divided into two sections: the header (or HEAD), which contains introductory information, and the body. Use the paired tags <HEAD>...</HEAD> and <BODY>...</BODY> to identify each section. In the case of our example, the HEAD consists of a TITLE, and the BODY contains the remainder of the text.

The <HEAD>..</HEAD> tags signal the header of the document. Usually, there's not much here, except the title (window heading) of the page.

The <TITLE>...</TITLE> tags indicate the name of the window.

The <BODY>...</BODY> tags surround the body (the majority) of the document.

No Comments?

As with other programming languages like BASIC and Pascal or C++, giving other users a clue about what you're doing so that they can easily interpret your script is a good idea. In most languages, we use what's called a *comment* to annotate the scripts. The comments are *not* seen by the Web browser or the user until he or she looks at the *source code* (HTML script) behind the scenes.

In HTML, you use the following format to insert a comment.

```
<!- This is a comment line. ->
<!- This is another comment line. ->
```

Note that the comment tags <!- and -> *must* be used for every comment line. You can slip these into your program anywhere except within another tag.

Remember that comments are designed as organizers or as information for you and your students or anyone else who reads your script. They will not show up on your final Web page.

Go ahead and type in a few comment lines. You might put the name of your Webmaster and creation date of the page. Here's a sample script:

```
<!- Jane Doe, Webmaster ->
<!- Created at Lanier Middle School, 1/1/96 ->
```

Save It!

Now's the time to save your work. If you're using a Macintosh:

1. **Choose File⇨Save.**

2. **Choose a folder on your hard drive.**

3. **Type a filename like** My First Page.html**.**

    (Note that your files should end with *html* to indicate to the browser program that the file is a readable script.)

If you're using a DOS/Windows computer:

1. **Choose File⇨Save.**

2. **Choose a subdirectory on your hard drive.**

3. Type a filename like Web1.htm.

(Note that your files should end with *htm* to indicate to the browser program that the file is a readable script.)

Breaking Up Is Easy to Do

The next thing we'll do to tweak our fabulous Web page is insert the tags that indicate paragraph formatting and line breaks. Add the <P> (skip to next line and begin filling text),
 (insert blank line) and <HR> (horizontal rule) tags to the end of the paragraphs as shown here:

```
<HTML>
<!- This homepage created by Mrs. Johnson's Sixth Grade
class. ->
<HEAD>
<TITLE>Munchkin Middle School</TITLE>
</HEAD>
<BODY>
<H1>Welcome to Munchkin Middle School!</H1>
<HR>
  This home page was created entirely by Mr. Templeton's Sev-
  enth Grade Science class in fulfillment of a science
  project...<P>
<BR>
  Our school is located in Anywhere, France and has 100 stu-
  dents and 45 teachers.
</BODY>
</HTML>
```

Note that the <P>, <BR>, and <HR> commands are formatting tags that do *not* require a closing tag. Also notice that I've embedded a descriptive comment for those who read your source code. The comment won't show up on the final Web page.

Making It Big

The last step in the initial setup of your school Web page is to add headings. Headings, you'll remember, divide text visually by enlarging headlines (or subheadlines) or changing the way the text appears on the screen. HTML supports six levels of headings that are placed within documents with a script command like this:

```
<H1> Welcome to Munchkin Middle School </H1>
```

Like other tags, heading tags need an open and close tag. The ⟨H1⟩...⟨/H1⟩ tag pair creates the largest text on the screen (about 24 point type, used for main headings), and the ⟨H6⟩...⟨/H6⟩ tags create the smallest text on the screen. Note that some browsers don't support heading commands; in that case, all your text will show up the same size.

Here's what your script would look like if you added the main heading tag pair ⟨H1⟩...⟨/H1⟩ to your document:

```
<HTML>
<!- This homepage created by Mrs. Johnson's Sixth Grade
        class. ->
<HEAD>
<TITLE>Munchkin Middle School</TITLE>
</HEAD>
<BODY>
<H1>Welcome to Munchkin Middle School!</H1>
<HR>
This home page was created entirely by Mr. Templeton's Sev-
enth Grade Science class in fulfillment of a science
project... <P>
<BR>
Our school is located in Anywhere, France, and has 100 stu-
dents and 45 teachers.
</BODY>
</HTML>
```

Tending your crops

Many Web pages wither away and die from lack of attention. As educators, we have a special duty to keep the information posted under the auspices of the school fresh and interesting. Don't be a "once and you're done" site!

Here are a few other "do's and don'ts" of Web design:

Do:

- use lots of navigational cues, like arrows and menus, to keep people from getting lost

- go for content over hype — "cool" is one thing; "cool and useful" is preferred

- minimize large graphics and/or have alternate graphics or text

- leave an e-mail address or a "mailto" link so people can write and give you compliments

Don't:

- let content get stale

- think more about format than content

- do what everyone else has done (you can do better!)

First Glance

Want to see what you've created so far?

1. **Save your file as a TEXT file with a filename like** Web1.htm.

   (Note that your files should end with htm—or html if you've got a Macintosh—to indicate to the browser program that it's a readable script.)

2. **Launch your Web browser—or the AOL browser from** *The World Wide Web For Teachers CD-ROM.*

3. **Choose File⇨Open file.**

4. **Select the template file you named in the steps above.**

Voilá! If all the planets are lined up and the sun is shining, you'll see something like the page in Figure 14-3.

Figure 14-3:
A first glance at your Web page opened with the *Netscape* browser.

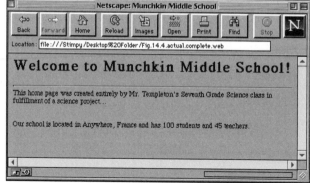

Graduation Day

If you've gotten this far, you're ready for graduation. You should understand four very simple things

✔ Web pages are created with a word processor (or Web-creator program).

✔ Web pages are read with a program called a Web browser (such as *Netscape Navigator* or the AOL web browser).

✔ Web pages consist of text surrounded by formatting commands called tags.

✔ This stuff is much easier than you expected!

In the next chapter, you'll move on to graduate school and add graphics and links to other pages based on a template on *The World Wide Web for Teachers CD-ROM*. Don't worry if your computer doesn't have a CD-player, however; you can also use any standard word processor and type in the full script yourself.

Beyond HTML

HTML 2.0 (HyperText Markup Language) is currently the coding language most used to publish Web documents. Your Web browser reads and translates the incoming HTML code and then displays the text, graphics, and links on a Web page. While the incoming language is the same, some browsers interpret the incoming code in different ways. *Netscape* can flow text around a graphic, for exampl, while *NCSA Mosaic* can't. (*Mosaic* will display the graphic and then place the text on the next available line.) *Lynx*, a non-graphical Web browser, prints alternate text and no pictures at all. You can read about HTML 2.0 standards at `http://www.w3.org/hypertext/WWW/MarkUp/html-spec/html-spec_toc.html`.

Next on the horizon is a new version of HTML called HTML 3.0. This update of the standard HTML 2.0 gives Web creators lots more control over content and graphics. The new code allows for stunning backgrounds, colored text, elegant tables, and more. In general, HTML 3.0 makes coding more-complicated pages easier. Get a heads up on HTML 3.0 by visiting `http://www.hpl.hp.co.uk/people/dsr/html/CoverPage.html`.

Chapter 15
Ready, Set, *PageMill!*

· ·

In This Chapter

▶ Why can't the computer write HTML?

▶ Open and shut

▶ Exploring *PageMill*

▶ Text and text goodies

▶ Graphics and links

▶ Wrapping the presents

· ·

*A*bout three-fourths of the people reading this book will read the word *code* (referring to learning HTML, HyperText Markup Language, which you can use to prepare your own Web page), will roll their eyes, and will feel like drop-kicking this book over the goal posts on the football field. Whoever thinks that educators have the time to learn whole new computer languages (when the principal's given them 72 hours to get a Web page up and running) has clearly never set foot in a classroom. "If this computer technology is so friendly," educators ask, "why can't the *computer* write the code for me?" Writing HTML code today is a little like the way things were in the early days of word processing when you had to embed print codes with the text. (Remember *AppleWriter*?) Nonsense!

Of course, I wasn't the only one thinking about Web development this way. The very creative folks at Adobe Systems stumbled upon an amazing development team at Seneca Software and discovered a program that allowed Web-page development with virtually no knowledge of HTML code. (Yippee!) The program was called *PageMill*. Adobe liked the program so much that they bought the whole company. (A cliché, perhaps, but it really did happen!)

PageMill to the Rescue

Programmers created Adobe *PageMill* so that novice Web authors could use a point-and-click environment to create error-free Web pages. The programmers' challenge was to make the process of creating error-free Web pages as easy as producing a word-processed document. The programmers clearly met their challenge. (And this is only the first release!)

With Adobe *PageMill,* users basically type in the text and use simple plain-English commands (in handy pull-down menus) and intuitive keystrokes to add everything from text emphasis (italics, boldface, and so on) to complex interactive forms (something that is a *pain* without *PageMill*!). After you've created your document, you can view it on the screen exactly as the page will appear when viewed with popular browsers — without ever seeing HTML code. Adding graphics is also a cinch. You can simply drag and drop the desired material to create links between files or to add images to text quickly. Adobe *PageMill* even supports advanced HTML features, including clickable image maps, fill-in forms, text/check boxes, and pop-up menus, all with WYSIWYG ease and accuracy.

Please note that the Windows version of *PageMill* wasn't available at the time that this book was published, but it is probably on the shelves by the time that you read this paragraph. To find out how to get other versions of *PageMill* or current updates, visit Adobe's Web page at `http://www.adobe.com/`. In the meantime, Windows users can use the easy and flexible HTML templates that accompany Chapter 14 (which are really just as quick to prepare) or search for other tools that might be developed for their operating systems.

Folks, *PageMill* is one of those programs that'll make you and your students look like Web gurus. I put a demo of *PageMill* on the CD for you. Try *PageMill*; you'll *love* it! You Word 6 for Windows users should try out *Internet Assistant,* which is also on the CD.

Zero to Web Page in Five Minutes

What follows is a step-by-step tutorial that helps you construct a simple Web page in *less than five minutes*. First you'll see a quick overview of the program and take a tour of some of the bells and whistles; then you'll create a page. When you've finished, you'll have something ready to slap on the Web server. Easy as pie!

Click to open!

First, open and browse a finished Web page so that you can learn a bit about how *PageMill* operates. Understanding the steps in the next few sections will make the job of creating a Web page for your school even easier. Start your stopwatch now!

1. **Double-click the *PageMill* icon on your hard drive to start the program.**

2. **Choose Open (⌘-O) from the File menu.**

3. **Locate and open the document called School1.html.**

This document is a very simple example of a complete Web page, very much like one that your school might create. The document opens in what *PageMill* calls Preview mode. *Preview mode* displays the page exactly as you'd see it while using *Netscape* or other Web browsers. The document will look much like the finished page that's shown in Figure 15-1.

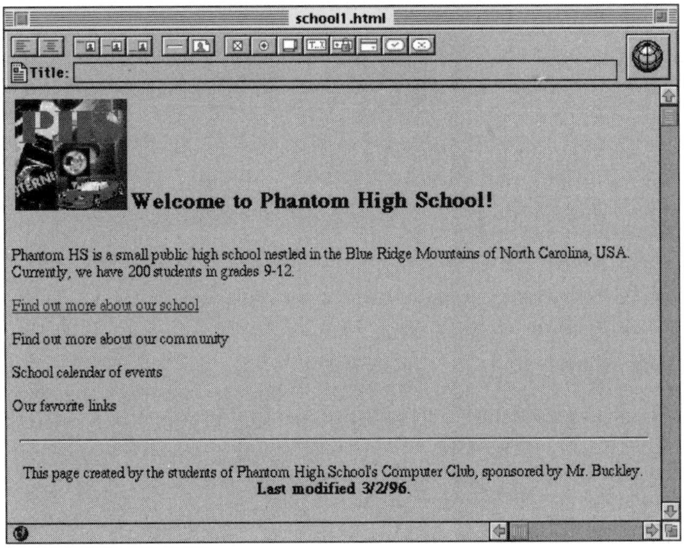

Figure 15-1: *PageMill's* Preview mode shows you what your finished page will look like when viewed with a Web browser.

school1.html

Title:

Welcome to Phantom High School!

Phantom HS is a small public high school nestled in the Blue Ridge Mountains of North Carolina, USA. Currently, we have 200 students in grades 9-12.

Find out more about our school

Find out more about our community

School calendar of events

Our favorite links

This page created by the students of Phantom High School's Computer Club, sponsored by Mr. Buckley. **Last modified 3/2/96.**

Finders linkers

Web pages are supposed to be interactive. Okay. So, interact! The following quick steps help you see how *PageMill* can help you create powerful interactive objects called *links*. For this example, use the School1.html file that you opened in the preceding steps. (See Figure 15-2.)

1. **Move the cursor around on the page.**

   Note that when you position the cursor over some words or pictures, the cursor's shape changes from an arrow to a pointing hand. The hand cursor indicates that you've discovered something *hot* — a link! These links can take you to other places on the same page as well as to other pages. Links can also cause a file to download or provide for the display of a graphic. (Links will actually do *way* more than that, but that's a topic for another book!)

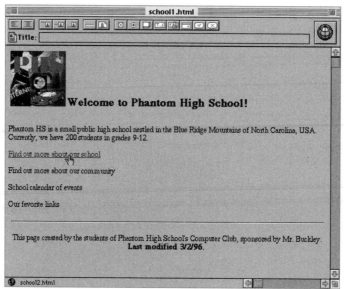

Figure 15-2:
In Preview
mode,
clicking
each link
opens a new
window,
allowing
easy editing.

Notice that when you pass the cursor over an object, a server address (also known as a URL) appears on the bottom of your screen.

2. Click on the *about our school* link.

Notice that a second Web page opens, in a window of its own, in front of the other page. These windows help you jump back and forth easily while you edit the content. (This capability is actually one of the big advantages of using *PageMill* instead of a word processor for creating Web pages.)

3. Click the Close Box in the upper left-hand corner of the open window to close the About Our School page.

Do it yourself

Next, explore *PageMill's* Edit mode. Unlike the Preview mode, Edit mode allows you to make changes in the way that the page looks and behaves.

1. Find the globe icon located on the top right-hand corner of the active window.

The globe indicates that you're in Preview mode. Remember, Preview mode enables you to sample how the finished Web page will appear when viewed with a browser like *Netscape*. (See Figure 15-3.)

Figure 15-3:
The globe
icon, at the
top right of
your
PageMill
window,
allows you
to toggle
from
Preview
mode to Edit
mode.

2. Click on the globe icon to change to Edit mode.

Edit mode, denoted by a pen-and-paper icon, allows you to enter and edit text, insert and manipulate pictures (images), and create hypertext links to other Web pages. Clicking on the pen-and-paper icon toggles the screen back to Preview mode.

Where the bold dare to go

In Edit mode, creating and editing text on your Web page is just like working with a word processor. You merely enter the text. Then you select text and choose commands from the pull-down menus to change text attributes (bold, italics, underline, and so on). (See Figure 15-4.)

To change text from regular to bold, do the following:

1. Move your cursor over the first sentence in the first paragraph of text and click and drag the mouse to your right to select the entire sentence.

2. Choose Bold (⌘-B) from the Style menu.

See? Easy, huh? Go ahead and play around by selecting and changing the style of some of the other text items on the page. If you're not happy with a particular style, select the text and reissue the same command again. That action puts things back the way they were before the most recent change.

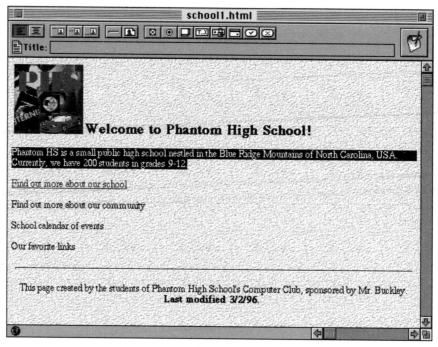

Figure 15-4:
Selecting
text in
PageMill is
as easy as
point, click,
and drag!

The drag strip

Because *PageMill* is a brand-new program, it supports the Macintosh OS's handy drag-and-drop feature. This feature makes adding text and graphics as easy as a mouse click. Here's how:

1. **Select the first sentence of text. Move the cursor on top of the selected text, hold the mouse button down, and drag the selected text to the end of the paragraph.**

   When you release the mouse, the text automatically moves itself to the last place that you directed your mouse. Is this cool or what?

2. **Replace the text on this Web page with similar text about your school.**

   Feel free to embellish the text with italics or boldface, and underline to your heart's content. (Remember, though, that *all* emphasis is *no* emphasis!)

Picture perfect

Manipulating images within *PageMill* is just as easy as manipulating text. You can move, resize, copy, paste, and delete images with the click of a mouse button. (See Figure 15-5.)

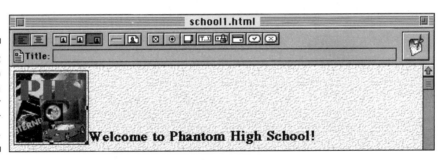

Figure 15-5:
Click to
select a
picture for
moving or
resizing.

To move and resize an image, try this:

1. **Click the picture of the school logo (upper-left corner) to select it.**

2. **Drag the image somewhere else on the page and drop it there.**

3. **Select Undo (⌘-Z) from the Edit menu to return the image to its last position.**

4. **To resize the image, select it and practice dragging the selection handles to make the image smaller or larger.**

To get a proportional scale as you resize the graphic, hold down the Shift key while you click and drag.

Creating hypertext links

Now's the time to find out how *PageMill* handles links. A link takes you from one page or location (*source*) to another (*destination*). The *PageMill* program allows you to insert links on a page in a number of ways. I show you two ways to insert links on a page, and you can investigate the documentation that comes with *PageMill* to find the rest of the ways. To get ready to explore links, first open a second sample page.

1. **Choose Open (⌘-O) from the File menu and open the file called School3.html. (Keep the School1.html file open in the background.)**

The School3.html page is really a placeholder. You can come back to this page later and put in lots of nifty and useful stuff.

2. **Position both windows so that you can see the contents of both windows.**

To resize the windows, use the window-resizing box in the lower right-hand corner of each window. To move the windows, click and drag the gray-shaded area in the title bar at the top of each window.

One way to link two pages is to select the text that you'd like to be hot. Then drag the page icon from the destination page over your selected text.

3. **Use your mouse to select the words *Return to Phantom Home Page* on the School3.html page.**

4. **Find the page icon (located just below the button bar) on the upper-left corner of the first page that you opened. Drag the page icon from the original page onto the selected text on the School3.html page. (See Figure 15-6.)**

Notice that the selected text turns blue and is underlined. These changes show that the text is *hypertext linked* back to some other page or text. Before you test the link in Preview mode, remain in Edit mode and link some other text another way:

5. **Select the words *about our community* on the original page. Type the address of your intended link in the Link Location Bar on the bottom of the window. In this case, type** School3.html **(the name of the separate page containing the community information) and press Return.**

You can also use the Copy and Paste commands to copy links.

That's it! You're *linked!*

Test drive

To test your links, switch to Preview mode and click the links to test them. As each linked page appears, close the other page to keep your screen from getting crowded. After you post your final page on the World Wide Web, your browser will automatically close each Web page window as you work.

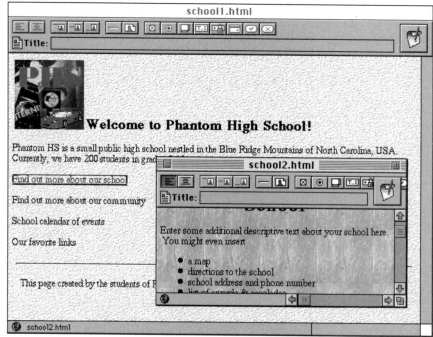

Figure 15-6:
One way to
link pages
together is
by dragging
the page
icon on top
of selected
text on
another
page.

Adding new graphics

Still not fancy enough for you? Okay. Here's how to add another graphic to the School2.html page.

1. **Either click on the hot link that you created above or use the Open (⌘-O) command in the File menu to open the School2.html page.**

2. **Click on the Apple Menu (top left-hand corner of your screen) and choose Scrapbook to open your Macintosh Scrapbook.**

3. **Choose any picture from the Scrapbook and Copy (⌘-C) and Paste (⌘-V) it anywhere you choose on the School2.html page.**

4. **Click the Close box in the upper-left corner of the window to close the Scrapbook.**

5. **Click the globe (upper right) until the pen-and-paper icon is displayed in order to return to Edit mode.**

6. **Click the image (picture) once to select it and click the Center button on the menubar to center the image on the page.**

There you go! A centered picture on your School2.html page! *PageMill's* drag-and-drop feature works with graphics types such as *jpg*, *gif*, and *pict* images and more. Because most browsers read gif files, *PageMill* automatically changes graphics into *gif* files as you drag them into a *PageMill* document. Neat, huh?

See-through images?

Next, you can make the background of the image transparent to allow it to better blend with the background of your Web page.

1. **Double-click the image.**

   PageMill's "out-of-place image view" window miraculously appears (as shown in Figure 15-7).

   The "out-of-place image view" window provides an easy way to change the size, transparency, background, and other characteristics of your image.

2. **Click the transparency tool and then click the background color of the image.**

   The background turns to the same color as the page background. (In this case, white.)

3. **Save (⌘-S) your changes by using the Save command from the File menu.**

4. **Close the "out-of-place image view" window.**

Figure 15-7:
Double-
clicking an
image
brings up
the image
view
window
where you
can make
changes to
the image.

The Attributes Inspector

Another powerful tool available to Webmasters is the Attributes Inspector. This Inspector allows you to choose attributes associated with the entire page, with selected text, or with specific objects (such as images, rule lines, or forms). In the following steps, you can experiment with changing the alignment and appearance of the text by using the Attributes Inspector.

1. **Select a block of text and choose Show Attributes Inspector (⌘-;) from the Window menu.**

2. **Display Page Attributes by clicking the page button (the button in the upper-left corner of the Attributes Inspector window).**

   Page Attributes control the color of the active, visited, and normal (plain) text on the screen. It's a good idea to use a different color for text that represents a link so that other users can tell the difference between hypertext and plain text.

   You can also control the color of the background by choosing a color from the pop-up menu next to the word *background*. Note that this system is much easier than calculating complicated hexadecimal commands — the way backgrounds are identified in raw HTML code.

3. **Choose a background color by setting the background pop-up menu to Custom and selecting a color from the color-picker dialog box.**

   See? The background color magically changes. Note that some browsers will automatically choose a color close to the one that you've selected if the user's computer won't display the color indicated.

Mighty morphin' text!

Of course, you probably want to make the text on your page even more attractive. Although Web pages are currently limited to standard fonts, you can highlight text by changing the style to bold or by aligning the text in different ways on your screen.

The following steps show you how *PageMill* uses the Attributes Inspector to alter the size and appearance of selected text. (See Figure 15-8.) In this case, you can change text from plain to bold and make the text larger.

1. **Select the text that you'd like to alter. (Make sure that you're in Edit mode.)**

2. **Open the Attributes Inspector (⌘-;) from the Window menu.**

3. **Click on the Text ("A") icon shown in the top-center in the Attributes Inspector window.**

4. **Click on the check box to the left of the word Bold. Note that the appearance of the text on your *PageMill* screen changes immediately (it's BOLD!).**

5. **Try clicking on the pop-up menu next to the word *Format* in the Attributes Inspector window. Choose the "largest heading" and watch what happens to your text.**

6. **Take a couple of minutes to click around on several of the check boxes to familiarize yourself with the other functions of the Attributes Inspector.**

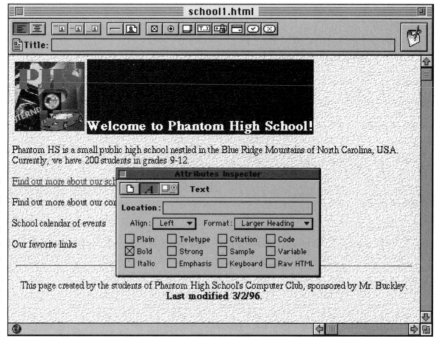

Figure 15-8:
Use the Attributes Inspector to change the style, alignment, and size of text.

One of *PageMill's* great strengths is its ability to stuff so many functions into such a compact dialog box. Note that, from this one menu, you can change the alignment of text and the text's style. (See the check boxes?) You can click on the pop-up menu next to *Format* to change the *size* of the text as well.

Whiz-bang backgrounds

As you visit other Web pages, you'll no doubt stumble on some pages that feature fancy backgrounds, displaying everything from faux granite to school logos. Before *PageMill,* background creation meant yet another series of HTML commands. Luckily, *PageMill* makes such things much easier. Here's how to add a background to your School1.html Web page.

1. **Resize your *PageMill* window until you can easily see your desktop and the contents of your *World Wide Web For Teachers CD-ROM.* Locate the file called paper1.gif within the *PageMill* folder.**

2. **Click the *PageMill* window to make it active.**

3. **Drag the paper1.gif icon from the Finder window into the *backgrd image* well in the Page Attributes Inspector.**

   (See Figure 15-9 for the Attribute Inspector window with the paper1.gif background pasted in.)

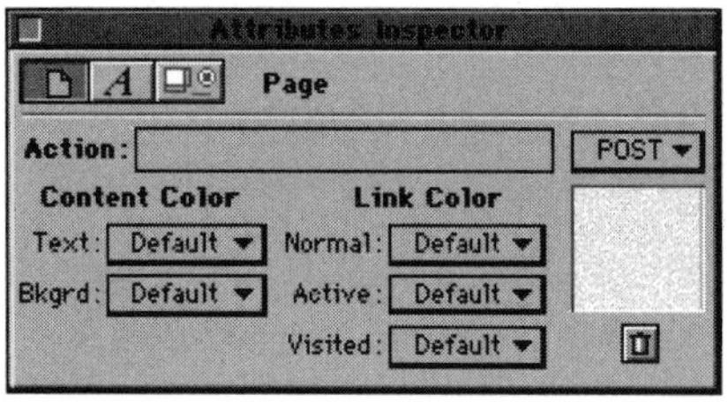

Figure 15-9:
Drag and drop images onto the Attributes Inspector background area to change the background of your Web page.

You'll immediately notice that your entire Web page has been "paperized"! Just about any image can be used as a background, just by dragging it onto the window. *PageMill* even converts the image to *gif* format on the fly!

You're done! You've now edited and added text, inserted graphics, and made a fancy background. Time for a well-deserved coffee break and a pat on the back. That wasn't too painful, was it?

Adding forms and buttons to your page, it turns out, is just as easy as creating a basic page. See *PageMill* documentation for step-by-step directions.

Stop the clock!

Okay. Check your watch. Maybe a bit more than five minutes have passed, but you were reading while you worked. *PageMill* can actually do much, much more than I've had time to share, so I encourage you to check out the documentation included on your copy of *The World Wide Web For Teachers CD-ROM*. In addition to many more bells and whistles (such as forms and charts), *PageMill* also fully supports the use of most standard HTML commands. In Edit mode, you can add your own HTML commands to the ready-made commands that *PageMill* has already entered for you.

PageMill menus and shortcuts

Here's a comprehensive summary of *PageMill* menu commands. See the *PageMill* documentation on your copy of *The World Wide Web For Teachers CD-ROM* for more information.

File Menu

Keystroke	*Function*
New Page (⌘-N)	Begin a new Web page
Open (⌘-O)	Open an existing Web page or image file
Close (⌘-W)	Close the window
Save (⌘-S)	Save the current file. Note that *PageMill* automatically appends the HTML suffix to the filename.
Save As...	Save the current page or graphic under a new name
Save A Copy As...	Save a copy of the current page or graphic
Revert to Saved	Restore the last saved version of the current page or image
Page Setup	Choose printing options
Print (⌘-P)	Print current page
Quit (⌘-Q)	Leave *PageMill*

Edit Menu

Keystroke	*Function*
Undo (⌘-Z)	Undo your last action
Cut (⌘-X)	Remove text or graphic from your page and place it on the Clipboard

(continued)

Edit Menu

Keystroke	*Function*
Copy (⌘-C)	Copy the selected item to the Clipboard
Paste (⌘-V)	Paste a cut or copied item from the Clipboard
Clear	Delete selected item(s)
Select All (⌘-A)	Select all text and graphic elements on the page
Remove Link (⌘-R)	Remove the link or disable the link while typing
Show/Hide Anchors (⌘-,)	Show or hide anchors on a page
Preferences	Change sounds, set line breaks, change default file suffix, change Save To folder, and more

Style Menu

Keystroke	*Function*
Plain (⌘-Shift-P)	Plain text (no special styles)
Bold (⌘-B)	Boldface text
Italic (⌘-I)	Italic text
Teletype (⌘-Shift-T)	Typewriter font
Strong (⌘-Shift-S)	Alternate boldface
Emphasis (⌘-Shift-E)	Alternate italic
Citation (⌘-Shift-C)	Alternate italic
Sample (⌘-Shift-A)	Display as monospace
Keyboard (⌘-Shift-K)	Display as monospace
Code (⌘-Shift-O)	Display as monospace
Variable (⌘-Shift-V)	Alternate italic
Raw HTML (⌘-Shift-H)	User-defined HTML code (will appear in red text enclosed by angle brackets "< >")

Format Menu

Keystroke	*Function*
Indent Left (⌘-[)	Align left (blockquote)
Indent Right (⌘-])	Align right (blockquote)
Paragraph (⌘-Opt-P)	Remove format from paragraph and return to Plain style
Heading	Set size of text
Preformatted (⌘-Opt-F)	Display in monospace font and leave spaces and returns intact

(continued)

Format Menu

Keystroke	*Function*
Address (⌘-Opt-A)	Alternate italic
List	Create bulleted, numbered, and other types of lists

Window Menu

Keystroke	Function
Show Pasteboard (⌘-/)	Display the temporary "holding area" for page elements
Show Attributes Inspector (⌘-;)	See and change the attributes assigned to a page, text, or object
Stack	Display open windows in cascading style, revealing the title bar of each window
Tile	Display all open windows as tiles so that you can see them all simultaneously
Close All	Close all open windows
Open Windows List	See list of open windows

Chapter 16
HTML 101

*N*ow that you've become familiar with basics of the user-friendly HTML code (if you skipped Chapter 14, you might want to take a glance at it now), it's time to make life more exciting. In this chapter, you and your students can learn how to "go graphic" (include graphics in your Web page), add specially formatted text, and use a few other useful HTML tags and hints.

Get ready! Writing your own Web page is just about as much fun as you and your students can have without breaking a law or two. Don't be thinking the little ones can't handle this either — I've taught third graders and college students to write Web pages. The only real difference is in the content that they include. In some ways, the third-graders' content is much more compelling. Repeat after me: "This stuff is easier than grading papers, finding the time to use the phone, and calculating your score on the National Teacher's Exam."

Remember that all you need to write a Web page script is a word processor. Just couldn't be any easier than this! Sharpen your electronic pencils and read on.

Web Weaver

On the disc that accompanies this book, I've provided a number of easy-to-adapt templates for your school's first Web page as well as a terrific Web-page-creation tool called *Web Weaver* for the Macintosh (Windows folks visit http://lal.cs.byu.edu/people/nosack/index.html-writer/index.html

for a great shareware tool called *HTML Writer* — perfect for educators!) that works just like a word processor but helps you add HTML code automatically. If you're creating a Web page, *Web Weaver* can save you time both in creating and in troubleshooting your Web page. Updates for *Web Weaver* can be downloaded from `http://www.northnet.org/best/Web.Weaver/WW.html`

Web Weaver is a handy tool written by Web wizard Robert C. Best, III. *HTML Web Weaver* allows you to create HTML documents easily and quickly by allowing you to write your document and then edit in your tags via a select-and-tag method. *HTML Web Weaver* also makes more complex HTML tags, such as those that link to other network services (for example, Gopher, FTP, WAIS, and WWW sites) by using a simple information form format.

Included with *Web Weaver* is an installation guide that explains both how to install, and how to use, the program. Although you don't need an HTML-creation program to do the exercises, having such a program helps. If you want to press on with your word processor, read on. If you wish to use an HTML "weaver" program, check out *Web Weaver* (on *The World Wide Web For Teachers CD-ROM*) or visit the Web site mentioned above for a quick download of a Web-creation tool for PCs running Windows.

In the section that follows, I show you another of the templates on *The World Wide Web For Teachers CD-ROM* and then delve into a bit more HTML code to help you and your students make your pages even more useful and attractive.

Here We Go!

Before you begin, open your word processor and load the template called *temp2.htm*. The HTML code looks like this:

```
<HTML>
<!- This homepage created by Mrs. Johnson's Sixth Grade
class. ->
<HEAD>
<TITLE>Munchkin Middle School</TITLE>
</HEAD>
<BODY>
<H1>Welcome to Munchkin Middle School!</H1>
<HR>
This home page was created entirely by Mr. Templeton's
Seventh Grade Science class in fulfillment
of a science project...<P>
<BR>
Our school is located in Anywhere, France and has 100
students and 45 teachers.
```

```
<BR>
Here are some cool links to Science sites:
Exploratorium
Yahoo Science
</BODY>
</HTML>
```

This HTML gibberish really will translate into a Web page. But before we do that, let's jazz up the text.

Webbing with Style

If you've used a computer for word processing, this next set of HTML tags should be very familiar. These tags deal with how your typefaces look. Think about the first time that you took your students to the computer lab to create a document with a word processor. After 15 minutes, students had created documents in which every word was a different font, style, or size. Remind your student Webmasters, and yourself, that *all* emphasis is *no* emphasis. Use formatting commands judiciously. Because HTML is designed to be cross-platform (used by different types of computers), it currently supports only style and size codes — no fonts — yet.

Style tags change the appearance of text on your Web page. There are tags for boldface, italics, strong emphasis, and more. There are two types of style tags: tags that are *browser specific* and that are *browser independent*. Browser-specific tags depend on each browser to interpret the style and display it according to whatever rules have been set for that browser. Browser independent tags look the same no matter what type of computer or what browser you're using.

Browser-specific style tags

As with other HTML tags (commands), each browser-independent style command has opening and closing tags. **Remember:** Using these tags is a bit risky because you never know exactly how other browsers (those not as hearty as *Netscape Navigator*) will read and interpret your script.

There are several browser-specific styles:

HTML Tag	Description
`<EM>...</EM>`	Emphasis. Each browser treats this text differently. Some browsers display as italic; some as underlined text.
`<STRONG>...</STRONG>`	Strong emphasis. Some browsers display as boldface; others as underlined text.
`<CODE>...</CODE>`	A code sample or Internet address. Appears in most browsers as Courier or as other monospace fonts.
`<SAMP>...</SAMP>`	Used for illustrative text or examples. Appears similarly to <CODE> text.
`<KBD>...</KBD>`	Used to indicate something to be typed by the user. Appears in monospace (Courier) font on graphical browsers.
`<ADDRESS>...</ADDRESS>`	Displays address information, usually in italics.
`<VAR>...</VAR>`	Used to name a variable. Some browsers show this text as italics or underline.
`<CITE>...</CITE>`	Citations for bibliographies. Usually shows text as italics.
`<DFN>...</DFN>`	Word or phrase to be defined. Usually shows the word as boldface.
`<BLOCKQUOTE>...</BLOCKQUOTE>`	Indents text to separate it from the surrounding text. For quotations.

Add one of these browser-specific styles to your template just so you can get the hang of what they do. In this case, we'll add the *emphasis* tags (`<EM></EM>`) to boldface the city and country where the school is located.

Edit your script to look like this (and Figure 16-1 shows the effect the $\langle$EM$\rangle$ (emphasis) tags had on the Web page):

```
<HTML>
<!- This homepage created by Mrs. Johnson's Sixth Grade
class. ->
<HEAD>
<TITLE>Munchkin Middle School</TITLE>
</HEAD>
<BODY>
<H1>Welcome to Munchkin Middle School!</H1>
<HR>
This home page was created entirely by Mr. Templeton's
Seventh Grade Science class in fulfillment
of a science project... <P>
<BR>
Our school is located in <EM>Anywhere, France</EM>
and has 100 students and 45 teachers.
<BR>
Here are some cool links to Science sites:
</BODY>
</HTML>
```

Figure 16-1:
Emphasis
tags help
you draw
attention to
specific
parts of your
Web page.

Take some time to play with the other formatting tags above by inserting them, in pairs, into your text and running your browser to see the effect.

To view the page with your browser:

1. **Launch your browser or the AOL browser from *The World Wide Web For Teachers CD-ROM.***

2. **Choose File⇨Open.**

3. **Select the template file that you created in the steps above.**

Browser-independent style tags

Because you can never be certain how browser-specific tags will display, you should use browser-independent tags for text that *must* be boldfaced, italicized, or set in monospace in order to have your presentation make sense.

Like the browser-specific tags, browser-independent commands consist of both opening and closing tags.

There are three styles that will display on virtually every browser (text or graphical) and one style, underline, that many (but not all) browsers support. These four styles are:

`<B>...</B>`	boldface
`<I>...</I>`	italic
`<TT>...</TT>`	monospace (like a typewriter)
`<U>...</U>`	underline (not supported by all browsers — yet)

The exception to the "compatible with many browsers" rule comes with text-only browsers, such as *Lynx*. The *Lynx* program interprets virtually any special character instruction as underline because the computers (typically terminals) can't handle boldface or italic type formats.

So that your text will be displayed on most graphical browsers, change your template script by replacing the `<EM>` (browser-specific, emphasis) tag with the `<B>` (browser-independent, boldface).

Your script will look like this:

```
<HTML>
<!- This homepage created by Mrs. Johnson's Sixth Grade
class. ->
<HEAD>
<TITLE>Munchkin Middle School</TITLE>
</HEAD>
<BODY>
<H1>Welcome to Munchkin Middle School!</H1>
<HR>
This home page was created entirely by Mr. Templeton's
Seventh Grade Science class in fulfillment
of a science project... <P>
<BR>
Our school is located in <B>Anywhere, France</B> and has
100 students and 45 teachers.
<BR>
```

```
Here are some cool links to Science sites:
Exploratorium
Yahoo Science
</BODY>
</HTML>
```

Whew! Okay. Now that you've gotten the template in a form that's readable by your Web browser (and you've *saved* it to your disk), go ahead and check out the effects of the boldface (`<B>...</B>`) command on your document by launching your Web browser and then using the Open command to open the template document you've revised.

Doing it your way

In an effort to keep space down, HTML commands typically instruct the browser to eliminate unnecessary white space. There are times, however, when you'd like to use typographic characters to draw pictures (remember your typing class?), create simple tables, or align text in a special way. HTML has a command that accepts text the way you type it. It's called the "preformatting" tag.

The `<PRE></PRE>` tags present a WYSIWYG (What You See Is What You Get) format, and all text appears in monospace (Courier) font.

Reverse engineering

Don't give me detention when I share a little secret. Most Web browsers allow you to take a peek behind the scenes and see the *source code* (actual HTML scripts) that created the page. You can learn much from analyzing the code and watching the way some of the more creative folks on the Net finesse graphics. Folks in Cybertown call the process of looking under the techno-hood *reverse engineering*.

To view behind-the-scenes action using the *Netscape Navigator* browser, choose View➪Source. The source code automatically downloads into a text file on your computer and pops up on your Mac or PC in a *SimpleText* or *Write* window.

You should be aware that each Web browser interprets HTML code in slightly different ways. Text-only browsers, for example, can't display graphics, so they'll show alternate text instead of all your wonderful graphics and colorful icons. In addition, some graphical browsers don't (yet) support some of the more recent bells and whistles such as tables, colored backgrounds, and other flashy, yet useful, options.

If you choose to copy code that's more than just basic syntax from someone's paper — uhm, I mean reverse engineer — it's a good idea to ask the author's permission before including the code on your page. Ultimately, you might find that this is the most useful tip in the book.

Online services and custom home page design

You won't be completely left out if you access the Internet via an online service and want to create your own home page. Both America Online and Prodigy have fill-in-the-blank forms that allow you and your students to create simple home pages without knowing any HTML language. Prodigy's Home Page Creator offers several template designs (which you can use at no extra charge) and makes creating a home page very simple. AOL's Personal Home Page uses a similar fill-in-the-blank method but allows more flexibility in the integration of graphics and sound and a few more templates. Of course, the meter's running all the while as you create your page; and when you are ready for more bells and whistles, you'll be wishing you could enter your own HTML code. But for beginners who just *have* to have their own home pages *now*, these online service home-page designers provide a great way to weave your own Web page.

Although there's no need for preformatted text in our sample template, here's an example of how the script lines might look. Note that the final table will look *exactly* as you type the text, blank spaces, blank lines, columns and all.

```
<H1> Collins Hill HS Eagles Scoreboard </H1>
<PRE>
Scoreboard

            Wins      Losses    Ties
Eagles      10        0         0
Tigers      8         1         1
Panthers    8         0         2
Cougars     6         4         0
<PRE>
```

More advanced commands are available to make neater, more readable tables. Check Chapter 17 for more information.

Linking to the World

The last line in our sample template reads:

```
Here are some cool links to Science sites:
Exploratorium
Yahoo Science
```

One of the last things we'll do before adding some graphics to our page is format the text in our script so that the words *Exploratorium* and *Yahoo Science* become hypertext links. *Hypertext links* are mouse-clickable pointers that whisk the user from one point to another. Sometimes the destination location is within your current document, and sometimes it's on someone else's Web page on another server somewhere else on the Net. You can hyperlink to different documents as well as images (pictures), sound files, and even movies!

Anchors aweigh!

The folks that wrote the HTML language call text or graphics that you click to get to other Web pages *links,* and they call the place that you're going an *anchor.*

To create a link and an anchor, use the ⟨A⟩...⟨/A⟩ tag pair. (*A* stands for *anchor.*) Anchor and link tags consist of an *HREF* (Hypertext Reference) attribute and the text between the opening and closing tags.

Linking to another Web page

Links basically have two parts: the link name and the actual URL of the location to which you'd like to link.

To add links to a document to take you to someone else's Web page, enter a script like this:

```
Here are some cool links to Science sites:<P>
<A HREF="http://www.exploratorium.edu/">Exploratorium</A>
<A HREF="http://www.yahoo.com/science/">Yahoo Science</A>
```

Note that the actual Internet URL goes before the link name and is set in quotation marks. The link names (*Exploratorium* and *Yahoo Science*) show up on your Web page, but the URLs don't. After the text is entered in this way, however, the resulting link names become "hot" links to the actual Web sites named. In other words, clicking on the word *Exploratorium* would zip you to San Francisco's Exploratorium Web site.

Linking two documents

Most of the links that you come across take you to another person's site. It's also possible to link a page to another page on the same server (at the same site). This feature is really helpful when you can't fit all your information on your home page, or you would like to access text documents or graphics.

```
Here are some cool links to other Web pages at our school:<P>
<A HREF="http://www.exploratorium.edu/">Dr. Craig Wall's
Class</A>
<A HREF="http://www.yahoo.com/science/">Mrs. Leni Donlan's
Class</A>
```

Linking to another spot within a document on the same page

You can also link to another spot within a document on the same page. The idea behind linking *within* a document is that you can have a "contents" list at the top of your page that, when clicked by a Web browser user, will jump the user to other items further down on the same Web page.

The spots to which you link are called *targets*. To indicate targeted text links, substitute NAME for HREF in the <A> tag line.

Here's an example. Say you want to list all the homerooms in your school on the top of one Web page and have the user jump to a class list by clicking the homeroom teacher's name. The class lists are further down the same page.

To create the link, use HTML code like this:

```
<A HREF="#Tyson">Mr. Tyson's Homeroom</A>
```

A code of this type might appear in a larger list of homeroom names on the top of your home page.

Further down in the document, at the location of the actual homeroom list, indicate the *target* name using the NAME command, like this:

```
<A NAME="Tyson">Tyson's Homeroom List</A>
```

The # character appears in the anchor statement (statements that start with <A> are anchor statements) that *links to* the target, not in the anchor that *names* the target.

When you click on "Mr. Tyson's Homeroom" in the list of homerooms at the top of the homepage, the browser will jump you to Tyson's homeroom list.

Going Graphical

The HTML language provides support for many different kinds of multimedia, including images (graphics). While not all Web browsers *support* (read) multimedia images, those that can't usually just ignore the code and skip right past the graphics to display the surrounding text.

To insert an image you must do two things:

- ✔ Enter the proper HTML code in your script
- ✔ Upload (copy) the image to your Web server using FTP (or some other file transfer method)

Web browsers read the scripts and then go searching for the graphics that you've programmed. The most important things are getting the file named correctly and making sure that the image is in the right format to be read by all Web browsers.

Inserting images

One of the most powerful things about the Web is its ability to display images that enhance the text and make your pages more exciting and interesting. The downside is that images usually slow down the process of loading Web pages because more data must be transmitted. The moral to this story is to use images with care. **Remember:** Some folks out there (mostly schools!) are still using slow dial-up connections.

To insert an image into your document, use an HTML tag called the ⟨IMG⟩ (image) tag. Here's the way that this tag is written:

```
<IMG SRC="imagename.gif">
```

The "imagename.gif" is the filename of the graphic that you wish to use. Graphics are usually provided in *graphics interchange format* (GIF) or *joint photographic expert group* (JPEG) format. Use your favorite graphics program to "Save As" these file types. Beware! Filenames are case sensitive.

Note that the ⟨IMG⟩ tag does not require a closing tag. Using one will make most browsers hiccup.

Depending on the pathway that you indicate, your image file can be on your own Web server, or you can point to a graphic loaded on a remote Web server anywhere on the Net. Be sure to get permission, however, before calling on someone else's graphics.

More "expert" HTML programmers also tack on another tag, the ALT tag, to indicate what text to show if users don't have a graphical browser or have the "display images" function on their browser disabled. If your school logo, for example, is on your home page, you can show alternate text like this:

```
<IMG SRC="imagename.gif" ALT="School Logo Picture Here">
```

Lining up

When images are included in a line combined with text, the bottom of the graphic is automatically aligned with the baseline of the text. The ALIGN command allows you to vary the position of the graphic relative to the surrounding text.

```
<IMG SRC="imagename.gif" ALT="School Logo Picture Here"
ALIGN="TOP">
```

The script line above would align your text with the top of the graphic. You can also use "MIDDLE" or "BOTTOM" as directions for image placement.

Note that the align command is browser specific. Some browsers, such as the ones used by most online services, may ignore these commands.

Making images into hyperlinks

To make your images *clickable* (that is, to allow users to click on graphics to whisk them away to other places on the Net), you combine the IMG and anchor tags. Use the following script:

```
<A HREF="www.cnn.com"><IMG SRC="cnnlogo.gif" ALT="CNN Logo
Picture Here"
```

Clicking on such a logo would launch a person who clicked on a picture of the CNN logo, for example, to the popular CNN Web site.

It's also possible to make different sections (parts) of a single graphic clickable links to other sites or to other places within a site. These pictures segmented into multiple clickable links are called *image maps*. Image maps are created using HTML code (a coordinate system). For more information on image maps, visit the *Netscape* home page at http://www.netscape.com/. In fact, the picture you see at the top of the *Netscape* home page is divided into several segments; clicking on different parts of the picture will result in different destinations. This is a great example of an image map.

More multimedia

You can include movies and sound in your Web site by using the HTML code to access those types of files. A hyperlink to a Macintosh-readable audio file, for example, might look like this:

```
<A HREF="file://starwars.AIFF">Click here</A> for the Star Wars
  theme (Macintosh).
```

A file readable by users of Windows might look like this:

```
<A HREF="file://starwars.wav">Click here</A> for the Star Wars theme
  (Windows).
```

Clicking on the link downloads the sound file to the user's hard drive and then launches a "helper" program, such as *Windows Media Player* or *SoundMachine* (Macintosh), and plays the file.

Digital video works the same way, only different tools (QuickTime, for example) are used to read the downloaded files. Note that some sound files, and most video files, are long and can significantly slow down the access process.

Here's a sample video file readable by any Macintosh. (Windows users should search for .avi- or .QTW-formatted files):

```
<A HREF="file://starwars.QT">Click here</A> for a Star Wars video
  excerpt.
```

Whoa, Nellie!

This chapter covered material that'll keep you and your student Webmasters busy for months. Take it slow and easy, and you'll be fine. Keep things simple in the beginning, and you'll stress less. If you're ready to press on — check out the next chapter for some really fancy stuff.

Want to see what the final script would look like for our sample template after our hypertext links and a dandy graphic were added? Here it is:

```
<HTML>
<!- This homepage created by Mrs. Johnson's Sixth Grade
class. ->
<HEAD>
<TITLE>Munchkin Middle School</TITLE>
</HEAD>
<BODY>
<IMG SRC="schlogo.gif" ALT="School Logo Picture Here"
ALIGN="LEFT">
<H1>Welcome to Munchkin Middle School!</H1>
<HR>
```

```
This home page was created entirely by Mr. Templeton's
Seventh Grade Science class in fulfillment
of a science project... <P>
<BR>
Our school is located in <B>Anywhere, France</B> and has
100 students and 45 teachers.
<BR>
Here are some cool links to Science sites:
<A HREF="http://www.exploratorium.com/">Exploratorium</A>
<A HREF="http://www.yahoo.com/education/">Yahoo Science</A>
</BODY>
</HTML>
```

Figure 16-2 shows what the script looks like when viewed with the *Netscape* browser.

Figure 16-2:
The completed sample template file viewed with *Netscape Navigator.*

Plenty of other books that'll help you increase your HTML vocabulary are out there on the market. One of my favorite resources is called *World Wide Web Secrets* by Paul J. Perry. It's a humongous book stuffed with great tips for creating Web pages and sites to visit. It's published by IDG Books Worldwide, Inc., of course.

Chapter 17

Achieving Hyperspace

Some of the greatest thoughts in history were first penned on (school lunchroom?) napkins, envelopes, tablecloths, and even matchbook covers. An idea popped into an author's head and ended up on a torn corner of an old magazine. When the ideas were flowing, the author didn't focus on how the text looked, but on what it said. Later, though, someone took the ideas and crafted them into a form that was more readable, attractive, and organized. This step was essential to ensure that the author's message was useful.

Web page organization and design help to

✔ Draw the reader into your page

✔ Highlight important information

✔ Provide easy navigation through the information that you've presented

This chapter gives you a heads-up on some HTML tags that can help you and your students organize content for easier reading and a more productive Web search session. If you haven't thought about what your content will be, stop reading now and jump back to Chapters 11 and 12 for a Web-design primer.

Making a List and Checking It Twice

Think about the lists you make each day — grocery lists, outlines, to-do lists — each list contains multiple items, but their formats are different.

Lists are a great way to organize information. Since people *browse* the Web (that is, pop in and out of sites), placing information in lists helps users see the value of your information quickly. You can use lists to organize student names, list menu items (subject areas), define terms, and more.

One of the neatest features of HTML is the ability to create and display items in a list. HTML list tags create preformatted lists that can be displayed as numbered lists, bullets, and more.

HTML supports five kinds of lists:

✔ Ordered or numbered lists (labeled with numbers)

✔ Bulleted lists

✔ Glossary lists (a highlighted term followed by a definition)

✔ Menu lists (lists of paragraphs)

✔ Directory lists (short lists of one- or two-word items)

Creating a List

Creating a list on your Web page is easy. Lists typically are created when you're listing Web links, people's names (or e-mail addresses), products in a catalog, and so on. As with most other HTML tags, lists begin and end with a tag that identifies the type and format of list that you'd like to use.

By the numbers

Ordered lists are used for items that are listed when sequence is important. An example would be a sequential list of steps to follow in order to register for classes at a local university. As the example shows, the tags for ordered (numbered) lists are <OL> and </OL>, and each list item begins with <LI> (list item).

<OL>

<LI> Log on to the university network.

<LI> Choose menu option "B"

<LI> Enter your student number...

</OL>

Bite the bullets

An unordered list is used when sequence isn't important, such as in a supply list. Unordered (bulleted) lists use the tags <UL> and </UL>, and each list item begins with <LI> (list item). (See Figure 17-1.)

School supplies for Ms. Jones' class:

<UL>

<LI> #2 pencil

<LI> 3-ring binder (green or black)

<LI> laptop computer

</UL>

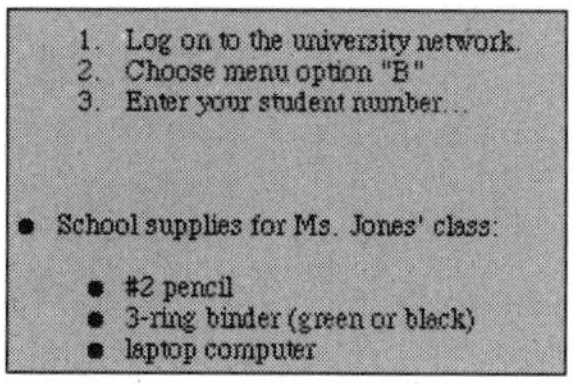

Figure 17-1:
Here's what the numbered and unordered lists will look like on most Web browsers.

1. Log on to the university network.
2. Choose menu option "B"
3. Enter your student number...

● School supplies for Ms. Jones' class:

  ● #2 pencil
  ● 3-ring binder (green or black)
  ● laptop computer

On the menu and directory assistance

Although rarely used, the MENU tag (<MENU>...</MENU>) and DIR tags (<DIR>...</DIR>) give you a modified indent within your listing. Like the bulleted list described before, begin each list item in a DIR or MENU sequence with <LI> (list item). **Caution:** Many Web browsers don't support these tags. Use them with care!

Look it up

Glossary lists are basically used to highlight a key word or phrase and display definitions in indented format. Begin and end the sequence with the `<DL>`... `</DL>` tags, precede every keyword with `<DT>` (defined term), and precede each term's definition with `<DD>` (definition). `<DT>` and `<DD>` do not need closing tags.

TIP

Netscape Navigator: leader of the pack

Usually, the folks who write Web browsers watch the developers of HTML and then write code to match. The folks at Netscape would be classified by teachers as, well, gifted overachievers. They decided to jump ahead of the current HTML standards (2.0) and create new features and tags before they were written into standards. As with any gifted student who jumps ahead in the curriculum, this both overjoyed and angered the developers.

Basically, Netscape's competitors will have to "get over it." Netscape's browsers are used by the vast majority of Web users, and the popularity of Netscape's browser, *Netscape Navigator,* continues to grow. Some of the additions to HTML 2.0 that work only on "*Netscape*-aware" browsers are:

✔ `<nobr>...</nobr>`	indicates text that must stay together with no line breaks
✔ `<center>...</center>`	centers text horizontally on the page
✔ `<font>` and `<basefont>`	creates 'drop caps' and adds emphasis to documents by varying font size
✔ bullet form	commands that allow you to change the kind of bullets you'd like (circles, squares, disks)
✔ list control	controls type and starting number of digits used to number a list
✔ special characters	&reg gets you a registered TM symbol; &copy, a copyright symbol

✔ `<isindex>`	adds words or phrases to searchable databases on your server
✔ `<list>`	flexibility in changing list types on the fly
✔ image control	new commands that add to the `<IMG>` command to control the alignment, size, and border of images
✔ `<hr>`	controls the thickness of a horizontal rule

... and there are more! For more information, check out the new specs at:

`http://www.netscape.com/`

Forms and tables

New HTML code makes it possible to create nicely formatted tables of information and forms for users to complete. In both cases, however, some browsers won't read the formatting commands, and you'll just see plain left-justified text on your screen.

The Sports Network features a formatted table with links highlighting different sports. Figure 17-2 shows a formatted table. For details on how to create your own table, check the source code at Netscape's home page (`http://www.netscape.com/`).

Figure 17-3 can give you a good idea of the potential for forms. To complete a form, simply position the cursor inside a blank and click your mouse button; then type away! To transmit the information on your form, look for a Search button on the Web page or press the Return/Enter key on your keyboard.

Figure 17-2:
Netscape Navigator allows you to create formatted tables.

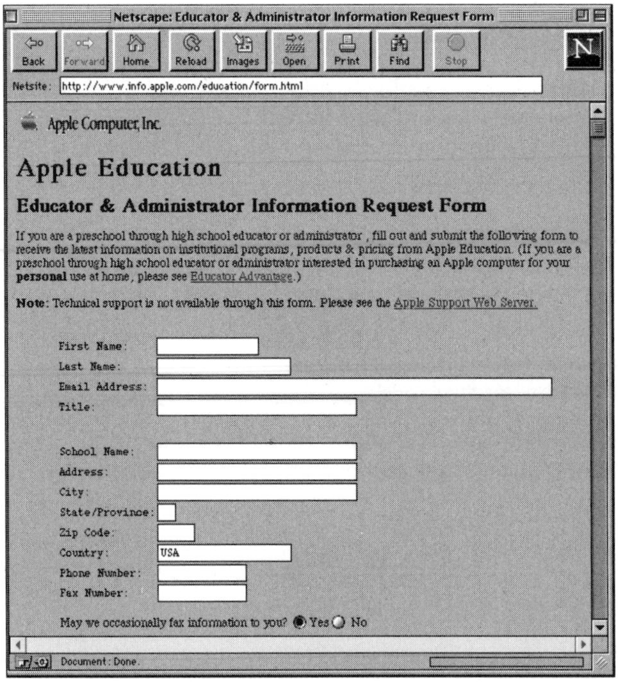

Netscape: Educator & Administrator Information Request Form
Back
Forward
Home
Reload
Images
Open
Print
Find
Stop
Netsite: http://www.info.apple.com/education/form.html
Apple Computer, Inc.
Apple Education
Educator & Administrator Information Request Form
If you are a preschool through high school educator or administrator, fill out and submit the following form to receive the latest information on institutional programs, products & pricing from Apple Education. (If you are a preschool through high school educator or administrator interested in purchasing an Apple computer for your personal use at home, please see Educator Advantage.)
Note: Technical support is not available through this form. Please see the Apple Support Web Server.
First Name:
Last Name:
Email Address:
Title:
School Name:
Address:
City:
State/Province:
Zip Code:
Country: USA
Phone Number:
Fax Number:
May we occasionally fax information to you? Yes No
Document: Done.

Figure 17-3: To complete a form, position your cursor, click, and type.

TIP

List tags

Lists help you keep information on your Web pages organized. Here are the most commonly used HTML tags and their functions:

List type	HTML tags	Note
ordered (numbered) lists	`<OL>...</OL>`	each list item begins with <LI> (list item)
unordered (bulleted) lists	<UL>...</UL>	each list item begins with <LI> (list item)
menu lists	<MENU>...</MENU>	each list item begins with <LI> (list item)
directory lists	<DIR>...</DIR>	each list item begins with <LI> (list item)
glossary lists	<DL>...</DL>	each list item begins with <DT> (defined term) and is followed with <DD> (definition); <DT> and <DD> do not need closing tags

Are Internet programs really free?

Well, some are; some aren't. You can sort the files on the Net into three categories: public domain software, freeware, and shareware.

✔ Public domain programs and files carry no copyright. There are no limits on redistribution, modification, or sale.

✔ Freeware programs and files are free for you to use and give away, but not to sell or modify. The author retains the copyright.

✔ Shareware programs and files allow you to road-test programs for a short evaluation period and then either pay the author a small

fee or erase the program from your computer. The author retains all copyrights; and although you can give shareware programs to your friends, all shareware information must accompany the program, and they have to pay the author, too.

You can set a good example for your students by always paying shareware fees and by discussing the issue of intellectual property rights with them. Most of the programs that come with this book are programs that wouldn't be available if there weren't lots of honest computers users, like you, out there.

Building forms can get pretty complicated because it requires action on *both sides* of the client-server connection. Simply put, an electronic information transfer method called the *Common Gateway Interface* (*CGI*) allows you to send scripts to and from a server and have the server act on information users write on their forms. The most popular CGI programs are *AppleScript* (for use with Apple Web servers), *Perl* (for use on computers that support a Perl interpreter/ compiler), and *C+* (for use on systems that support C compilers).

For *lots* more information about CGI and programming your own forms, check out IDG's *HTML For Dummies* by Ed Tittel and Steve James. This book is a great reference for advanced Webmasters (such as you and your students!).

Setting a background color or graphic

Users of *Netscape Navigator* Version 1.1 or greater can add a splash of color behind their Web pages using the powerful `<BGCOLOR>` tag. Here's the HTML code, for example, to set the background color to black and the text color to white; clickable links will look red, and already-clicked-on links will appear blue:

```
<body bgcolor="000000" text="ffffff" link="ff0000" vlink="0000ff"
alink="0000ff">
```

(continued)

(continued)

The numbers in these HTML codes come from the hexadecimal equivalent for colors. To see more colors or read more about how these hex equivalents are derived, visit the following URL:

`ackhttp://www.ohiou.edu/~rbarrett/webaholics/ver2/colors.html`

HEX		Color	HEX		Color
000000	-	black	808080	-	60% gray
0000FF	-	navy blue	8C8C8C	-	55% gray
003D84	-	speckled cornflower	92C000	-	light speckled green
0063A4	-	light speckled cornflower	999999	-	50% gray
874000	-	dark speckled green	A6A6A6	-	45% gray
008F93	-	speckled teal	B3B3B3	-	40% gray
00A0DD	-	speckled medium blue	BFBFBF	-	30% gray
00FF00	-	neon green	C40026	-	dark red
00FFFF	-	neon blue	C5004C	-	medium red
1C0B5A	-	dark purple	C50067	-	dark pink
262626	-	dark gray	CCCCCC	-	gray
333333	-	90% gray	D9D9D9	-	20% gray
404040	-	85% gray	DC6000	-	dark orange
4D4D4D	-	80% gray	E6E6E6	-	off-white
4DA619	-	speckled grass green	EC9800	-	light orange
53005D	-	purple	FF0000	-	bright red
595959	-	75% gray	FF00FF	-	bright purple
666666	-	70% gray	FFEB00	-	speckled dark yellow
737373	-	65% gray	FFFF00	-	neon yellow
7C005F	-	speckled purple	FFFFFF	-	white

You can insert background artwork behind your Web page by saving the files in GIF (or JPEG) format, uploading the artwork to your Web server, and calling it within the `<BODY>` of your script with the following HTML code:

`<BODY BACKGROUND="imagename.GIF>`

The `<Body Background>` tag isn't supported by some other browsers. Readers accessing your page with older browsers won't see the background art. Be careful to use background art that is subtle enough to allow foreground text to be readable. Also, be aware that loading background art, like any other art, slows down access time to your Web page. Use background art and color sparingly.

Chapter 18

Getting Your Web Page Online

● ●

In This Chapter

▶ Search for a server

▶ FTP and me

▶ Maintaining your Web page

▶ Getting the word out

● ●

*H*ere it is: the moment of truth! Now that you and your students have crafted the world's most awesome Web page, it's time to share it with several million other Internet users.

The first goal in your quest to publish your Web page is to find a Web server. *Web servers* are machines on the Internet that run programs that "listen" to the Internet and wait for inquiries to the Web pages they contain. As requests are submitted from Web clients (see Chapter 2 for a heads-up on clients and servers), the Web server locates files and other resources and sends them over the Net.

Web servers come in all shapes and sizes. A Web server can be anything from a mainframe or mini-computer running UNIX to a friendly Macintosh. Clients and servers communicate using a communication language called HyperText Transfer Protocol (HTTP). This protocol allows computers of all kinds to tap information from your Web server.

Uh, oh . . . I feel the propeller on my beanie spinning. That's a signal that the techno-speak is getting a bit rough. Hang in there, though; this chapter isn't as bad as you might expect. Most of the hundred-dollar words you've already seen!

UNIX daemons

A *daemon* is a UNIX program that sits around and waits for someone to access it. When requests come in to the server, the program jumps in and processes each request and then hustles back to the corner to wait for another request.

Daemons are similar to Windows *TSRs* (Terminate and Stay Resident) and Macintosh OS Extensions (things that hide in the System folder). Daemons are dandy because they grab processing power only while they're active.

The Search for Servers

Your search for a fileserver on which to post your Web page could be as simple as a call to your school system's district office. Many schools (especially colleges) have Web servers and allow students, teachers, and staff members to create and publish their own Web pages. Most such sites even offer classes, or online assistance, in creating Web pages. The major benefits to publishing on your own Web server are cost and space availability. Typically in this situation, your school won't be charged by the minute to access the Web, and plenty of space is available for any Web ideas that you and your students can conjure.

If your school or school system doesn't have its own Internet node with a Web server, you've got a couple of other options. Nowadays, more and more commercial online services are offering users space for Web pages on their huge Net-connected computers. America Online, for example, not only offers subscribers space, but has a dandy tool called *NaviPress* for helping novice users develop their own pages.

The benefit of using an online service is that online services are likely to offer the latest in development tools and lots of online assistance as you create your pages. The downside is cost. As you develop and post your home pages, you're charged standard online access fees. Although your pages will be available to non-AOL subscribers, if you use AOL's hearty browser to access your Web page (or other Web pages), the meter's running all the time, unlike when you use your local Internet node where time is essentially free.

Another option is to contact an Internet Service Provider (ISP). ISPs are another way, besides using commercial online services, to connect to the Internet. Most ISPs offer their subscribers a few megabytes of space on which to store their Web pages. The biggest benefit of relying on an ISP is that the ISP is responsible for the maintenance of the Web server, not you. It's a little like having a housekeeper come in and clean your classroom windows (Who has windows?) and blackboard every night (We can dream, can't we?).

The Great 1995 Web Site explosion!

Web66, the education Web site that's cornered the market on tracking other education Web sites, hosts the Internet's oldest and most comprehensive list of school Web home pages. In calendar year 1995, we saw a 1249 percent increase in the number of K-12 school Web home pages registered in the Web66 International Registry of School Web Sites.

A breakdown of the increase shows huge gains in every category:

Date	Elementary	Secondary	Total	Districts
Jan 1 1995	47	107	154	48
Dec 31 1995	618	1305	1923	404
Increase:	1315%	1220%	1249%	842%

These statistics are a great addition to your school's technology plan! For more statistical and historic information about school Web sites, visit:

`http://web66.coled.umn.edu/schools/stats/stats.html`

Would You Like Fries with That? (Self-Serve Web)

If your school has it's own Internet node, you may choose to set up your own Web server. To set up a Web server you need four things:

- A fast connection to the Internet (56 Kbps minimum)
- A computer running Macintosh OS, Windows, or UNIX
- A person (or people) who can wear the Webmaster beanie and maintain the Web server
- A program that instructs your computer how to act like a Web server

Because the Web was born on a UNIX system, there are lots of ways to set up a Web server on a computer running UNIX. Two are freeware programs, *CERN HTTPD* and *NCSA HTTPD*. (*HTTPD* stands for HyperText Transfer Protocol Daemon. See the sidebar in this chapter for a description of what a daemon is.) These programs are full of great features, but they are a bit hairy to install. Here's where your beanie-wearers come in handy. UNIX is about as friendly as a bus driver on the last day of school. You can find CERN's HTTPD by jumping to their site from `http://www.netscape.com/`

One server solution

In the beginning, Web providers were forced to endure the confusing world of UNIX servers. Nowadays, smart folks, like many associated with schools, are flocking to an easier solution — Apple's Internet Workgroup Server bundle. All you need is a PowerMac Workgroup Server (they come in several flavors) and supporting software. Apple's server comes with *WebStar* (formerly known as *MacHTTP*), *Netscape Navigator* (the best browser on the planet), *BB Edit* (for writing Web pages), *PageMill* (for creating Web pages in a user-friendly, drag-and-drop, point-and-click Mac environment), and lots of other goodies.

The bundle includes the ability to build a secure Web site, and no *firewall* (a software blockade to keep prying eyes away from your server resources) is needed. The Mac software has fewer security holes than UNIX does; but just in case, plan to dedicate a server to Web tasks instead of using your LAN's major server.

Apple's solution is about half the price of a UNIX solution and is much easier to administer. The downside? PowerMacs don't currently support multitasking, so some processor-intensive tasks may slow down network access. One solution is to *daisychain* a number of servers and post the same information on each server. When the load gets too large, each server will then pass along users to the next server.

Grabbing a Macintosh is one of the easiest ways to create a Web server at your school. A Mac freeware program called *MacHTTP* can be up and running inside of 15 minutes. Most anyone can do it, beanie or not. You can find *MacHTTP* at `http://www.apple.com`

In the interest of equal time, there are also some dandy, fast, Pentium Internet servers out there. If your school or district has lots of Windows gurus, and you want to give them a challenge, there are places on the Web (`http://www.ibm.com/`) that will show you the way.

Leave the Driving to Them

If your school or district doesn't have its own Web server, don't worry; many Internet providers allow subscribers to publish their own Web pages with little or no cost beyond their monthly Internet access fee. In Atlanta, for example, a company called Mindspring (`http://www.mindspring.com/`) uses revenue from corporate customers to allow it to give one free dial-up account, with accompanying space for a Web page, to practically every Georgia public or private school that wants one. These folks at Mindspring have the right idea. Call your local Internet provider and wave that in their face!

To find a listing of providers in your areas, check out the Internet Access Providers links on the popular Yahoo Internet catalog (http://www.yahoo.com/Business/Corporations/Internet_Access_Providers/).

You can also publish Web pages on commercial online services, although right now, access, space, and creativity are limited with commercial service Web-page authoring systems.

FTP and Me

After you've established a site for your Web page, the next step is to actually publish your Web page to the Internet provider's Web server. Basically, this involves four easy steps:

- ✔ Determine which subdirectory on the Web server you will use to post your Web page
- ✔ Use FTP to send a TEXT version of your HTML script file to the Web directory on your Web server
- ✔ Use FTP to send all associated GIF (image), sound, or movie files to the same subdirectory on the Web server
- ✔ Test your Web page (for the hundredth time) by logging into the Web server and accessing your Web page

To determine the subdirectory to use, contact your network administrator or information provider. They can give you the *path* that you'll need in order to post your Web pages to the proper place. After you've gotten the path to follow, using FTP programs like *Fetch* (Macintosh) makes the data transfer pretty effortless (see Figure 18-1). Just be sure that the file that you transmit has the letters *htm* appended to the filename (which, itself, should be eight characters or less, if you're not a Mac or Windows 95 user). When sending graphics (image files), make sure that you've named them *exactly* the way that you named them in your main HTML Web page script. Note that if your Web page is also access-ing documents from other sources, you may have to edit your HTML script so that it knows where to look for those resources when it needs them.

Don't forget to try accessing your brand new Web page from several different types of computers using several different Web browsers. Sometimes you might be surprised at what you see. (Pleasantly or not.)

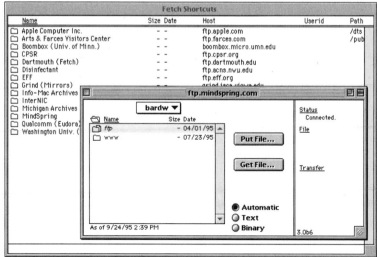

Figure 18-1:
Use *Fetch* or some other file transfer program (FTP) to move your Web scripts to the Web server.

Getting the Word Out

Because nobody administers the entire Internet, there's no "district office" to which you submit the name of your Web server for broadcast to the rest of the Internet. There are, however, a few simple ways to get the word out:

- ✔ Post to newsgroups
- ✔ Send e-mail to **news@ncsa.uiuc.edu**
- ✔ Get your URL posted on the What's New page on your Internet provider's home page
- ✔ Visit **www-announce@info.cern.ch**
- ✔ Check out CERN's Visual Library at `http://info.cern.ch`
- ✔ Write an article for your local (or national) paper
- ✔ Create a business card containing your school's Web address
- ✔ E-mail to everyone that you know and have them pass the word along

A Final Word

You might be wondering how much it costs to publish a Web page. The best answer to that question is, "How much do you have?" Depending on whether you work with a current Internet service provider or an online service, or you opt for your own Web server, the cost can be from pennies to thousands per month. The toughest part of cranking up your own server is paying the monthly maintenance fees for ISDN, T-1, T-3 or other high-speed lines. Most schools and districts balk at the $60 — $2,000 monthly fee. Wait! Before you fall out of your chair, know that ISDN and other lines are:

- ✔ Becoming more common
- ✔ Becoming less expensive
- ✔ Often discounted for educational institutions
- ✔ Becoming easier to set up
- ✔ Becoming easier to manage

With all this good news, how can you help but jump online?

At first, I'd definitely recommend that you work with a service provider. Having your own server is a little like buying that hundred-acre farm that you always wanted — it's great until you have to get up at 5:00 a.m. and milk the cows. Web servers require expertise and maintenance. Might as well let someone else get udderly frustrated!

Part IV
The Web Meets the Classroom

"No, Thomas Jefferson never did 'the Grind', however this does show how animation can be used to illustrate American history on the Web."

In this part . . .

Here's a survival guide for using the Web in the classroom. This is the part where I tackle the tough stuff (such as what to do with one computer and 30 students, and what to do when you get that inevitable "what about the porno" call from a parent or board member) and provide you with some great strategies for helping fellow educators get cyber-literate.

Chapter 19

Managing Instruction

• •

In This Chapter

▶ One computer, 30 students

▶ Jumping in feet first

▶ Evaluation and the Net

• •

*1*f you're an educator, chances are that at one point in your teaching career you've been involved in that wonder-of-wonders science project — creating a volcano. As a newbie science teacher back in eighty-something (that's *nineteen* eighty-something!), I distinctly remember breezing past working with my students to build a stream table to simulate water erosion (and a mighty river it was) and reaching Volcano Day. You know the drill: get all the materials together, set the stage for the grand event by placing the experiment in the context of your learning goals, then make the earth tremble.

When the class began, the students were already bustling with excitement. As I carefully explained the experiment, they were already anticipating outcomes. The ingredients were measured, the data tables were drawn, and the lab notebooks were poised for the big event. When the final ingredient was added, the baking soda volcanoes began to dribble forth a fizzing river of white goo. That's when it happened. One of my better science students, Christy, raised her hand and said, "Mr. Williams, this is boring. Why didn't it blow up?" Gulp.

As I was adeptly explaining how some volcanoes dribble and don't go off with a shower of sparks and ejecta (that's flying rocks for non-science folks), I realized Christy had a point. The little science guy sitting on my shoulder whispered in my ear that proper volcanoes really do show the power of nature, effortlessly blasting molten rock and boulders from here to there.

I'll bet you know where *this* is going. I tripped back into my lab cabinet and selected various volcano-making chemicals and other goodies (small quantities, of course) and proceeded to build a volcano. To make a long story short, I built another volcano, lit the fuse, and proceeded to experience a small, and safe, *boom* that (to the delight of the class) had the requisite sparks and flames. Unfortunately, the experiment also created what was described by science-whiz Christy as a "cloud of stink" that floated lazily out of the classroom and down the hallway, creating what might only be described as a panic.

Teachers complained. Students complained. The principal visited. The smell was sulfur, of course (not something that any self-respecting scientist would crinkle a nose at, but something that, to most folks, smells worse than yesterday's tuna). The experiment had been a success, sort of, and had created at least one unexpected outcome that was good (a few extra sparks and flame that fizzled safely away) and one that was not so good (the amazing stinking cloud).

Chances are that you and your students will experience varying degrees of success with every Internet journey. You'll quickly learn to expect the unexpected and be equally prepared for positive and negative outcomes.

The moral? The first time that you surf with your students, think about the stinking cloud *before* you click that unknown source link or allow students to go surfing into unknown territory.

Success with the Net

There are a number of parallels between Volcano Day and your experiences in the classroom with the Internet. Here's a quick list of things to think about before you and your students begin Net-surfing:

- ✔ Make sure that you have a plan (establish a reason for logging into the Internet)

- ✔ Make sure that you've prepared your students (frame your reason in the context of your instructional goals and objectives)

- ✔ Make sure that you've completed a "pre-volcano" (or in this case, a pre-surf) checklist (log on to the Net and establish a few places where you can anticipate that students will be successful in reaching your desired outcomes)

- ✔ Make sure that you're prepared for unexpected outcomes (the good ones — and the not-so-good ones)

- ✔ Lead, follow, or get out of the way (know when to give direction, when to jump on the surfboard with students and ride to another resource, and when to step back from your computer and let students explore on their own)

This last item in the list will probably be the most difficult item at first, but you'll quickly get the hang of deciding what role is most appropriate for each learning activity. Getting out of the way empowers students with the freedom to browse for their target information and experience the same joy that you have found in discovering unknown Internet treasures. I know: you've heard a great deal about not-so-appropriate things on the Internet, but there's really relatively little to worry about as long as your surfers stay goal-focused.

One word of caution. If you present a model to students that they can aimlessly wander around the Internet as a reward for completing their other assignments, you're setting yourself up for more not-so-good outcome possibilities. Many students can use their at-home Internet connections (read: under parental supervision) for random surfing. If students are browsing "just to discover," at least have them give you a topic ("rock and roll on the Internet") or an outcome ("finding out if there's a skateboard magazine on the Net").

Think about keeping a log of "successful Internet journeys" next to your computer. You may even create a form that students or teachers can complete so that others can benefit from their experiences. The form might include questions like:

- ✔ What was the name of the Web page?
- ✔ What was the Internet address (URL)?
- ✔ List four positive things about this page.
- ✔ How might the content on this page be improved?
- ✔ What topic/subject area might this page be most useful for?
- ✔ The best thing about this Web site is . . .

As a follow-up, suggest that a small group of students sort through the logs and create a "Top Tips for Using the Internet" in your classroom.

Flying Solo

If your school's like most, you don't have Internet access in every room. In fact, chances are that if you have a connection at all, it's in your school's media center or tucked away in a computer lab. No matter where the phone lines are located, it's also likely that your school has only one computer on-ramp to the info superhighway.

One computer connected to the Internet is kind of like having one set of encyclopedias for an entire class. It's not an ideal configuration, but (crafty, innovative teachers that we are) we can usually find a way to make it work.

Here are a couple of ideas for using the Internet when you're computer and phone-line restricted. Think about your goals for the Net activity; then read on. These are, of course, only a few of the possibilities for working with the Internet.

TIP

Limiting Internet access

Because the Net offers access, both as consumer and producer of information, to millions of people worldwide, content is as varied as the users. You'll find things that'll make you chuckle, cry, and cringe. Recently, several commercial products have emerged that will make limiting Net access, if that's what you feel is appropriate, easier than ever.

Currently there are more than 200 Internet newsgroups that contain sexually explicit material. Sites on the Web also contain pictures and text that depict sexual situations. Until recently, there has been no way to control access to this information . . . until *Surfwatch*.

Surfwatch is a software product for the Macintosh and for PCs running Windows that allows you to be responsible for blocking access to sexually explicit sites from individual computers *or* through networks. A password-protected on/off switch enables you to allow or prevent access.

Surfwatch comes with an initial listing of hundreds of sites containing Internet addresses that the folks at Surf-Watch believe might be objectionable to your kids. They also offer a subscription program that updates the list of unwanted sites automatically. Their standards are admittedly subjective, but you can request customized

lists for your particular setting. *Surfwatch* controls access to specific WWW, FTP, Gopher, and chat sites, and it can restrict access to select newsgroups. *Surfwatch* works with any Macintosh or Power Macintosh with System 7.x or higher and with any modem, ISDN, or high-speed Internet link. *Surfwatch* is not designed to work with commercial online services. If a program like this interests you, contact Surf-Watch via e-mail: `info@surfwatch.com`

Another program, called *CyberPatrol*, offers blocking at the page or file level. Unlike *Surfwatch*, which screens files at the Net-address level, *CyberPatrol* allows more flexibility in screening students from viewing resources within a single site. *CyberPatrol* also offers the ability to limit a user's access to the Internet to specific times of the day and specific days of the week. With the product, users get *CyberNOT Block List,* a directory of researched Internet sites containing material deemed objectionable by a group of Microsystems' employees, a group composed of parents and teachers. The resulting list is fully customizable and is updated weekly on *CyberPatrol's* Web page. For more information, surf to: `http://www.microsys.com`

The Internet learning center

One strategy for using the Net in a resource-limited environment is the creation of a learning center. Meet with fellow teachers and develop short, meaningful excursions that are step-by-step oriented and focus on a specific learning goal with some kind of written product. With this configuration, you can easily rotate students of just about any age through the learning center and have them be successful.

Carefully written directions and a whole-class discussion of the technical aspects of the activity will prevent Net-floundering and frustration on everyone's part. Have students write *something* about their journey and/or print data to share with you and the rest of the class as evidence of success in their learning adventure.

Control their time-on-task by using clocks or timers and make sure to give them a "starting point" (Internet URL) from which to explore. Allow students to work in pairs, if possible, to encourage synergy and reduce the likelihood that they will float past unanswered questions.

One more thing: If students don't make good use of their time, restrict their access to the Web. You'll quickly find that this is just as effective as the "no video games until you do your homework" rule at home.

Splashing the Net on your walls

Sometimes exploring the Net with your entire class makes sense. Hook your computer to a good-quality LCD panel and project your Internet session on your classroom walls. This strategy for whole-group instruction makes good sense, especially when you're all just learning to surf.

Write down ten or twelve random topics related to your subject area (or not) and have students draw them from a hat. Use these topics as a starting point (and goal) for your on-the-wall activity. I usually model that by beginning with a *search engine* (a site on the Internet that allows you to search other sites), such as the WebCrawler (`http://webcrawler.com/`), and show students how moving from link to link until you find the information that you need is an exercise in hit and miss.

To keep the entire class involved, frequently question students about what they're seeing and how the surfing expedition is proceeding. Try questions like:

- ✔ Does this Internet site contain information that is credible, truthful, and helpful for our learning goal?

- ✔ Does this Internet site contain *all* the information we need? If not, what are the unanswered questions?

- ✔ Now that we've gotten the information, what should we *do* with it?

Having one or more students keep a log of all sites that you've visited is also helpful. After the activity is complete, create a "road map" that shows where you surfed and helps students understand the dynamic nature of the Internet. This activity also helps students to think about the complexity and vastness of the Internet as a classroom resource.

Working without a Net

If you don't have access to the Net via a direct Internet connection, remember that most online services offer Internet connection. If you don't have *any* access to the Internet, try asking a friend who does to print samples of data mined from the Net, including screenshots and URLs, and share these with your students to give them a taste of what Net-surfing is like.

Here are few more activities to heighten awareness of the Net while you await your connection:

✔ Have students collect newspaper and magazine articles focusing on the Net and create a bulletin board.

✔ Test student knowledge of the Internet by challenging them to draw a picture of the Internet (this activity can be lots of fun — who knows *what* you'll get!).

✔ Invite a parent or a local business to give a presentation to your class using their Internet connection.

✔ Invite students to create a classroom dictionary of terms found in books and periodicals relating to the Internet.

Meanwhile, put on your best lobbying face and begin to work behind the scenes to make sure that your Internet connection will be a reality. For some statistics that'll help you in your quest, check out *The Internet For Teachers* (IDG Books Worldwide, Inc.).

Objective Realities

As you plan for the use of the Web (or the Internet) in general, it's important to take a lesson from some of our underwater friends. SCUBA divers have a saying: Plan your dive and dive your plan. It's obvious that good planning is essential to any classroom activity, and following those plans will lead your students to the projected outcomes as efficiently as possible.

When planning to use the Internet with students, think about using the Internet to:

✔ Expand and enhance problem-solving skills (throw out a topic and see what resources can be identified)

✔ Build critical-thinking skills through focused, outcome-based activities

✔ Evaluate what students see/hear/read based on a predetermined set of parameters

Reread the last bullet above. This is a biggie. It's scary to think that there are folks out there who believe everything that they read in a newspaper or everything that they see on television. It's more scary to think that students will be surfing the Internet, where there is even *less* journalistic control and fewer folks who might be guided by truth and other desirable virtues. Talk with your students early in the process of using the Internet about taking a careful look at the *source* of the information that they're reading and work to develop a list of "essential questions" about the credibility and truthfulness of each source they stumble upon.

It's also a great idea to have students cite Internet resources when they use the information for classroom assignments, presentations, or other research activities. Check out the sidebar in this chapter that shows you what the good folks at the APA said about citing resources.

How to cite electronic media

After your students find information on the Net, how do they properly give the author credit when they use material? Here's a set of standards modeled on the *1994 APA guidelines*.

- Electronic mail messages:

    Author (Year, month day). <u>Subject of message</u> [e-mail to receiver's name], [Online]. Available e-mail: receiver's e-mail address.

Here is an example:

    Templeton, P.K. (1995, June 5). <u>Project Deadline</u> [e-mail to fred.flintstone@slate.com], [Online]. Available e-mail: fred.flintstone@slate.com.

The following examples show other kinds of citations:

- Articles available via mailing lists:

    Root, C. (1994). ESL and learning disabilities: A guide for the ESL practitioner. <u>TESL-EJ 1</u>. Available e-mail:LISTSERV@CMSA.BERKELEY.EDU Message: GET TESLEJ01 A-4 TESLEJ-L F=Mail

- FTP or telnet:

    Kehoe, B.P. (1992). <u>Zen and the art of the Internet</u> (2nd. Ed.), [Online]. Available FTP (Telnet): quake.think.com Directory: pub/etext/1992. File: Zen10.text.

- Computer programs:

    Sandford, J.A. & Browne, R.J. (1985). Captain's log: Cognitive Training System (Version 1.0), [Computer program]. Indianapolis: Psychological Software Services, Inc.

- Online databases:

    <u>The educational directory</u>. [Online]. (1992). Available: Knowledge Index File: The Educational Directory (EDUC6).

These guidelines are available via an e-mail message to `LISTSERV@CMSA.BERKELEY.EDU` with the message `get TESLEJ-L APAGUIDE TESLEJ-L F=MAIL` (leave the Subject line blank).

Making the Grade

What is a successful outcome from an Internet session? It's important to think about your expectations before you set about surfing the Internet. Because of the dynamic nature of the medium, every session may not be successful. The Net is vast, but it still doesn't have quality, credible information on every topic imaginable. More often than not, the session will have to be supplemented with good ol' books and other print media to produce a clear picture of the topic. All this presents some interesting challenges when it comes time to evaluate student progress and assess outcomes.

How do you evaluate students on Internet projects? The answer depends largely on your goal. Think about whether the goal of your lesson is to do one or more of the following:

- Teach something *about* the Internet
- Teach how to *use* the Internet
- Teach something by *using information gained from* the Internet

Regardless of whether you're focusing on the Internet, the process of using the Internet, or the way the resulting information is used, you can use the same techniques of evaluation that you use for other classroom projects. Checklists, rubrics, peer-evaluation, pen-and-paper exams — they all work just fine.

Want to find some great evaluation activities and checklists? Launch your WWW browser and get to the Wentworth Communications Web site (http://www.wentworth.com/). There you'll find lots of sample articles, hyperlinks to valuable education sites on the WWW, and even some home page links to schools on the Internet. The Wentworth folks publish what I believe to be the best monthly education resource for Net-surfers, *Classroom Connect* magazine. To get on the *Classroom Connect* mailing list, send e-mail to **crc-request@wentworth.com.** In the body of the message, type **subscribe**. Leave the subject of your message blank. You also can visit their FTP site for some great educational software and documents. Use FTP to get to ftp://ftp.wentworth.com/

Chapter 20
Acceptable Use Policies

*1*t's halfway through your third-period class, and a tall, lanky student shuffles into your room. The student quietly walks directly up the middle aisle. A hush falls over the room. He hands you a note and turns to walk away, but not before flashing an all-knowing little grin.

You open the note and it says, "Call Mr. Jones about the Internet ASAP. Then see me." Signed, "The Principal." Gulp!

It's inevitable, folks. Sooner or later, someone in your school will be called upon to defend the use of the Internet in the classroom, just as many before them have been called upon to defend the use of certain textbooks, movies, audio-visual aids, computers, even the quill pen (back in the younger years of progressive education). How you feel at the moment you see the note will be directly affected by one simple question: What is your school/district policy on Internet use? If your answer is "we don't have one" or "I don't know," you're in for a hefty case of indigestion, far worse than the feeling that you had when you ate the green hot dog by mistake last week in the school cafeteria.

You Need an AUP!

Let's face it: most people get most of their knowledge of the Internet from television, newspaper, and radio reports. These reports seem to work hard to flush out every tiny negative thing about the Internet. You can't turn on a television these days without seeing a news story about a kid in Paducah downloading a picture of a naked something-or-other. Few people really understand the Net. That's why it's important for you and your school to help educate your community about the positive aspects of the Internet. An *Acceptable Use Policy* (AUP) is a great way to help both your peers and your community understand how and why you use the Internet in the classroom.

Although there have been some highly publicized cases of abuse involving computers and online services (or the Internet), reported cases are infrequent. The fact that crimes are being committed online is not a reason to avoid using online services. A better strategy is to help kids become "street smart" about what they can do to safeguard themselves against possible problems.

Who's the Boss?

One issue you should think about right off the bat is *who* should lead the effort to develop the AUP. Should the policy be developed by your school's media and technology committee? (You *do* have a media and technology committee, don't you?) Should parents and other community members be involved in the creation of the policy? Or should the policy be created at the district level and approved by your local Board of Education?

This is a big issue. It could be a bigger issue than *Catcher in the Rye* was. (When did *you* first check out that book?) In general, most educators would prefer a district-wide policy. In many school systems, an Internet "rider" is added to the same policies and procedures that govern textbook adoption and curriculum material review. One difficulty in the implementation of a district-wide policy is that, in order to encompass all uses of the Net in your school system, the policy will likely be very broad. Sometimes, however, schools feel the need (either because of their community or their school culture) to make a more specific policy.

The benefit of a district-wide policy? District policies tend to promote consistency among schools in your district, are usually more broad, and if things go wrong, *you* don't take the blame. Hmm . . . Something to think about! Discuss this issue with all parties involved before deciding who should take ownership of the policy, if there is a policy at all.

Keyword: Flexible

A flexible policy contains general guidelines about who can use the online service, under what circumstances they can use the service, and what (if any) restrictions are placed upon that use. Be advised, though (for you overachievers out there), that *flexible* does not mean that you should generate a 40-page document. A brief, well-constructed, collaboratively developed document is the best bet.

Before you develop a policy, put together a group of parents, teachers, students, and other community members. Don't forget to invite a representative from your local public library (the library's support could be critical if the policy is challenged).

Spend some time educating the committee about the positives of the Internet, partly to counteract the nasties in the media, partly just to make sure that everyone's on the same (home) page. Next, shoot for a policy that can fit on one page (don't let the wordy people use nine-point type either!).

Ready to write?

I'm a big fan of not reinventing the wheel. To that end, I've slipped in a couple of AUPs in Appendix C of this book. Neither are perfect, and both are very different in style, language, content, and the limitations that they place on users. However, some of the stuff in there is really great. The folks at the Utah State Department of Education and those at Western Connecticut State University get a big gold star for being very proactive. Ready to share those kudos?

Intelligence inside

Based on the issues raised in the sample Acceptable Use Policies in Appendix C and a few from newsgroups on the Net, what follows is a handy little checklist of things you might include in your policy.

An effective AUP may cover several topics. They may include statements that:

- ✔ Address adherence to state, local, and federal laws
- ✔ Outline the limits (if any) of access
- ✔ Provide a definition of *authorized use* and *authorized access*
- ✔ Explain the responsibility of the student, parent, and teacher/administrator
- ✔ Set forth a penalty for not abiding by the rules
- ✔ Declare who can grant/revoke privileges of Net access
- ✔ Caution against revealing personal information or establishing face-to-face meetings with other people who are online

Don't forget signature lines for parent, student, and school representative signatures!

Rules for online safety (for kids)

As part of a project supported by all the major online services, the National Center for Missing and Exploited Children (1-800-THE-LOST) and the Interactive Services Association developed a great pamphlet entitled *Child Safety on the Information Highway* (1994). The pamphlet contains, among other things, a list of items entitled "My Rules for Online Safety." These rules are excellent for use as part of, or as an addendum to, an acceptable use policy. They are written in terms that both parents and children can understand. Here are the rules recommended by the NCMEC:

✔ I will not give out personal information such as my address, telephone number, parents' work number or address, or the name and location of my school without my parents' permission.

✔ I will tell my parents right away if I come across any information that makes me feel uncomfortable.

✔ I will never agree to get together with someone I "meet" online without first checking with my parents. If my parents agree to the meeting, I will be sure that it is in a public place and bring my mother or father along.

✔ I will never send a person my picture or anything else without first checking with my parents.

✔ I will not respond to any messages that are mean or in any way make me feel uncomfortable. It is not my fault if I get a message like that. If I do, I will tell my parents right away so that they can contact the online service.

✔ I will talk with my parents so that we can set up rules for going online. We will decide upon the time of day I can be online, the length of time I can be online, and the appropriate areas for me to visit. I will not access other areas or break the rules without their permission.

Sharing Your Policy

Don't let the protocol monster bite you in the node. Before you even think of sharing your policy with external audiences, make sure that your district media and/or technology coordinators get the chance for input. Remember that their input can be critical in defending the policy later on.

When you're ready to publish the policy, remember that the reason you created a policy in the first place was to be proactive. Introducing the policy to external audiences before something happens might save you stress, time, and (in some cases) your job. Whether the policy is created at the district level or the local level, there are several ways to spread the word, and if you're really shrewd, you can end up with some much-needed "fundage" to help you with your school's technology needs.

Here are a few ideas from schools around the nation for spreading the word about your policy or your use of the Internet:

- ✔ Educate your community about how the Net is used (hold open houses and/or seminars, or offer training for parents).
- ✔ Make sure that teachers and administrators know and understand the policy (another faculty meeting agenda item!).
- ✔ Make the policy readily accessible to all teachers and students (plaster it *everywhere!*).

Now, one last thing to do. Be sure to share your policy with the Internet education community. Who knows; your AUP could end up in a book like this some day! Share via online services (check the EdConnection library in the Electronic Schoolhouse [Keyword: **ESH**] on America Online) or post it to an education newsgroup.

C'mon. Creating an AUP was a lot of work, but it promoted dialog and educated lots of your peers and community; and now you can help others. I'd call that a lasting contribution to education as we know it!

The 5th Wave   By Rich Tennant

"Awww jeez- I was afraid of this. Some poor kid, bored with the usual chat lines, starts looking for bigger kicks, pretty soon they're surfin' the seedy back alleys of cyberspace, and before you know it they're into a file they can't 'undo'. I guess that's why they call it the Web. Somebody open a window!"

Chapter 21

Spreading the Word

● ●

In This Chapter

▶ Vogue: the staff development way

▶ Doing the right thing the right way for the right reasons

▶ Net by teacher: Internet training tips

● ●

*R*emember when computers first began to appear in schools? I remember teaching hundreds of fellow teachers to be "computer literate." Back then, computer literacy meant knowing the difference between RAM and ROM and knowing that, to insert a $5^1/_4$-inch floppy into a disk drive, you "put your thumb on the label." We all sat through courses in BASIC programming. We went to sleep at night thinking about:

```
20 for x=1 to 10
30 flash
40 print "I Love <fill in the blank>"
50 next x
60 end
```

We gave "computer licenses" to students and personal floppy disks to teachers. Not too distant memories, right? We spent countless hours focusing on *the machine*, not on what we'd *do* with the machine.

As the years rolled on, we discovered that teaching *with* computers was more important and valuable than teaching *about* computers. Courses in *applications* appeared, and suddenly we were learning about word processors, spread-sheets, and databases. No longer did we have to learn, or care to learn, about what's under the hood of our computer. We learned to use basic tools, both for instruction and for personal productivity. Then someone figured out that we still weren't focusing on the *educational outcomes* or *educational objectives*.

Now the winds of technology-staff development have shifted again (this time toward *interdisciplinary* instruction), with the computer as a *tool* to achieve an *educational objective*. Courses in creative writing, for example, now include instruction in using a word processor. Finally, the technology is becoming easier to use — more transparent. Now we can get back to the business of focusing on the subjects at hand and not the technology.

We can learn much from these lessons on the introduction of computers. Look around. Do you see "Internet literacy" classes offered? Why not teach a course in "How to Teach Biology 101's Frog Dissection" and include information about how to access the Web's "virtual frog" page as a part of the course?

(The URL for virtual frog is `http://george.lbl.gov:80/vfrog/`)

Models for Staff Development

Everybody's talking about the Internet. Everybody wants to learn more about it. Here's your chance to light a fire under your peers and really make some exciting things happen!

Many models for sharing knowledge about the Internet with fellow teachers are available. Here are four methods that I think might be effective for you. Each of these methods is teacher-tested and can net (no pun intended) some really amazing results!

Teachers teaching teachers

Think about centering your instruction on teaching teachers how to teach other teachers. Focus classroom activities on (1) developing (or modeling) a scope-and-sequence for instruction about the Net and (2) producing a variety of activities, written in lesson-plan form, that you can use to ensure that teachers feel comfortable using on their first Net-ventures.

As with any staff development, make sure that you consider follow-up activities ("refresher courses") as you plan, to ensure that folks can keep up with the dynamic Internet marketplace.

Summer camp

Try CyberCamp! Yep — we're talking tee-shirts, camp counselors, off-the-computer activities (the wellness people will love this!), and lots of focused Internet-and-computer-based activities that are driven by surveys of your camp's participants. Don't be afraid of asking your school's business partner, or the local PTA, to cosponsor the event. Summer camps might run for a week and would be a great way to develop a Net-surfing wonder-team!

To be sure that the campfire doesn't fizzle, make sure to create a notebook of activities that participants can carry back to their classrooms. Stick the materials in a three-ring binder and have participants add to the package during the year. It goes without saying that these activities should be shared via e-mail or newsgroups with the Internet community as well!

After-school blitz

Offer a couple of hours a week of *open* instruction for teachers in your school. Keep the atmosphere light (there's nothing more tired and stressed than a teacher after the final bell) and the content focused on real-world activities that are immediately useful in the classroom. In general, a ten-hour course, taught over five consecutive weeks, works well. Don't forget to plan for a "class reunion" later in the year to see how your class time has paid off.

Be sure to take the time to apply for continuing education credit for the participants. Look for instructors at your local college or university or your regional education agency.

Weekend cyberwarriors

Want to have some *real* fun? Try a casual roundup of teachers on an *Internet Saturday*. About eight hours of instruction on a Saturday can do wonders for getting teachers and administrators fired up about the possibilities of using the Internet for instruction or personal productivity. The Internet, it seems, is one of the few topics that teachers will actually give up a Saturday for. Try it. More than you think will apply!

Keep the curriculum focused, the atmosphere fun, and allow frequent breaks. Begin your day with a short overview of the Internet (puh-leeeese keep the Net history part *very* short!) and then jump immediately on the Net for a topic-based activity like planning a trip to an exotic resort, finding a good seafood restaurant in Boston, or searching for information on education reform in the archives of the U.S. Department of Education.

Again, it's imperative that you create a structure for documenting great activities, useful Internet addresses, and tips for teaching. Don't forget to add a bit of time at day's end for general questions and a discussion about classroom management.

Your Responsibility as a Cyberteacher

Before you launch off on teaching your first Internet course for your peers, take a tip from a friend who conducts staff development for vocational education teachers and "know the tools of the trade before you trade the tools." You'll be much more successful if you have a good understanding of what the Net *is*, what it *does*, and the *challenges* you might face in using the Net with students. Setting up rules and discussing ethics with students (no matter what their age) is an important part of your responsibility as a purveyor of Internet wisdom.

Even though the Internet is still the "wild, wild west" of Cyberspace (itself a virtually lawless and totally free environment), people have been talking about Internet ethics and rules since the Net's inception. Groups such as the Division Advisory Panel of the National Science Foundation's Division of Network Communications Research and Infrastructure (is that a mouthful or what?) have formalized thoughts about unethical and unacceptable activities. They define these activities as those that purposely do any of the following:

- ✔ Seek to gain unauthorized access to the resources of the Internet
- ✔ Disrupt the intended use of the Internet
- ✔ Waste resources (people, capacity, computer)
- ✔ Destroy the integrity of computer-based information
- ✔ Compromise the privacy of users

These guidelines can provide a platform for discussion with your peers (and students) about ethics and responsibility as well as serve as a jumping-off point for anticipating the questions of parents and administrators. Take the time to incorporate a discussion of ethics and responsibility into every Internet staff-development session. Focus on what effective Internet citizens should *know, do,* and *be like*. You might even have your class work in small groups to develop their own Code of Internet Ethics and share the results with your district technology coordinator or college dean — you won't be sorry that you did.

After you've taken your students on a tour of the Net and discussed the previously mentioned list of Internet don'ts, ask them to work in small groups to develop their own Code of Internet Ethics and post each group's work in your classroom.

The top ten ways to be a good Internet citizen

Want people to smile at you when they see you on the information superhighway? Think about these ten tips before you surf!

1. Never knowingly post or forward information that's not true.

2. Have good manners.

3. Tell people when you like their work.

4. Be creative, not destructive.

5. Always obey copyright laws.

6. Think before you send.

7. Be yourself.

8. Don't use someone else's account or password.

9. Ask for help when you need it.

10. Think before you upload.

(Adapted from *"Ten Commandments for Computer Ethics,"* Computer Ethics Institute.)

Staff Development Tips

The Internet learning curve is a bit steep, but you can overcome it easily. The best way to learn is to ask someone who's already an Internet surfer to show you the way. And guess what: these mentors don't even have to be in the same country as you are! They can be anywhere in Cyberspace. You can use telecommunications such as e-mail, LISTSERVS, and so on, to communicate. Someone recently called this relationship *telementoring.* I think that's a nifty way of saying, "Find a mentor, and have that person teach you about the Net."

I like to think of Internet tools as "stumbleware." One of the best things about the Internet is that you very often stumble onto resources or ideas that you'd never dreamed of finding. The best way to learn about the Net is just to dive right in and try it. An easy introduction through a commercial online service is a great way to begin.

During your first visits, focus on *one* tool or *one* type of information. Think about how you can make your next visit more productive as you explore. As with any technology, the more you use it, the better you become.

As a practical matter, using a good-quality overhead display makes sense for large group instruction. Multiple phone lines also help. Don't be bashful in asking local colleges or universities to let you use their facility if you don't have access to these important tools.

Beyond pen pals . . .

E-mail can be a very powerful tool in your classroom. The first thing you'll probably think of is simply finding electronic pen pals for your students. Finding electronic pen pals is nice and can be interesting; but I've found, particularly with K–8 students, that the quality of pen-pal writing often degrades to something such as the following excerpt from a fifth grader's pen-pal writing:

> How old are you? What do you look like? Which is your favorite Teenage Mutant Ninja Turtle?

Wouldn't you rather have this excerpt from a fifth grader's essay on "A Special Person in My Life"?

> My grandmother is the nicest person I know. She cares about me, about my mom, and about my puppy, Joker. I like the way her cheeks turn red when she laughs. That always happens when we play together on the porch. She always takes time for me. She must have been a great mommy.

As you think about using the Internet with your students, you'll discover many projects that focus on higher-order thinking skills such as analysis and evaluation. A teacher in New York developed a writing project that featured student-authored biographies created from interviews with an "everyday person on the street." She exchanged the biographies with teachers at other schools; and together, the collected biographies create a "Profile of America." A media specialist from Canada built a database of children's book reviews, collected from students all over the world via e-mail. The final product was posted to a Web site that features children's literature and other resources (`http://www.ucalgary.ca/~dkbrown/index.html`).

Sigh. I had a nice grandma, too. Think about moving your students *beyond* pen pals.

Finally, be sure that you focus your instruction on teaching *with* the Internet, not teaching *about* the Net. Be sure to link your instruction to curriculum-focused activities and think about possible *tangible* products and the ways in which you might evaluate those products.

You'll find that well-conducted staff development is a great opportunity to motivate teachers, however *veteran* they are; and you'll quickly see the wheels turning in the minds of even the staunchest techno-phobe.

It's fun and worth the effort! Happy surfing!

Part V
The Part of Tens: Places to Go, Things to Do

The 5th Wave   By Rich Tennant

"Children- it is not necessary to whisper while we're visiting the Vatican Library Web site."

In this part . . .

As of the end of 1995, more than 3,000 schools have made the jump to Cyberspace and have posted their own Web pages. Far more schools now have access to the Web through local information providers, through online services, or through colleges, universities, or libraries with big hearts and fileservers.

As you might guess, people e-mail me "cool Web site" addresses just about every day. So, I've collected these sites (and added a bunch more that I've stumbled upon) and use this part of the book to present them as starting points for your Internet journeys. You'll find something for the media center, something for teachers, something for parents and students, and even something for "after the homework is done" (fun stuff).

Chapter 22

Ten Web Sites for Your Media Center

In This Chapter

▶ Why can't I use that content?

▶ Surfing libraries

▶ Meandering through museums

▶ Tapping reference resources

▶ Seek and ye shall find!

*O*ne place in which the Internet should be a fixture in your school is the media center (or *library* to use an archaic-but-still-wonderful term!). The richness, quality, and timeliness of research and reference resources on the Internet is increasing daily. Think of the Internet as your *third line* reference resource, after print and local electronic media (such as CD-ROMs) are explored.

Libraries are really one perfect place for an Internet connection because:

✔ If there's anyone on the planet who knows how to narrow a broad topic, it's a school media specialist

✔ In many schools, the media center is a technology hub (there are great books there, too)

✔ There's often someone there to give individual attention to the floundering students who come to use the Net

✔ It's very often located in the center of the school

✔ Media specialists will nag you to death if you don't install it there (after all, the Internet *is* the world's most up-to-date reference tool!)

The Internet is a great source for information that might be too specific, or too current, to be included in the encyclopedias or periodicals at your disposal. No matter where you locate the connection, you'll often need someone to help surfers who run aground. Examining issues like copyright and identifying some terrific Net sites in advance can really save students, teachers, and other educators (such as media specialists) lots of time.

Media Issues

Acceptable use policies

Take a look at AUPs at the resource-rich Armadillo site.

Address: `http://www.rice.edu/armadillo/acceptable.html`

Copyright bonanza

A self-described "aging exile from the Copyright Office" offers up information on copyright issues.

Address: `http://lcweb.loc.gov/copyright`

Virtual Libraries

Virtual Library

Address: `http://tecfa.unige.ch/info-edu-comp.html`

Internet Public Library

Address: `http://ipl.sils.umich.edu`

Library of Congress

Browse the stacks of the Mother of All Libraries. (See Figure 22-1.)

Address: `http://www.loc.gov`

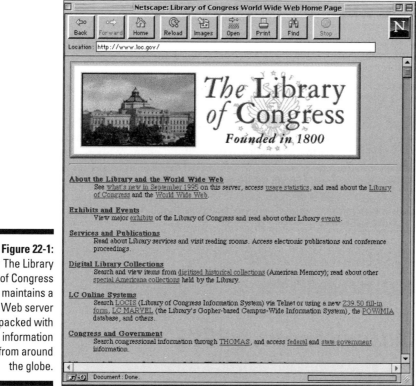

Figure 22-1:
The Library
of Congress
maintains a
Web server
packed with
information
from around
the globe.

Virtual Museums

Museum of Natural History, Smithsonian Institution

A Web site almost as vast as the museum it represents!

Address: `http://nmnhwww.si.edu/nmnhweb.html`

Exploratorium home page

Take a virtual visit to San Francisco's Exploratorium.

Address: `http://www.exploratorium.edu/`

Great Museum Index — NSTA

One-stop shopping, if it's museums you'd like to browse (courtesy of our friends at the National Science Teachers Association).

Address: http://www.nsta.org/misg/museumg/

Have your students create their own virtual museum. Choose a time period, a country, a type of art, or an industry, and have your students mine the Net for sites containing information useful in understanding more about the world around them. Collect the URLs and put them together in a custom Web page file. (See Chapters 14 through 16 for information about creating your own Web pages.) After the file is created, post it to your school's Web server under a thematic heading, or make the information available to teachers and students on disk for use with their Web browsers at home.

Reference Resources

CIA World Factbook 1995

Address: http://www.odci.gov/cia/publications/95fact/index.html

Maps, maps, maps

If it's on the Earth, there's a map here for it.

Address: http://pubweb.parc.xerox.com:80/map/

US Census Information Server

Address: http://www.census.gov/cgi-bin/popclock/

Hello, Mars!

Get a great view of the solar system.

Address: http://bang.lanl.gov/solarsys/

The Corporation for Public Broadcasting

An amazing source for education links. This Web site includes schedule information and special projects for teachers and students. (See Figure 22-2.)

Address: http://www.cpb.org/

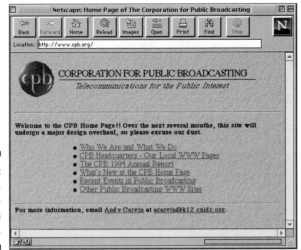

The Internet is teeming with electronic magazines and rich sources of information from media moguls worldwide. Challenge your students to a scavenger hunt where they identify Web sites with content supplied by the "biggies" in media content such as CNN, *National Geographic, USA Today, The New York Times,* and so on. Have them create a chart that indicates the URL, cites the media source, and briefly describes the type of reference information found at the site.

Time Magazine

Read it (and search it) on the Net *before* it hits the newsstands!

Address: http://www.timeinc.com/time/timehomepage.html

Search Engines

You've got to have a place to begin any task. When you visit your library, you usually begin at the card catalog, er, computer circulation station, and enter keywords to search for the book or periodical that will help you complete your task. The Internet offers a number of "electronic Internet catalogs," driven by special software (called *search engines*) that searches the Internet for specific content. These electronic catalogs that can be your (and your students') first stop on the information highway.

The good news is that these search sites offer some very powerful search tools — most support *Boolean* (*and, or, not*) searches, and some even offer full-text searches. The bad news? No single site can search the entire volume of the Internet (so visit more than one site!). There is no more valuable place on the Net to begin your search. Encourage your students to focus on these sites first!

Yahoo	`http://www.yahoo.com/`
WebCrawler	`http://webcrawler.com/`
Lycos	`http://lycos/cs.cmu.edu/`
Galaxy	`http://www.einet.net/cgi-bin/wais-text-multi/`
InfoSeek	`http://www2.infoseek.com/`

It's important to encourage students to visit more than one search site when researching, because no one site contains the one, all-encompassing search tool. One activity sure to liven things up is to offer up a topic of interest to your students (you know: something like Nintendo or chocolate, vices shared by most of the inhabitants of planet Earth), and send them off to find out how many sites contain information about the topic. Give each group the URL for only *one* of the aforementioned search sites, and see how different the results can be. Spend some debriefing time, discussing why the sites produced different results and debating the plusses and minuses of each search engine.

Chapter 23

Ten Web Sites for Parents and Kids

L iterally thousands of sites on the Net are stuffed with information that is perfect for students who are working on school projects or parents who are searching for the latest information on everything from parenting to polo. The ten (or so) links below are great places to begin.

 Remember that URLs (Net addresses) change as often as the direction of the wind, so don't be too disappointed if your surfboard hits a dead end now and then. To find the "change of address," simply visit one of the many Internet search sites (such as Yahoo located at `http://www.yahoo.com/`) and enter the site name as a search term. You'll be back surfing in no time.

Surfing Schools

Atlantic View Elementary School

A great student-created home page focusing on social studies.

Address: `http://fox.nstn.ca/~nbarkhou/avshome.html`

Ralph Bunche School

The Ralph Bunche School in Harlem, NY — a nice Web page. (See Figure 23-1.)

Address: `http://mac94.ralphbunche.rbs.edu/`

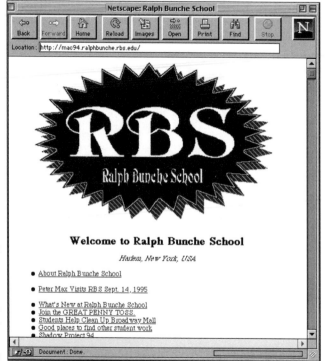

Figure 23-1:
This school
in Harlem is
known for
its super
Web pages!

Create your own list of schools on the World Wide Web. It's a great way to help everyone realize the growth and potential of the Internet. All you need is a map of the world, some pushpins to indicate the geographic locations of Net sites, and a place for students to contribute the URLs that they've found. With over 2,100 schools already on the Web, there's plenty out there to find. The following site is a great jumping-off point:

Address: `http://www.wentworth.com/`

Learning Sites

Safe site for kids

Address: http://www.webfeats.com/illusion/index.html

Children's literature

Address: http://www.ucalgary.ca/~dkbrown/

Kids' site

Address: http://www.sju.edu/~milliken/demos/hot-educ.html

(See Figure 23-2.)

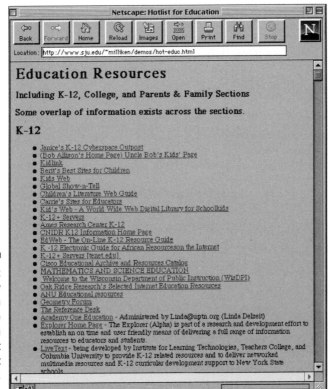

Figure 23-2:
One of many places on the Web packed with sites that are great for kids.

The Young Scientist Program

Address: `http://pharmdec.wustl.edu/YSP/`

Projects and Resources

National Air and Space Museum

Address: `http://ceps.nasm.edu:2020/NASMpage.html`

U.N. Youth Summit

Address: `http://tdg.uoguelph.ca/un50/`

Need Alaskan?

Alaskan Web site!

Address: `http://www.customcpu.com/`

Midlink

An electronic magazine for kids in the middle grades — generally ages 10 to 15 — *Midlink* is published bimonthly, and each issue has a new and exciting theme. *Midlink* is sponsored by Discovery Middle School in Orlando, FL.

Address: `http://longwood.cs.ucf.edu:80/~MidLink/`

Chapter 24

Ten Web Sites for Teachers

In This Chapter

▶ Oodles of online projects

▶ Electronic teacher resources

▶ Content-rich sites

▶ Resources for productive teachers

▶ Research-R-Us

*1*n the process of writing *The World Wide Web For Teachers,* I sent a survey (via e-mail, of course) to 20 of my online friends and asked the simple question: "What would you like to see in the book?" The overwhelming reply came almost immediately: "Lots of Web links!" (I also got some great jokes and a few recipes for German chocolate cake.) So . . . I got the surf team together, and we spent hours combing the Net for sites that would be great for teachers, students, and anyone else interested in education. The first ten (or twenty) are right here in this chapter; the rest, on the accompanying CD.

This book and the accompanying CD contain more links than you'll see anywhere thanks to the hundreds of folks on the Net who sent me their favorites and thanks to the wizardry of my Web-surfer buddy, Craig Wall.

One caution, however: Sometimes links change because their Webmasters (creators) change the pathway of their Web site, and sometimes links just disappear. Chances are that you'll encounter some "404" (not found) errors along the way; but at press time, all of 'em worked.

Online Projects

You're in luck ! There are literally thousands of places on the Net and on online services where you can find rich, interesting projects for students at all levels. Each of the sites below features instructions about enhancing and enriching your curriculum objectives through interactive exchanges of writing, data, or pictures. Surf them all and you'll get the flavor of the wide variety of projects available on the Internet.

Projects galore!

An information-rich source of online projects and classroom-implementation strategies. (See Figure 24-1).

Address: `http://gsn.org/gsn/gsn.home.html`

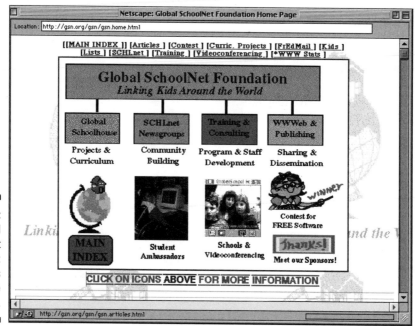

Figure 24-1:
The Global
SchoolNet
Foundation:
Linking Kids
Around the
World.

Tons of teacher topics

Access this site only when you have lots of time! You will sink into a deep pit of rich resources never to return again!

Address: `http://www.asd.k12.ak.us/Andrews/TeacherTopics.html`

JASON Project

This site features interactive explorations around the globe. It's a must-see for science lovers!

Address: `http://seawifs.gsfc.nasa.gov/scripts/JASON.html`

Electronic Teacher Resources

Australia online

Here you can get a glimpse of the ambitious and well-developed I*EARN site from "down under."

Address: http://www.peg.apc.org/~iearn/

U.S. Department of Education

A humongous listing of education-related Internet resources is available on this site.

Address: http://www.ed.gov/EdRes/EducRes.html

Educational technology

This site has a fine summary of electronic journals and links to sites that discuss issues in educational technology.

Address: http://tecfa.unige.ch/info-edu-comp.html

HyperStudio Journal

This is an online "e-journal" that features information and projects that use *HyperStudio* from Roger Wagner Publishing.

Address: http://www.hsj.com/HSJ.html

Educom

Educom is a daily newsletter featuring news about education-oriented Web sites. Get it via Web or e-mail — instructions on how to get the information via e-mail are available on the Web sites. (See Figure 24-2.)

Address: http://educom.edu/

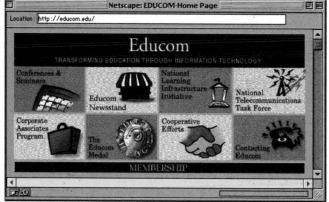

Figure 24-2:
One of the best collections of education resources on the Net.

SyllabusWeb

SyllabusWeb is a popular higher-ed journal packed full of curriculum and technology ideas and research.

Address: http://www.syllabus.com/

Subject Area Content

Look for lots more of these on *The World Wide Web For Teachers CD-ROM*!

NASA K-12 Internet Initiative

This is one of many quality Web pages from the great folks at NASA.

Address: http://quest.arc.nasa.gov/index.html

Geometry Forum

For those of you who are thinking mathematically, this page is great!

Address: http://forum.swarthmore.edu/~steve/

Shakespeare

Here's a great Web page dedicated to the "other" Bard.

Address: http://the-tech.mit.edu:80/Shakespeare/works.html

National Science Foundation

This site is a great source for research, lesson plans, projects, and more.

Address: http://www.nsf.gov/

Challenge your fellow teachers to a subject-based lesson plan contest! After an overview of the Web and a lesson or two on navigation, turn them loose to browse for content related to their own subject areas. Supply a short, easy-to-use, Net-lesson-plan form (perhaps in electronic form). Have one or more of the participants share a sample lesson at your next department or faculty meeting to help others realize the potential uses of the Net. Don't forget to use your school-wide or district-wide network (or snail-mail) to share this great resource!

Teacher Productivity

All the information on the Net isn't just for students. There is a wealth of information posted *by* teachers and *for* teachers. From accessing ERIC for your grad-school class to browsing lesson plans, you'll find plenty of resources to help you burn the midnight oil.

Cool School Tools!

An amazing collection of resources from reference sources to projects to lesson plans — a must-see on the information super highway! (See Figure 24-3.)

Address: http://www.bham.lib.al.us.cooltools/

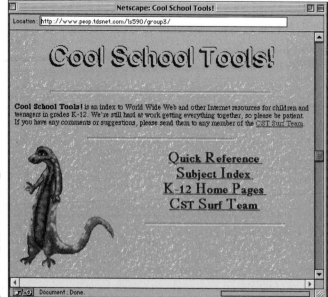

Figure 24-3:
Cool School Tools has a great collection of education resources.

Research and Education Issues

Want more information about outcome-based instruction, portfolio management, and lots more? Check the Net! Here are a few starting points.

Instructional Technology Research Online

You'll find bunches of links, technical information, bibliographies, and FAQs for educators interested in instructional technology.

Address: http://129.8.48.23/InTRO/InTRO.html

Magpie

Here's a great educational resource/database.

Address: http://www.dcs.aber.ac.uk/~jjw0/index_ht.html

Access ERIC

Check out this site if you're interested in:

- ✔ Searching the ERIC database
- ✔ Tapping the subject expertise of the 27 ERIC components
- ✔ Finding out how to use the ERIC system
- ✔ Receiving publications about the latest ERIC services and products, such as *A Pocket Guide to ERIC, All About ERIC,* and *The ERIC Review* (a *free* journal on current education topics)
- ✔ Gaining direct access to the education community's premier electronic services, AskERIC, and the National Parent Information Network (NPIN)

Address: http://www.aspensys.com/eric2/welcome.html

EdWeb

Managed by the Center for Public Broadcasting, this is a great periodical for those seeking to understand the Internet and its role in education.

Address: http://k12.cnidr.org:90/resource.cntnts.html

AIMS

AIMS is Activities Integrating Math & Science — a gold mine for integrated-curriculum activities K–12.

Address: http://204.161.33.100/AIMS.html

Chapter 25
Ten Web Sites for after Your Homework

• •

▶ Free Willy?

▶ Dig the robot

▶ Leader of leaders

▶ The Science Guy

▶ Go where no teacher has gone before

▶ Miss Piggy goes hi-tech

▶ TV on the Web

▶ DisneyWeb

▶ Elvis lives!

▶ Useless, but fun

▶ Mysterious bonus site!

• •

*T*his chapter contains places to go after all the papers are graded, parents are called, homework is done, and dinner is over. Some of the Web sites in this chapter are educational, some are for professional growth, and some are just plain fun. Whether you're an educator or a student, these Web sites will keep your surfboard in the big waves for hours.

SeaWorld

Summer vacation is a long way away. You can enjoy a sample *now* with just a click of the mouse!

Address: `http://crusher.bev.net/education/SeaWorld homepage.html`

Robot Farmer

This tele-robotic installation allows WWW users to view and interact with a remote garden filled with living plants, as shown in Figure 25-1. You and your students can plant, water, and cultivate a garden from thousands of miles away!

Address: http://www.usc.edu/dept/garden/

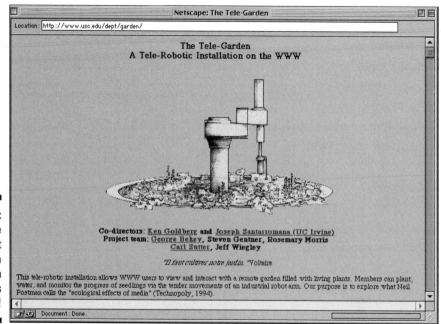

Figure 25-1:
Help the robot cultivate a garden from 2,000 miles away!

Student Leader

Currently, the site has a fascinating blend of material useful not only to student activity advisors, but also to those in any organization who are trying to develop skills in fundraising, public speaking, listening, creating enthusiasm, elections, and leadership styles.

Address: http://www.sentex.net/~casaa/

This site provides a great resource for student groups, faculty advisors, and anyone else interested in building professional and leadership skills. Schedule some surfing time for your student council, sports teams, or other groups for the purpose of finding information that will help them build skills to achieve their personal goals.

Use this site as the fuel for a hot lesson in leadership and management. Ask your students (your student government?) to visit the site and prepare an Internet-assisted presentation for other students at your school. Make sure that they cite the site!

Bill Nye: The Science Guy

From the popular TV show to the World Wide Web, this Science Guy will keep you guessing for hours. (See Figure 25-2.)

Address: `http://www.seanet.com/Vendors/billnye/nyelabs.html`

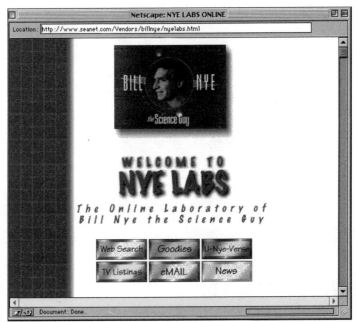

Figure 25-2:
A fellow mad scientist and teacher on the Web.

Star Trek: The Next Generation (ST:TNG)

Warp factor three! Stellar graphics.

Address: http://www.ugcs.caltech.edu:80/~werdna/sttng/

Pigs in Cyberspaaaaaaaaace . . .

Miss Piggy gets Webbed. (See Figure 25-3.)

Address: http://www-leland.stanford.edu/~rosesage/Muppet.html

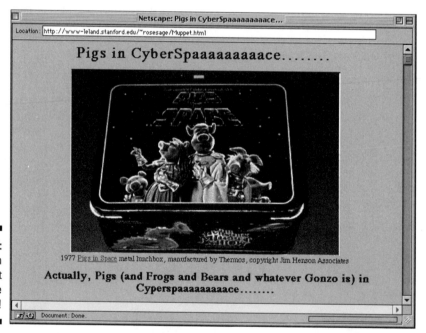

Figure 25-3:
Just when
you thought
it was safe
to fly!

The Ultimate TV List

I know: TV is mindless, but when *is* that great movie on?

Address: http://www.tvnet.com/UTVL/utvl.html

Buena Vista MoviePlex Marquee

This site features a movie extravaganza that you won't want to miss.

Address: `http://bvp.wdp.com:80/BVPM/MooVPlex.html`

History of Rock 'n' Roll

See Elvis! He's alive and well and living in his own home-on-the-Web.

Address: `http://www.hollywood.com/rocknroll/`

Useless WWW Pages

The title says it all. Bet you can't resist!

Address: `http://www.primus.com/staff/paulp/useless.html`

And one last bonus site:

Strawberry Pop-Tart Blow-Torches

Had to list this one, folks. A great example of intelligent students with *way* too much idle time!

Address: `http://www.sci.tamucc.edu/~pmichaud/toast`

Chapter 26

Ten Cool Ideas for Hot Web Projects

In This Chapter

▶ Activities that challenge students to research

▶ Activities that challenge students to communicate

▶ Activities that challenge students to produce and publish new knowledge

▶ Projects for the really young ones

1 can think of only about three reasons why you'd not want to do a project by using the Internet:

✔ You don't have easy access to the Internet (It's a money thing.)

✔ You don't understand the Net (It's a learning thing.)

✔ You have 120 kids at school, 3 kids at home, and a spouse that thinks that going to the hardware store for a Phillips-head screwdriver — or to the mall for a tube of lipstick — is an online objective (It's a time thing.)

Folks, this Internet stuff is easier than you think. No matter what the reason, a way can be found to get around every problem — learning more about the Net ensures that you can jump these hurdles like an Olympic athlete rather than a beginning runner. The toughest problem, the *time* thing, really involves the toughest change for you: rethinking teaching and learning and figuring out how (and *if*) the Internet fits into what you wish to accomplish each day.

As you scan the project descriptions below (and these descriptions are just a fraction of the ideas that are out there for the taking), think about the potential benefits to learning (either to your own learning or your students' learning) and try to determine whether or not the activity fits with the learning objectives that you're currently trying to help your students achieve.

After each project, I've given you an Internet address that may serve as a beginning point for students. Feel free to use your own places to start searching! Make a New Year's resolution to try just one of the addresses I've included. You'll find that using the Web is addictive.

Talking to the World

The first way most people use the Internet is to communicate. Think of the Internet as a bunch of boxes (computers) connected by wires (networks) and driven by lots of people (users, all of whom bring their knowledge and wisdom to bear). Online projects that allow you and your students to communicate with your peers (or with experts — or just with other citizens of Planet Earth) can bring big rewards. Using the Web is a gestalt sort of thing — the whole is greater than the sum of the parts.

Animal magnetism (zoo searches)

Lots of animals are roaming the Net. From the London Zoo to national forests, a wealth of information is available about everything from endangered species to the rare birth of a white panda in China. Have students choose an animal and visit these online zoos to collect information about that animal. Also suggest that your students find pen pals that live in cities that have zoos. Ask your students to contact these pen pals and conduct interviews, exchange pictures (digitally!), or post information about their own personal experiences at the zoos. After your students have found the information, have them create a mobile, a bulletin board, or a brochure about their animal. Be sure to add the project information (and some of the student products) to your school's Web page!

Starting point: `http://www.yahoo.com/Science/Museums_and_Exhibits/Zoos/`

Recipe exchange

Close your eyes and think about the best home-cooked meal that you've ever had. Don't you wish you could recreate that magic recipe? Here's a great idea to combine communication, research, and fundraising in your school.

Challenge your students to poll their families and friends, both on the Internet and off, and get their favorite recipes. Use the final recipes to create a *yummy* Web page that features a new recipe each week. (Be sure to create a "recipe release" form for your participants to sign!)

If you want to get really creative, try publishing your own cookbook and *advertising* the book on your new Web page. (One school in Michigan earned more than $2,500 in three weeks with their cookbook!)

Starting point: `http://www.indi.net/welcome.html`

You're moving where?

I recently moved from the sunny South to the snowy North. You wouldn't believe how useful the Net has been in helping me get comfortable. I can sign on to the Net and find subway maps, restaurants, and libraries. I've even discovered Bunker Hill!

Have your students draw the names of large cities from a hat. Explain to your students that they will soon move to the city that they picked and they need to find enough information so that they can decide in what area of the city they would like to live. Then they need to get directions to that area of the city from the airport.

Starting point: `http://www.neosoft.com/citylink/`

Hitting the Electronic Books

Bosnia

A hot spot always seems to be popping up somewhere in the world. These days, things in Bosnia are getting steamy, and many dynamics are at play there. Staying abreast of breaking news stories is a great reason log on to the Net.

Have your students work in groups to search popular search engines, such as Yahoo! (`http://www.yahoo.com/`) or CNN's Web site, for articles and information about Bosnia. Be sure to have students search for background material (weather, climate, geography, culture, and the like). Then ask your students to write a news story about some aspect of the country. Ask your students to exchange the stories with each other and to edit them until they're worthy of publication. The final newsletter that contains their stories can then be shared with other students around your school.

Starting point: `http://www.cnn.com/`

For younger students, find a map and point out Bosnia. Then ask them to search for information about clothing, major cities, and the like and encourage them to relate that information to their own surroundings.

ERIC

We educators can't seem to do anything in educational research without our good buddy ERIC. These days, ERIC not only lives in the voluminous binders on library shelves, but also lives in a CD-ROM and on the Net. Here's a starting point for educators on the long road to conducting research. You may also want to check with your local college for telnet addresses that you can use.

Starting point: `http://www.ericir.syr.edu/`

The market basket (food price comparison)

How much does a loaf of bread cost in Alaska? Here's a chance to help your students integrate communication skills with higher-order thinking skills while they research and compare prices on ten well-known products.

First, have students visit a supermarket and get the prices on ten "commodity" items: bread, Coca-Cola, apples, and the like.

Second, arrange to exchange e-mail with a school in another state (or country) and have students practice their graphing and analysis skills as they answer questions such as these:

✔ What items are more expensive where you live?

✔ What items are less expensive where you live?

✔ How much difference is there in the price of each item?

✔ List three reasons why the same item might cost a different amount depending on where you live.

✔ What products are grown or produced in your town, city, county, or state? Are these products less or more expensive where you live? Why?

✔ How might the information you collected be used to advise a person looking to move to your area? If your prices are more expensive than those at the comparison sites, how can you justify the extra expense to a prospective home buyer?

Other projects like market basket are available through mailing lists — or try Keyword: **ESH** on America Online.

Starting point: `http://pixel.cs.vt.edu/melissa/projects.html`

Which source is best?

Is everything that is published on the Net true? Here's a chance for a great lesson for students. Have small groups of students choose a topic of interest and collect information about the topic from four different sites on the Net. As they collect the information, have them note where they visited (the URL). After the information is collected, have the students in each group rank-order the sources based on their perceptions of the credibility of each source. Have each group present their sites to the class and discuss their rankings.

Starting point: http://www.cnn.com/

For younger students, discuss some easy tips for determining when information is true or false. This exercise provides a great opportunity for a values lesson on being a good "Internet Citizen" as well!

A taxing situation (search for forms on the Net — visit the IRS)

Imagine that it's 10:00 p.m. on the night before tax returns are due to Uncle Sam. You still need one more form to complete your return: the form that lists dependent income. Have your students surf the Web and find the IRS Web page, download the file for this form, and print it. Extend the activity by discussing the context in which the form might be used and some strategies for better tax planning.

Starting point: http://www.irs.ustreas.gov/prod/

Raising Arizona (search for American Indian cultural heritage)

We're lucky enough to live in a country with a very heterogeneous population. This "melting pot" helps ensure a constant opportunity for global thinking, producing new, creative ideas, and fostering an understanding of doing business around the world. Imagine that you and your students have just become ethnographers. First, have your students find out what an ethnographer is and what an ethnographer does. Next, have your students choose a culture. Finally, have them search the Internet for specific information that might be used to give a picture of that culture or of famous people from that culture.

Starting point: http://www.dreamcatchers.org/

WebCo, Ltd.

Have students list their favorite soft-drink company, computer company, fast-food company, book company, or any combination thereof. Explain that they have just been hired to create a Web page for that company and that the Web page is to be aimed at their own age group as a target market.

To create the Web page, your students should first search the Web to see if they can locate a Web page for a company similar to the one that they have chosen. After they have found a similar page, have them note what elements the company's Webmaster has chosen to include, such as graphics, advertisements, coupons, and so on.

Next, have students consider the demographics of the group of people who might be likely to purchase your company's product. What age groups might buy the product? Would the product appeal more to males or to females (or equally to both)?

Finally, have your students use *PageMill* or their favorite word processor to create a mock-up of a Web page for the business that they have selected. See Chapters 14 and 15 for lots of hints.

The icing on the cake might be to have students create a screen print of the Web page and enclose it with a letter explaining the process to the vendor. Who knows; they might write back and offer your students a job!

Starting point: `http://www.pizzahut.com/`

Breaking New Ground

The following Web activities will engage students in the process of evaluating and creating new knowledge.

I want to take a vacation in . . .

Have students use the Net to collect information about the vacation spot of their choice. Next, have them create a simple brochure telling the reason for their choice, describing highlights of the spot, and relating other facts about it. As an extension to the activity, see if they can search the Net or online services and find out about the actual travel and lodging costs at each site, or invite students to interview others via e-mail about their travel experiences. Post the final brochures in an "Around the World on the Net" area in your school's media center.

Starting point: `http://www.bookport.com/htbin/publishers/`
`thomasfilms/yah/`

Shopping on the Net

You thought telephone shopping was easy? Wait until you see how easy it is to shop on the Web! Have students search the Web for sites that are selling such items as clothing, music, food, and the like. Ask students to evaluate and analyze each site for content, organization, and "sales appeal." Then ask them to draft a note to the Webmaster explaining their rankings.

Starting point: `http://www.shopping2000.com/`

My own catalog of URLs

Here's a chance to have your fellow teachers construct a list of their favorite URLs. Post a log beside each Net-connected computer in your school. As each person enters a URL that they like, ask them to record it in the log to share later. Issue an "Internet Teacher of the Month" award for the educator who enters the most URLs.

Starting point: `http://www.yahoo.com/`

What's next on the Web (search key sites for ideas — from Java to sound to multimedia)

Virtually nothing is changing more quickly than the information on the Internet. With the Internet's explosion of content, plenty of creative people are looking for new ways to search for and display the information. You can now use the Internet as a telephone, movie projector, interactive conference tool, and CD-player.

Challenge your students to write a short paragraph about what they believe the Internet will be like in ten years. Then invite them to search the Web to find initiatives or companies that are working to push the Web to its next level. Here are a few URLs to get you started:

Apple Computer, Inc.: `http://www.info.apple.com/`

International Business Machines (IBM): `http://www.ibm.com/`

Netscape Communications, Inc.: `http://www.netscape.com/`

Sun Microsystems, Inc.: `http://www.sun.com/`

A Word about Web-Surfing Activities for Younger Students

If I were to hand you a lump of clay and ask you to design an activity for high school students, would you think that clay is for *little* kids? Probably not. After a day or so of pot-throwing, ink-stamping, and Sanskrit-writing, you'd probably think that the possibilities found within a lump of clay were endless. Think of the Internet as putty in your hands. (Okay. The phrase is a bit hackneyed, but I think that it works!) No matter what the age of your students is, information that they (or you) can use to enhance, enrich, or remediate is available.

In general, the greatest hurdle to using the Net with younger students is that much of the medium requires reading skills. However, a very graphical part of the Net exists that kids of practically any age can understand. Try the activities above, as appropriate, by using parent "coaches" or older student "buddies." You'll be surprised at how successful the young ones can be!

Part VI
Appendixes

"WELL, I NEVER THOUGHT I'D SEE THE DAY I COULD SAY I TELNETTED TO A BRAZILIAN HOST, THEN USED THE WORLD WIDE WEB TO GET A GOPHER MENU, ONLY TO FIND OUT I HAVE TO ANONYMOUS FTP."

In this part . . .

*H*ere's a place to go when you're cyber-stumped. You'll find a glossary of terms written in `plain` English, a handy dictionary of HTML tags (for the advanced Web page creator), and a sample of a policy of acceptable use that you might use as a framework for your own policy.

Appendix A
Glossary of Terms

• •

address (e-mail, mail server, Web server)

A bunch of letters and/or numbers that tell the world *who* you are followed by more letters and numbers that tell them *where* you are. Your Internet address will look something like this: `username@domain_name`. The username is your login name or account number. The domain name is the name of the computer through which you're connected to the Internet. The domain name can be a few words strung together with periods. An Internet address usually doesn't have any spaces between words or symbols, but when there are spaces, they are indicated by an *underscore* character as in `fredf@bedrock_slate.com`

alt

A newsgroup that deals with "alternative" topics. This newsgroup is often thought of as the place where topics are born. When they grow up, they move to other classifications. Beware when you are stomping around in `alt.` territory; some things in the bushes shouldn't be in your classroom.

America Online (AOL)

A public online service that has access to the Internet. AOL has the largest U.S. subscription base of any of the commercial online services. Many of its subscribers are educators.

anonymous FTP

When you log on to someone else's computer, you may need to provide a login name and password. On some systems, logging in as "anonymous" and using your e-mail address as a password is enough to give you access to public files.

ASCII

American Standard Code for Information Interchange. Another word for characters (letters and numbers) in a text file.

baud

A unit of transmission speed. The greater the baud rate, the faster data moves from point to point.

BBS

Bulletin Board System. A system that lets people post messages and read others' messages. USENET newsgroups are kinda' like the world's largest distributed BBS.

binary file

A file that may contain words, sounds, pictures, even movies, in their *raw* form.

BinHex

A program that converts a binary file, specific to a particular machine, to a text file so that it can be transferred over the Net. The program can then be used to convert the file back to binary for use on your computer.

bounce

When you send e-mail and it comes back marked as undeliverable.

browser

A program that enables you to explore the World Wide Web (WWW).

chat

The electronic equivalent of CB radio. Person-to-person, real-time conferencing.

communications program

A program that enables you to dial through a modem and access another computer. Examples are *Microphone* and *Z-Term* for Macintosh computers and *CrossTalk* and *Procomm Plus* for computers that are running Windows.

CompuServe

The granddaddy of all online communications networks. Focuses mostly on the business user.

Cyberspace

The digital world of computers and the information that passes between them. Comes from the sci-fi novel *Neuromancer* by William Gibson.

Delphi

An online service that was one of the first out of the box with Internet connections.

dial-up connection

You've got one of these if you access a network or the Internet by dialing a telephone number. The opposite, a *direct* connection, means that the computer is always hooked into the Net.

digest

A compilation of a bunch of messages posted to a mailing list. The mailing list's moderator puts all the messages together periodically, by topic, and sends them out to all the mailing list's subscribers.

domain

Internet-speak for a computer on the Net. The part of an Internet address that comes after @.

dotted quad

The techno-weenie words that describe a numerical Internet address such as this one: `128.33.43.55`

download

To move data from another computer to yours. Compare with *upload.*

e-mail

Electronic mail. Messages sent via modem or over a network.

e-World

A terrific online service from Apple Computer that's one way to get onto the information superhighway.

edu

An Internet identifier for a college, university, or K–12 school.

Eudora

A great mail program for Macintosh or Windows computers. Both a shareware and a commercial version are available.

FAQs

Frequently Asked Questions. Commonly asked questions about a variety of topics, including learning about the Internet. Reading FAQs will save you a great deal of time and embarrassment. You'll find FAQs in public areas of most FTP sites and in the Internet areas of commercial online services.

Fetch

A handy Macintosh FTP program from Dartmouth that enables you to transfer files.

firewall

Software or hardware protection for areas of a Web server computer that protects against unauthorized access.

flame

A sarcastic, critical, or obnoxious message posted to a newsgroup or sent via e-mail. Flames are neither nice nor necessary.

forms

Sections of HTML documents that accept input from users. Forms are used for user feedback, ordering, password protection, and searching.

FTP

File Transfer Protocol. A method of transferring files across the Internet from one computer to another. Also refers to the name of a program that transfers files.

GIF

Graphics Interchange Format. A kind of universal picture file that Macintoshes, computers that are running Windows, and most other computers running most other operating systems can read by using a program called a *GIF Viewer*.

Gopher

A program that runs on Internet host computers and helps you find information on the Net. The results are displayed via menus and can include documents and links to other computers. To get to Gopher, either launch a program such as *TurboGopher* or telnet to a Gopher server.

home page

The first page you see when you log on a Web site.

host

A computer that offers resources that are usable by Internet users. You can access a host computer via telnet, FTP, or the World Wide Web. Technically, in TCP/IP, any machine connected via IP is considered to be a *host* computer.

HTML

HyperText Markup Language. The language used to create pages for the World Wide Web. The commands enable users to specify different fonts, graphics, hypertext links, and more. You can use a word processor to create a Web page if you know the HTML commands to embed.

HTTP

HyperText Transfer Protocol. The way World Wide Web pages are transferred over the Web. Every Web address begins with `http://`.

hypertext

Text found on Web pages that you can click to go to another location, page, or document, or be linked to sounds, graphics, or movies.

image map

A special type of graphics file that allows Web users to click on a section of an image that links to other documents, other images, or other Web pages on the Internet.

information superhighway

This is a goodie. It means lots of things. Most people think that the Internet _is_ the information superhighway. They're mostly right. Stuff such as cable TV and phone company networks also qualify, though.

Internet

A bunch of computers hooked together by high-speed telephone lines and networks. The whole is greater than the sum of the parts.

IP

Internet Protocol. Techno-speak for the language that computers use to route information from computer to computer on the Internet.

IRC

Internet Relay Chat. A system that enables Internet users to chat, or talk in real time, by using an Internet link (rather than after a delay, as with e-mail messages).

JPEG

A compressed file format for pictures.

LISTSERV

A family of programs that automatically controls, sorts, and distributes incoming messages on a mailing list server.

MacTCP

An extension that allows a Macintosh to connect to the Internet.

modem

A marvelous piece of electronics that translates what you type and create on your computer into a signal that can be sent through a phone line and recreated by another modem on the other end of the line.

network

Basically, a bunch of computers strung together by wire. They can be wired together at one site (local area networks, or *LANs*) or can be connected via telephone or satellite (wide area networks, or *WANs*).

newbie

Someone who's new to the Internet. I must still be a newbie, because I discover something new every time I log on.

newsgroup

A bulletin board system on the Internet that's organized by topic.

newsreader

A program that enables you to read and respond easily to newsgroups on the Internet.

node

A computer that's hooked to a network.

NREN

National Research and Education Network. An effort to bring high-speed computing to schools everywhere.

PKZIP

A file-compression program for DOS and Windows.

PPP

Point-to-Point Protocol. An alternative to SLIP for dial-in access to the Internet. PPP is more reliable (and sometimes faster) than SLIP. For Macintosh users, a control panel called MacPPP is used to connect to the Internet if you have a dial-in connection.

protocol

A set of rules that controls communications on or between networks.

service provider

A company that supplies you with the connection that you need to access the Internet.

shareware

Software that you download and try out. If you keep the software, you're honor-bound to send the author a small fee.

SLIP

Serial Line Internet Protocol. A way to connect directly to the Internet so that programs you download come to your local hard drive and not to your information service provider's hard drive. If you have a SLIP account, you computer is actually *on* the Internet and is not just a dumb terminal. If you're SLIP (or direct, or PPP) connected, others can telnet to *your* computer, too, if you have the software to allow this. A control panel called MacSLIP (or InterSLIP) is used to connect to the Internet, if you have a dial-in connection.

spam

Posting commercial messages to lots of unsuspecting users. A huge no-no on the Internet. (Also a mysterious luncheon meat and the topic of Monty Python skits.)

StuffIt

A Macintosh file-compression program.

TCP/IP

Transmission Control Protocol/Internet Protocol. The system or language used between computers (hosts) on the Internet to make and maintain a connection.

telnet

A way to log into someone else's computer and use their computing resources.

terminal

A stupid, brainless front-end machine that relies on the computing power of a host computer. You can run programs on your computer that will make it act like a stupid, brainless terminal to enable you to dial into some host computers.

TurboGopher

A program that allows Macintosh users to access Gopher servers with a familiar (and friendly) point-and-click interface.

UNIX

A computer operating system. Get *UNIX For Dummies* (IDG Books Worldwide, Inc.) to become an instant expert.

upload

To move data from your computer to a host computer. Compare with *download*.

URL

Uniform Resource Locator. Basically, the address of any Gopher, FTP, telnet, or WWW site. URLs for Web pages look like this: `http://www.domain.top-domain`. For a Gopher site, a URL might be `gopher://domain.top-domain`.

USENET

A collection of thousands of newsgroups.

uuencode/uudecode

Programs that encode and decode newsgroup (and some other) files for sending over the Internet.

WAIS

(Pronounced *wayz.*) Wide Area Information Servers. A system of servers that enables you to search for documents on the Internet.

WinSock

A program that conforms to a set of standards called the Windows Socket API. *WinSock* programs control the link between Windows software and a TCP/IP program. You'll need this API (software driver) if you're using a computer running Windows to connect to the Internet.

World Wide Web (WWW)

A graphics-rich hypermedia system that enables you to move from site to site with the click of a mouse, collecting great (and not-so-great) information at every step.

Appendix B
HTML/HTML + Dictionary

● ●

*H*ere are the most-commonly used HTML tags. They're not case sensitive, so caps-on or caps-off, they work the same way.

Structural Tags

`<HTML>...</HTML>`	Indicates the beginning and ending of an HTML document.
`<HEAD>...</HEAD>`	Beginning and end of a document header.
`<TITLE>...</TITLE>`	Page (window) title.
`<BODY>...</BODY>`	Beginning and end of body of document.
`<!- ... ->`	Comment (does not show up when viewed by browser).

Formatting Tags

`<p>`	Paragraph.
`<H1>...</H1>`	Sets size of text. Lower is larger. Range is from H1 to H6.
`<PRE>...</PRE>`	Preformatted (WYSIWYG) text.
`<HR>`	Horizontal line.
` `	Line break.

Browser-Independent Tags

`<B>...</B>`	boldface
`<I>...</I>`	italic
`<TT>...</TT>`	monospace (like a typewriter)
`<U>...</U>`	underline (not supported by all browsers — yet)

Browser-Specific Tags

`<EM>...</EM>`	Emphasis. Each browser treats this text differently. Some browsers display as italic; some as underlined text.
`<STRONG>...</STRONG>`	Strong emphasis. Some browsers display as boldface; others as underlined text.
`<CODE>...</CODE>`	A code sample or Internet address. Appears in most browsers as Courier or other monospace font.
`<SAMP>...</SAMP>`	Used for illustrative text or examples. Appears similar to `<CODE>` text.
`<KBD>...</KBD>`	Used to indicate something to be typed by the user. Appears in monospace (Courier) font on graphical browsers.
`<ADDRESS>...</ADDRESS>`	Displays address information, usually in italics.
`<VAR>...</VAR>`	Used to name a variable. Some browsers show this text as italics or underline.
`<CITE>...</CITE>`	Citations for bibliographies. Usually shows text as italics.
`<DFN>...</DFN>`	Word or phrase to be defined. Usually shows the word as boldface.
`<BLOCKQUOTE>...</BLOCKQUOTE>`	Indents text to separate it from the surrounding text. For quotations.

Hypertext Links

`<A HREF=`"**destination URL**"`>`**link description** `</A>`
Link to another Web page, different server.

`<A HREF=`"#**target name**"`>`**destination description** `</A>`

`<A NAME=`"**target name**"`>` **destination** `</A>`
Link to another place, same Web page.

Lists

`<UL>...</UL>`	bulleted list
`<OL>...</OL>`	numbered list
`<MENU>...</MENU>`	menu list
`<DIR>...</DIR>`	directory (horizontal) list
`<DL>...</DL>`	glossary list
`<DT>`	definition text (for glossary lists)
`<DD>`	definition description (for glossary lists)
`<LI>`	list item

Images and Sound

`<IMG SRC=`"**filename.gif**"`>`
Inserts image (graphic).

`<IMG SRC=`"**filename.gif**" `ALIGN=TOP>`
Inserts image (graphic) and aligns top of accompanying text with top of image (*middle* and *bottom* work, too).

`<IMG SRC=`"**filename.gif**" `ALT=`"**alternate text**"`>`
Inserts image (graphic) and alternate text for non-GUI browsers.

`<A HREF=`"**file://filename.mov**"`>` **click for movie** `</A>`
Link to sound, movie, or other external file.

Appendix C

Acceptable Use Policies

● ●

*T*he following are several excerpts from acceptable use policies published on the Internet and on online services. Use the policies as you decide what is appropriate for your school's policy. Consider the tone and complexity of the policy and design one that fits your school.

UtahLink Use by the Public Schools

(Excerpted from material provided by the Utah State Department of Education.)

All use of UtahLink shall be consistent with the purpose, goal, and mission of the network. Successful operation of the network requires that its users regard UtahLink as a shared resource, and cooperate to form a community of diverse interests in an effort to promote educational excellence and provide world-class education throughout the state of Utah. It is therefore imperative that UtahLink members conduct themselves in a responsible, decent, ethical, and polite manner while using the network. Further, they must abide by all local, state and federal laws. To ensure the smooth and continued operation of this valuable resource, members must accept the responsibility of adhering to high standards of professional conduct and strict guidelines.

. . . it is important to recognize that with increased access to computers and people all over the world also comes the availability of controversial material that may not be considered of educational value in the context of the school setting.

. . . UtahLink recognizes the importance of each individual's judgment regarding appropriate conduct in maintaining a quality resource system. And while this policy does not attempt to articulate all required or proscribed behavior by its members, it does seek to assist in such judgment by providing the following guidelines:

    I. Any use of UtahLink for illegal or inappropriate purposes or to access materials that are objectionable in a public school environment, or in support of such activities, is prohibited.

Language that is deemed to be vulgar is also prohibited. Illegal activities shall be defined as a violation of local, state, and/or federal laws. Inappropriate use shall be defined as a violation of the intended use of the network, and/or purpose and goal. Objectionable is defined as materials that are identified as such by the rules and policies of the Utah State Board of Education that relate to curriculum materials and textbook adoption.

II. All use of UtahLink must be in support of a world class public education and educational research in Utah and consistent with the purposes of the network;

III. The following uses are also prohibited:

- Any use for commercial purposes or financial gain;
- Any use for product advertisement or political lobbying;
- Any use which shall serve to disrupt the use of the network by other users;

IV. UtahLink accounts shall be used only by the authorized owner of the account. Account owners are ultimately responsible for all activity under their account;

V. Unbridled and open-ended use of the network in terms of access time cannot be accommodated due to cost. Users are cautioned to exercise prudence in the shared use of this resource;

VI. All communications and information accessible via UtahLink should be assumed to be private property. Great care is taken by the UtahLink's administrators to ensure the right of privacy of users. However, it is recommended that users not give out personal information like home addresses and/or telephone numbers. Also, passwords should be kept private and changed frequently;

VII. Neither the USOE nor the UEN have control of the information on the Internet. Other sites accessible via the Internet may contain material that is illegal, defamatory, inaccurate or potentially offensive to some people;

VIII. Under prescribed circumstances, public school student use may be permitted, provided proper supervision is maintained by school officials and parents;

IX. Under prescribed circumstances,* non-educator use may be permitted, provided such individuals provide evidence that their use furthers the purpose and goal of the network and public education in general;

X. As necessary, the Utah State Office of Education will determine whether specific Public Education uses of UtahLink are consistent with this policy. The State Office shall be the final authority on use of the network and the issuance of public education user accounts;

XI. Each school district and school shall define and adopt an Acceptable Use Policy that identifies the standards and guidelines that are appropriate to their local circumstances. However these local policies may not permit uses that are outside of the guidelines of this policy;

XII. All accounts for the school professionals within a district will be issued and managed by the local node administrator(s). The issuing of these accounts will be coordinated with the UEN Network Operations Center;

XIII. Extensive use of the network for private or personal business is prohibited;

XIV. This is a legally binding document and careful consideration should be given to the principles outlined herein;

XV. Violations of the provisions stated in this policy may result in suspension or revocation of network privileges.

* Such prescribed circumstances and uses shall be defined in writing by the Utah Department of Education and from time to time are subject to change.

Western Connecticut State University

(From Regional School District 12, Western Connecticut Superintendents Association.)

Internet Network Access Agreement

ACCESS Project Student Form

Name _____

School_____

Home Address _____

Sponsoring Teacher _____

I accept responsibility to abide by the Internet Network Access policies of Regional School District 12, the Western Connecticut Superintendents Association, and Western Connecticut State University as stated in this agreement.

I agree:

✔ To use the Internet Network in support of education and research, consistent with the educational objectives of Regional School District 12.

✔ To use the Internet Network only with the permission of the responsible teacher.

✔ To be considerate of other users on the network and use appropriate language for school situations as indicated by the school codes of conduct.

✔ Not to knowingly degrade or disrupt Internet network services or equipment, as such activity is considered a crime under state and federal law; this includes, but is not limited to, tampering with computer hardware or software, vandalizing data, invoking computer viruses, attempting to gain access to restricted or unauthorized network services, violating copyright laws.

✔ To immediately report any problems or breeches of these responsibilities to the responsible teacher.

I understand that any conduct that is in conflict with these responsibilities is unethical and will result in termination of network access and possible disciplinary action.

Student Signature _____

Date _____

As a parent/guardian of this student, I have read the responsibilities for Internet Network Access. I understand that Internet access is designed for educational purposes and that Regional School District 12 and the Western Connecticut Superintendents Association have taken all available precautions to eliminate access to controversial material.

I understand that any conduct, by the above named student, that is in conflict with these responsibilities is unethical and such behavior will result in the termination of access and possible disciplinary action as indicated by the school codes of conduct.

I have reviewed these responsibilities with my child and I hereby give permission to Regional School District 12 to provide Internet network access.

Parent/Guardian Signature _____

Date _____

Read All About It

Everything You Need to Know (But Were Afraid to Ask Kids) About the Information Highway (Item No. S9501-06) is available from the Computer Learning Foundation for $5.95 (plus $4 shipping and handling). Computer Learning Foundation, Dept. EIH, P.O. Box 60007, Palo Alto, CA 94306-0007.

Appendix D

About the CD

• •

What's on the CD?

Hello, humble reader! This file gives you a great idea of all the educational
jewels hidden away in the goldmine of software on your *World Wide Web For
Teachers* CD. The tools really fall into several broad categories:

- Tools that help you access the Internet
- Tools that help you create your own Web page
- Tools that help you as you work through the examples in the book
- Tools that are very cool and that I had to include just for grins
- A set of BONUS files (created by teachers for teachers) that'll keep you so
  busy that you'll miss two days of school and forget to pay the power bill

I've sorted them into nice little nuggets (directories/folders) based upon
whether you're a Macintosh user or you're using a Windows machine.

This CD works happily on Windows machines as well as Macintosh computers.
I've also designed the CD so that programs designed only for Windows don't
show up if you're using the disk on a Mac. Likewise, programs meant only for
the Mac don't show up on the CD if you're using Windows.

Here's a basic listing of everything that you'll find on the CD, appropriately split
up in three categories:

- For all computers
- For Windows only
- For Macintosh only

I talk more in detail of the CD's contents after this listing. I tell you how to install
everything later, as well.

Important note for users: Be sure to check the software licensing agreements
on the CD for all software you plan to use.

For All Computers

✔ **America Online**

Sign on to America Online. For folks using Macs or PCs, I've included the newest version of America Online, the granddaddy of online services. (The special card included in the CD-ROM package gives you additional instructions as well as a special registration number and password to use to access your ten free hours.)

I stuck *AOL* on the disk because it's the first way most users sign on to the Net, mostly because it's quick and easy and doesn't require forty purchase orders. There's a *huge* amount of educational content on AOL as well. Don't forget to visit the Electronic Schoolhouse (Keyword: **ESH**) on Sunday nights at 8:30 EST for a spirited educator's online chat!

You can also use AOL's easy FTP (file transfer protocol) interface to retrieve the newest copy of *Netscape,* something that you'll need if you're going to visit the Web on a regular basis.

✔ **Eudora Light**

I've included *Eudora Light* (Macintosh and Windows versions) for your electronic mail-reading pleasure. *Eudora* is the software standard in e-mail sending and receiving, and it will help you and your students keep your heads above water as when the almost certain e-mail waterfall comes your way as you begin actively using the Net. More than 3,000,000 users can't be wrong! (Eudora Light™ is a trademark of Qualcomm, Incorporated. Eudora® is a registered trademark of the University of Illinois Board of Trustees.)

✔ **StuffIt Expander**

Chances are that you'll encounter files that are way too large and take way too long to send across the Net. (Too long is defined in school terms as the time it takes to snarf down a corndog in the school cafeteria. Approximately five minutes, by my last estimate.) That's why I've included Aladdin's incredible *StuffIt Expander* for Macintosh and Windows. *StuffIt Expander* will allow you to "unStuff" (decompress) any archive file you download that's been "stuffed" (compressed) by most of the popular compression programs. It even unstuffs ZIP files. (Note for Windows 95 users: *StuffIt Expander* doesn't understand Windows 95's long file names. If you decompress files that contain things that use Windows 95-length filenames, *StuffIt Expander* for Windows and Macintosh will twist the filenames back into the clunky DOS 8-character format.)

✔ **The Super-Fantastic Web Page!**

This is the best part of the CD! Located in the EDWEB directory/folder is a master Web page called MAIN.HTM. If you open it using a Web browser, you can access some Web sites that you and your students will find quite cool.

I've put my Web elves to work, and they've managed to create a most amazing set of Web pages packed with more than a thousand Web sites for use in your classroom. To access these pages, just fire up your favorite WWW browser (AOL, Netscape, Mosaic, whatever) and use the Open File command to open the file called MAIN.HTM. Then you and your students can point-and-click your way to educational nirvana. Beware, my testers (teachers just like you and me) had to be pried away from the computer. It was their suggestion (a good one, I think) to sort the files according to subject area. I hope that you'll enjoy these files!

Note: Because Web sites come and go more often than school board members (no offense!), you're likely to get an error message or two as you visit these sites. They were all tested and valid during the publishing process, though, so you should surf effortlessly most of the time.

I also made 11 additional Web pages that are linked with the MAIN.HTM document. You don't need to open these with your Web brower directly. The MAIN.HTM Web page has links to every one of these pages.

Finally, in the TUTORIAL directory, I included three HTML documents as well as a graphic file for use with the lessons I provide with this book.

For Windows Users Only

For those of you who are Windows gurus, I've included the *Internet Assistant,* an incredible HTML translator/editor that works with *Microsoft Word For Windows* (both Windows 3.1 and Windows 95 flavors).

If you don't own *Microsoft Word for Windows,* you can't use *Internet Assistant.* (*sob*). The programs, located on the CD in the \WIN\TOOLS\NETASST directory, are:

WORDIA.EXE	The *Internet Assistant* for *Microsoft Word for Windows* versions 6.0a and 6.0c only
WORD60.EXE	This program updates your copy of *Word* from 6.0 to 6.0a so you can use Internet Assistant.
WORDIA2B.EXE	The *Internet Assistant* for users of *Microsoft Word for Windows 95* (version 7.0)

Internet Assistant for *Word* 6.0a and 6.0c (note the wee letters at the end of the version numbers) doesn't work with *Word for Windows* 6.0. That's why I've included WORD60.EXE, which will update your 6.0 version to 6.0a so that you, too, can enjoy the benefits of *Internet Assistant.*

To check the version number of your copy of *Word for Windows,* open *Word,* and then choose Help⊅About Microsoft Word. A cute window appears that shows your version number. If the version number shows 6.0, you need to use the **Word 6.0 Updater** before using *Internet Assistant.* If you see version 6.0a or 6.0c (there's no "6.0b". . . don't ask us why), feel free to install *Internet Assistant* for *Word for Windows* 6.0a and 6.0c. If you see version 7, slap yourself on the back for being a Windows 95 user and use the installer for *Internet Assistant* for *Word for Windows 95.*

In the future, you can also look on AOL (Keyword: **Microsoft**) for the update.

For Macintosh Users Only

✔ **PageMill** Demo

Adobe PageMill gives you the tools to create your Web page without any knowledge of HTML or any other strange interplanetary computer languages. The demo version lets you do everything but save and print your file, but you can still practice with this demo while you're saving your pennies to buy the full commercial version. Adobe® and PageMill™ are trademarks of Adobe Systems Incorporated.

✔ **PageMill** Tutorial Files

This folder contains additional Web pages and graphics for use with the book and *PageMill* Demo.

✔ **CyberFinder**

Ready for a surprise? I've also scored one of the first copies of Aladdin's *CyberFinder* demo (with a 15-day trial period). *CyberFinder* makes the process of locating Net resources simple and elegant.

✔ **HTML Web Weaver 2.53**

HTML Web Weaver is the complete version of a terrific little utility for those of you who would like to create a Web page and who have just a smidgen of knowledge about that wondrous Web-language called HTML. The guy who thought up this software gem is gonna win a Nobel prize for creativity one day.

✔ **TurboGopher 2.0.3**

For Macintosh users, I've gotten you a fresh, new copy of *TurboGopher.* You and your students will use *TurboGopher* when you're ready to search worldwide Gopher server databases for information, articles, or other print resources.

You say you want to license *TurboGopher?* Just read on. . . .

TurboGopher: copyright 1993-1995, University of Minnesota

TurboGopher is copyrighted software and is owned by the University of Minnesota. You can obtain a license to use the software by sending (US)$25 to:

Distributed Computing Services
Attn: TurboGopher Licensing
190 Shepherd Labs
100 Union Street SE
University of Minnesota
Minneapolis, MN 55455
U.S.A.

The license granted for this software is limited to USE only. You may not modify, sell, distribute, or incorporate any part of *TurboGopher* in any other piece of software. The license fee applies to the current version of the software. The University of Minnesota may, in its sole discretion, require an additional license fee for future versions of the software. The University of Minnesota is not promising to create future versions. This includes, but is not limited to, the correcting of bugs in the current version.

The University of Minnesota makes no warranty about the software. In particular, THERE IS NO EXPRESS OR IMPLIED WARRANTY, NO WARRANTY OF MERCHANTIBILITY, AND NO WARRANTY FOR FITNESS FOR A PARTICULAR PURPOSE. The software is licensed as is. The software contains bugs. These bugs may be corrected in future versions of the software, but the University of Minnesota does not promise such corrections will be made. You agree that you will use the software at your own risk and will not hold the University of Minnesota liable for any damage that may be caused by this software.

Installing the CD Programs on Your Computer

Just follow the following sets of directions to get started.

Macintosh users

Every file included on the CD can either be copied onto your hard drive or comes equipped with an easy-to-use install program. To use the installers, just double-click their icons. Most of the programs come with more Read Me files that detail how to properly install things; just follow their directions and you and your students will be surfing in no time. To install software that is shown inside a folder on the CD, copy the entire folder to your hard disk.

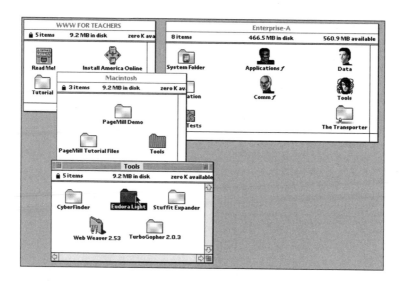

Windows 3.1 users — installing anything EXCEPT America Online

The first thing you need to do is to get the File Manager set up to copy files or activate installers.

Set up the File Manager

1. Close all other programs in Windows. Most of you will need the extra memory when using the File Manager and the installers that you'll activate from there.

2. Insert the *World Wide Web For Teachers* CD in your CD-ROM drive.

3. Open the File Manager. An icon to open File Manager is in the Main program group.

4. Choose Window⇨New Window to create a new window.

5. Choose Window⇨Tile Vertically to reorganize the windows to make it easier to see things.

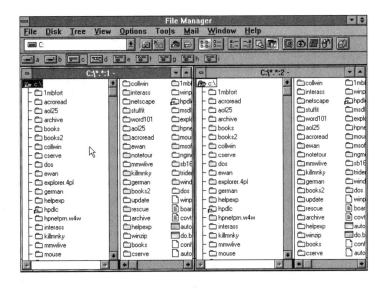

Do you see more than two windows? If so, close all but two of the windows, and then choose Windows⇨Tile Vertically again.

6. Click the title bar of the first window.

7. In the toolbar located just below the menu, click on the button that represents your computer's CD drive.

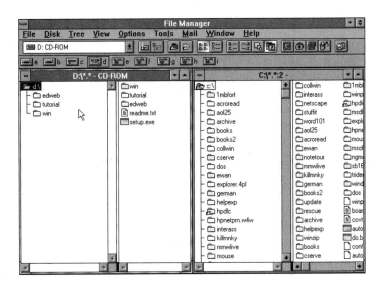

8. Click the title bar of the second window.

9. In the toolbar located just below the menu, click on the button that represents your computer's hard disk drive.

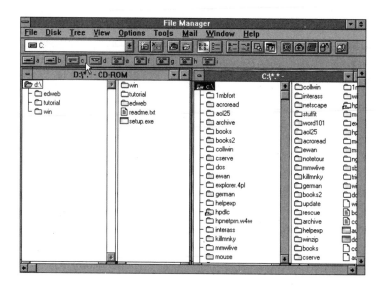

The second thing is to double-click or copy files from the CD drive to your computer drive. I'll go about this for each program and set of files that you'll find.

Copy EDWEB and TUTORIAL folders

1. Click and begin dragging the folders (one at a time) from the CD window to the folder called C:\ in your computer's hard drive window (this is your computer's top directory).

2. Still keeping that button down, place your mouse pointer over the C:\ folder so that it's highlighted (with a box!), and then release your mouse button.

   This copies the files from one drive to the other.

   To drag, click your mouse pointer on the folder to highlight it. Then, while still holding down the mouse button, move your mouse pointer. A tiny outline of the folder will move with the pointer.

   Depending on your File Manager settings, you may get messages from the File Manager asking you if you really want to copy files. Click on the OK button to confirm this.

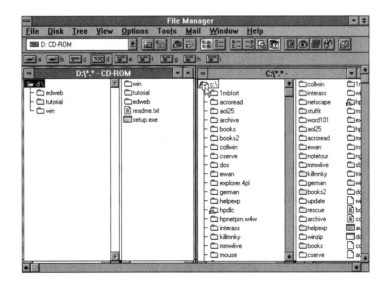

Copy Internet Assistant and Eudora Light

1. In the CD window of the File Manager, open the WIN folder. You should see the NETASST folder.

2. Drag the NETASST folder from the CD window to the C:\ folder in your computer's hard disk window (this is your computer's top directory). This copies the files from one drive to the other.

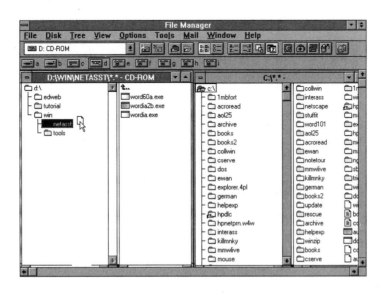

To drag, click your mouse pointer on the folder to highlight it. Then, while still holding down the mouse button, move your mouse pointer. A tiny outline of the folder will move with the pointer. Still keeping that button down, place your mouse pointer over the C:\ folder so that it's highlighted, and then release your mouse button.

In the CD window of the File Manager, open the TOOLS folder (located inside the WIN folder). You should be able to see the EUDORALT and STUFFIT folders.

Repeat steps 1 and 2 for the EUDORALT folder. (**Don't copy the STUFFIT folder.**)

Install Internet Assistant

Ask yourself, "Have I read the section about the *Internet Assistant* for *Word* 6.0a and 6.0c under the section 'Tools that help you build your own Web pages'"? If you haven't, do it now, or you'll end up unhappy because you didn't follow instructions.

Make sure that *Microsoft Word* is **not** running, or your computer may lock up harder than an Edsel without motor oil.

3. Now that you've read the stuff about using *Internet Assistant* (you have, haven't you?) open the NETASST folder that you just copied to your computer's hard disk drive window by double-clicking its folder.

4. Next, if you're using *Word* 6.0 (NOT 6.0a or 6.0c), double-click on the file named WORD60.EXE to update your version of *Word* to 6.0a.

5. Finally, double-click the file WORDIA.EXE to install *Internet Assistant* for *Word for Windows* 6.0a and 6.0c.

Install *Eudora Light* for *Windows*

1. First open the EUDORALT folder that you just copied to your computer's hard drive window by double-clicking its folder.

2. Next, double-click on the file called EUDOR152.EXE. This activates a program that installs *Eudora Light* in the EUDORALT folder.

3. Click on the file 15MANUAL.EXE to install the manual for *Eudora Light*. This is a large file (over 3 MB), and it's a *Microsoft Word* document, so don't bother installing this if you don't own *Word* or a word processing program that can read *Word* documents (hint: *Write* or *Notepad* won't cut it!).

   Also included is a *Word* document that talks more about *Eudora Pro,* the commercial version of *Eudora Light*. If you have a few pennies to spare, *Eudora Pro* has quite a few features to make your Internet e-mail management easier than what's available in its freeware version.

Install StuffIt Expander for Windows

1. Open the STUFFIT folder in the CD window by double-clicking its folder.

2. Next, double-click the file SITEX10.EXE to start the *StuffIt Expander* Installer.

3. Follow the installer's directions on screen, and you're all set.

   Here's a tip: Just click the Install button and don't change any of the installation settings.

Install America Online for Windows 3.1

1. Insert the *World Wide Web For Teachers* CD in your computer's CD-ROM drive.

2. Close all programs that you're running. Installers work best when no other programs are running.

3. From the Program Manager, click on the File menu and choose Run.

4. In the Run dialog box, type in **D:\SETUP** (most computers use "D" as their CD-ROM drive. If your CD drive letter is different, type it in instead of "D").

5. Click on OK and follow the on-screen instructions. (See the card enclosed in the CD-ROM envelope for more instructions as well as a password and registration number.)

Windows 95 users — installing everything EXCEPT America Online

First, get your windows open so that you can easily copy files from the CD to your computer.

1. Insert the *World Wide Web For Teachers* CD in your computer's CD-ROM drive.

2. Close all other windows on your desktop to make it easier to see which window does what.

3. Double-click the My Computer icon (if you've called it something else, well, click the icon that displays icons for all your computer's drives — particularly, your computer's hard disk and CD-ROM drive).

4. From the My Computer window, double-click your CD icon to open its window.

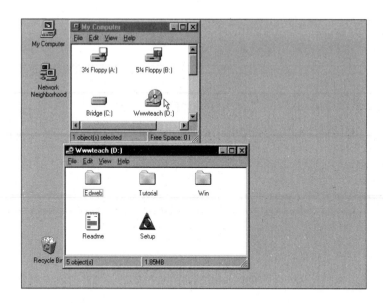

5. Double-click the C: drive icon to open its window. You'll see the contents of your hard disk drive.

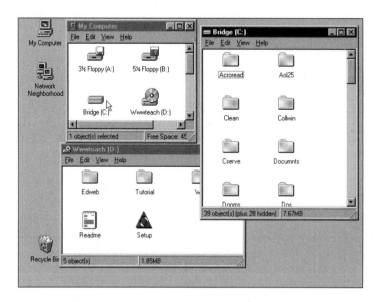

6. Move the CD window to the left of your screen, and move the hard disk drive window (C:) to the right side of the screen.

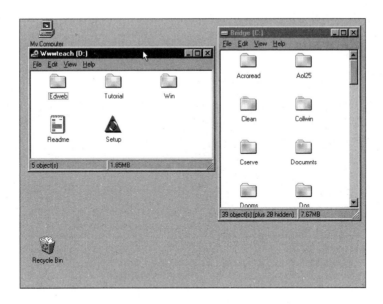

Copy EDWEB and TUTORIAL folders

1. Click and drag the Edweb and Tutorial folders from the CD window to the hard disk drive window (C:). This copies the folders to your computer's hard disk drive.

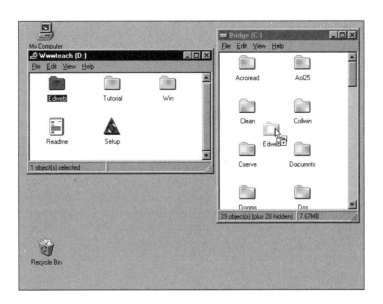

To drag, click your mouse pointer on the folder to highlight it. Then, while still holding down the mouse button, move your mouse pointer. A tiny outline of the folder will move with the pointer. Still keeping that button down, place your mouse pointer on an empty part of the hard disk drive window, and then release your mouse button.

2. Depending on your settings, you may get messages from Windows asking you if you really want to copy files. Click on the appropriate buttons to confirm this.

Copy *Internet Assistant and Eudora Light*

1. In the CD window, open the Win folder. You should see the Netasst folder.

2. Drag the Netasst folder from the CD window to your computer's hard disk window. This copies the files from one drive to the other.

To drag, click your mouse pointer on the folder to highlight it. Then, while still holding down the mouse button, move your mouse pointer. A tiny outline of the folder will move with the pointer. Still keeping that button down, place your mouse pointer over the C:\ folder so that it's highlighted, and then release your mouse button.

In the CD window, open the Tools folder (located inside the Win folder). You should be able to see the Eudoralt and Stuffit folders.

Repeat steps 1 and 2 for the Eudoralt folder. (**Don't copy the Stuffit folder!**)

Install *Eudora Light for Windows*

1. Open the Eudoralt folder that you just copied to your computer's hard disk drive window by double-clicking its folder.

2. Next, double-click on the file called EUDOR152. This activates a program that installs *Eudora Light* in the Eudoralt folder.

Click on the file 15MANUAL to install the manual for *Eudora Light.* This is a large file (over 3 MB), and it's a *Microsoft Word* document, so don't bother installing this if you don't own *Word* or a word processing program that can read *Word* documents. (*WordPad,* included with Windows 95, can open *Word* documents for you.)

Also included is a *Word* document that talks more about *Eudora Pro,* the commercial version of *Eudora Light.* If you have a few pennies to spare, *Eudora Pro* has quite a few features to make your Internet e-mail management easier than what's available in its freeware version.

Install *Internet Assistant for Word for Windows 6.0a and 6.0c, or for Word For Windows 95*

Ask yourself, "Have I read the section about the *Internet Assistant* under the section, 'Tools that help you build your own Web pages'"? If you haven't, do it now, or you'll end up unhappy because you didn't follow instructions.

Make sure that *Microsoft Word* is **not** running, or your computer may freeze faster than a Vermont lake in January.

1. Now that you've read the stuff about using *Internet Assistant* (you have, haven't you?) open the Netasst folder that you just copied to your computer's hard disk drive window by double-clicking its folder.

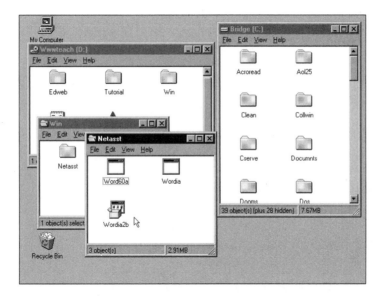

2. Next, if you're using *Word* 6.0 (NOT 6.0a or 6.0c), double-click on the file named WORD60 to update your version of Word to 6.0a.

3. If you're using *Word for Windows 95* (version 7.0), double-click the file WORDIA2B to install *Internet Assistant* for *Word for Windows* 6.0a and 6.0c. If you're running *Word* 6.0a or *Word* 6.0c, double-click the file WORDIA to install *Internet Assistant* for *Word* 6.0a and 6.0c.

Install *StuffIt Expander for Windows*

1. Open the Stuffit folder in the CD window by double-clicking its folder.

2. Next, double-click the file SITEX10 to start the *StuffIt Expander* Installer.

3. Follow the installer's directions on screen, and you're all set.

   Here's a tip. Just click the Install button and don't change any of the installation settings.

Remember: *StuffIt Expander* for Windows doesn't understand the long filenames of Windows 95. *StuffIt Expander* will still open archives which contain long filenames, but it will shorten the names to the icky 8-character DOS file name format.

Install *America Online for Windows 95*

1. Insert *The World Wide Web For Teachers* CD in your computer's CD-ROM drive.

2. Close all programs that you're running. Installers work best when no other programs are running.

3. Click on the Start button, and then choose Run.

4. In the Run dialog box, type in D:\SETUP (most computers use "D" as their CD drive. If your CD drive letter is different, type it in instead of "D").

5. Click on OK and follow the on-screen instructions. (See the card enclosed in the CD-ROM envelope for more instructions as well as a password and registration number.)

A Note to Those with Guilty Consciences

TurboGopher 2.0.3 and *HTML Web Weaver* (both Macintosh programs) are *shareware* products. By shareware, the program's author freely places programs on the Internet and other places in hopes that you'll play with it awhile. Aladdin's *CyberFinder* program is also on the CD, with a 15-day trial period. If you like using the program, you can choose to pay the author for the software, or you can remove it from your computer. This is a nice "try-it-before-you-buy-it" concept that works well because the authors don't have to pay a middleman to distribute their software, and as a result, you'll pay a lot less for a shareware product. If you don't pay up on shareware that you're using, you're doing a disservice to the shareware's author (why should the author make more programs if you'll snatch them up without paying for them) and other paying users of the software (why should they miss out on future releases of a good program because you didn't pay?). So, *pay up* or face your coworkers with a guilty face and very bad karma!

Index

• X •

• Y •

• Z •

The Internet For Macs® For Dummies® 2nd Edition	by Charles Seiter	ISBN: 1-56884-371-2	$19.99 USA/$26.99 Canada
The Internet For Macs® For Dummies® Starter Kit	by Charles Seiter	ISBN: 1-56884-244-9	$29.99 USA/$39.99 Canada
The Internet For Macs® For Dummies® Starter Kit Bestseller Edition	by Charles Seiter	ISBN: 1-56884-245-7	$39.99 USA/$54.99 Canada
The Internet For Windows® For Dummies® Starter Kit	by John R. Levine & Margaret Levine Young	ISBN: 1-56884-237-6	$34.99 USA/$44.99 Canada
The Internet For Windows® For Dummies® Starter Kit, Bestseller Edition	by John R. Levine & Margaret Levine Young	ISBN: 1-56884-246-5	$39.99 USA/$54.99 Canada

MACINTOSH

Mac® Programming For Dummies®	by Dan Parks Sydow	ISBN: 1-56884-173-6	$19.95 USA/$26.95 Canada
Macintosh® System 7.5 For Dummies®	by Bob LeVitus	ISBN: 1-56884-197-3	$19.95 USA/$26.95 Canada
MORE Macs® For Dummies®	by David Pogue	ISBN: 1-56884-087-X	$19.95 USA/$26.95 Canada
PageMaker 5 For Macs® For Dummies®	by Galen Gruman & Deke McClelland	ISBN: 1-56884-178-7	$19.95 USA/$26.95 Canada
QuarkXPress 3.3 For Dummies®	by Galen Gruman & Barbara Assadi	ISBN: 1-56884-217-1	$19.95 USA/$26.99 Canada
Upgrading and Fixing Macs® For Dummies®	by Kearney Rietmann & Frank Higgins	ISBN: 1-56884-189-2	$19.95 USA/$26.95 Canada

MULTIMEDIA

Multimedia & CD-ROMs For Dummies® 2nd Edition	by Andy Rathbone	ISBN: 1-56884-907-9	$19.99 USA/$26.99 Canada
Multimedia & CD-ROMs For Dummies®, Interactive Multimedia Value Pack, 2nd Edition	by Andy Rathbone	ISBN: 1-56884-909-5	$29.99 USA/$39.99 Canada

OPERATING SYSTEMS:

DOS

MORE DOS For Dummies®	by Dan Gookin	ISBN: 1-56884-046-2	$19.95 USA/$26.95 Canada
OS/2® Warp For Dummies® 2nd Edition	by Andy Rathbone	ISBN: 1-56884-205-8	$19.95 USA/$26.99 Canada

UNIX

MORE UNIX® For Dummies®	by John R. Levine & Margaret Levine Young	ISBN: 1-56884-361-5	$19.99 USA/$26.99 Canada
UNIX® For Dummies®	by John R. Levine & Margaret Levine Young	ISBN: 1-878058-58-4	$19.95 USA/$26.95 Canada

WINDOWS

MORE Windows® For Dummies® 2nd Edition	by Andy Rathbone	ISBN: 1-56884-048-9	$19.95 USA/$26.95 Canada
Windows® 95 For Dummies®	by Andy Rathbone	ISBN: 1-56884-240-6	$19.99 USA/$26.99 Canada

PCS/HARDWARE

Illustrated Computer Dictionary For Dummies® 2nd Edition	by Dan Gookin & Wallace Wang	ISBN: 1-56884-218-X	$12.95 USA/$16.95 Canada
Upgrading and Fixing PCs For Dummies® 2nd Edition	by Andy Rathbone	ISBN: 1-56884-903-6	$19.99 USA/$26.99 Canada

PRESENTATION/AUTOCAD

AutoCAD For Dummies®	by Bud Smith	ISBN: 1-56884-191-4	$19.95 USA/$26.95 Canada
PowerPoint 4 For Windows® For Dummies®	by Doug Lowe	ISBN: 1-56884-161-2	$16.99 USA/$22.99 Canada

PROGRAMMING

Borland C++ For Dummies®	by Michael Hyman	ISBN: 1-56884-162-0	$19.95 USA/$26.95 Canada
C For Dummies® Volume 1	by Dan Gookin	ISBN: 1-878058-78-9	$19.95 USA/$26.95 Canada
C++ For Dummies®	by Stephen R. Davis	ISBN: 1-56884-163-9	$19.95 USA/$26.95 Canada
Delphi Programming For Dummies®	by Neil Rubenking	ISBN: 1-56884-200-7	$19.99 USA/$26.99 Canada
Mac® Programming For Dummies®	by Dan Parks Sydow	ISBN: 1-56884-173-6	$19.95 USA/$26.95 Canada
PowerBuilder 4 Programming For Dummies®	by Ted Coombs & Jason Coombs	ISBN: 1-56884-325-9	$19.99 USA/$26.99 Canada
QBasic Programming For Dummies®	by Douglas Hergert	ISBN: 1-56884-093-4	$19.95 USA/$26.95 Canada
Visual Basic 3 For Dummies®	by Wallace Wang	ISBN: 1-56884-076-4	$19.95 USA/$26.95 Canada
Visual Basic "X" For Dummies®	by Wallace Wang	ISBN: 1-56884-230-9	$19.99 USA/$26.99 Canada
Visual C++ 2 For Dummies®	by Michael Hyman & Bob Arnson	ISBN: 1-56884-328-3	$19.99 USA/$26.99 Canada
Windows® 95 Programming For Dummies®	by S. Randy Davis	ISBN: 1-56884-327-5	$19.99 USA/$26.99 Canada

SPREADSHEET

1-2-3 For Dummies®	by Greg Harvey	ISBN: 1-878058-60-6	$16.95 USA/$22.95 Canada
1-2-3 For Windows® 5 For Dummies® 2nd Edition	by John Walkenbach	ISBN: 1-56884-216-3	$16.95 USA/$22.95 Canada
Excel 5 For Macs® For Dummies®	by Greg Harvey	ISBN: 1-56884-186-8	$19.95 USA/$26.95 Canada
Excel For Dummies® 2nd Edition	by Greg Harvey	ISBN: 1-56884-050-0	$16.95 USA/$22.95 Canada
MORE 1-2-3 For DOS For Dummies®	by John Weingarten	ISBN: 1-56884-224-4	$19.99 USA/$26.99 Canada
MORE Excel 5 For Windows® For Dummies®	by Greg Harvey	ISBN: 1-56884-207-4	$19.95 USA/$26.95 Canada
Quattro Pro 6 For Windows® For Dummies®	by John Walkenbach	ISBN: 1-56884-174-4	$19.95 USA/$26.95 Canada
Quattro Pro For DOS For Dummies®	by John Walkenbach	ISBN: 1-56884-023-3	$16.95 USA/$22.95 Canada

UTILITIES

Norton Utilities 8 For Dummies®	by Beth Slick	ISBN: 1-56884-166-3	$19.95 USA/$26.95 Canada

VCRS/CAMCORDERS

VCRs & Camcorders For Dummies™	by Gordon McComb & Andy Rathbone	ISBN: 1-56884-229-5	$14.99 USA/$20.99 Canada

WORD PROCESSING

Ami Pro For Dummies®	by Jim Meade	ISBN: 1-56884-049-7	$19.95 USA/$26.95 Canada
MORE Word For Windows® 6 For Dummies®	by Doug Lowe	ISBN: 1-56884-165-5	$19.95 USA/$26.95 Canada
MORE WordPerfect® 6 For Windows® For Dummies®	by Margaret Levine Young & David C. Kay	ISBN: 1-56884-206-6	$19.95 USA/$26.95 Canada
MORE WordPerfect® 6 For DOS For Dummies®	by Wallace Wang, edited by Dan Gookin	ISBN: 1-56884-047-0	$19.95 USA/$26.95 Canada
Word 6 For Macs® For Dummies®	by Dan Gookin	ISBN: 1-56884-190-6	$19.95 USA/$26.95 Canada
Word For Windows® 6 For Dummies®	by Dan Gookin	ISBN: 1-56884-075-6	$16.95 USA/$22.95 Canada
Word For Windows® For Dummies®	by Dan Gookin & Ray Werner	ISBN: 1-878058-86-X	$16.95 USA/$22.95 Canada
WordPerfect® 6 For DOS For Dummies®	by Dan Gookin	ISBN: 1-878058-77-0	$16.95 USA/$22.95 Canada
WordPerfect® 6.1 For Windows® For Dummies® 2nd Edition	by Margaret Levine Young & David Kay	ISBN: 1-56884-243-0	$16.95 USA/$22.95 Canada
WordPerfect® For Dummies®	by Dan Gookin	ISBN: 1-878058-52-5	$16.95 USA/$22.95 Canada

Fun, Fast, & Cheap!™

NEW!

The Internet For Macs® For Dummies® Quick Reference
by Charles Seiter

ISBN:1-56884-967-2
$9.99 USA/$12.99 Canada

NEW!

Windows® 95 For Dummies® Quick Reference
by Greg Harvey

ISBN: 1-56884-964-8
$9.99 USA/$12.99 Canada

SUPER STAR

Photoshop 3 For Macs® For Dummies® Quick Reference
by Deke McClelland

ISBN: 1-56884-968-0
$9.99 USA/$12.99 Canada

SUPER STAR

WordPerfect® For DOS For Dummies® Quick Reference
by Greg Harvey

ISBN: 1-56884-009-8
$8.95 USA/$12.95 Canada

Title	Author	ISBN	Price
DATABASE			
Access 2 For Dummies® Quick Reference	by Stuart J. Stuple	ISBN: 1-56884-167-1	$8.95 USA/$11.95 Canada
dBASE 5 For DOS For Dummies® Quick Reference	by Barrie Sosinsky	ISBN: 1-56884-954-0	$9.99 USA/$12.99 Canada
dBASE 5 For Windows® For Dummies® Quick Reference	by Stuart J. Stuple	ISBN: 1-56884-953-2	$9.99 USA/$12.99 Canada
Paradox 5 For Windows® For Dummies® Quick Reference	by Scott Palmer	ISBN: 1-56884-960-5	$9.99 USA/$12.99 Canada
DESKTOP PUBLISHING/ILLUSTRATION/GRAPHICS			
CorelDRAW! 5 For Dummies® Quick Reference	by Raymond E. Werner	ISBN: 1-56884-952-4	$9.99 USA/$12.99 Canada
Harvard Graphics For Windows® For Dummies® Quick Reference	by Raymond E. Werner	ISBN: 1-56884-962-1	$9.99 USA/$12.99 Canada
Photoshop 3 For Macs® For Dummies® Quick Reference	by Deke McClelland	ISBN: 1-56884-968-0	$9.99 USA/$12.99 Canada
FINANCE/PERSONAL FINANCE			
Quicken 4 For Windows® For Dummies® Quick Reference	by Stephen L. Nelson	ISBN: 1-56884-950-8	$9.95 USA/$12.95 Canada
GROUPWARE/INTEGRATED			
Microsoft® Office 4 For Windows® For Dummies® Quick Reference	by Doug Lowe	ISBN: 1-56884-958-3	$9.99 USA/$12.99 Canada
Microsoft® Works 3 For Windows® For Dummies® Quick Reference	by Michael Partington	ISBN: 1-56884-959-1	$9.99 USA/$12.99 Canada
INTERNET/COMMUNICATIONS/NETWORKING			
The Internet For Dummies® Quick Reference	by John R. Levine & Margaret Levine Young	ISBN: 1-56884-168-X	$8.95 USA/$11.95 Canada
MACINTOSH			
Macintosh® System 7.5 For Dummies® Quick Reference	by Stuart J. Stuple	ISBN: 1-56884-956-7	$9.99 USA/$12.99 Canada
OPERATING SYSTEMS:			
DOS			
DOS For Dummies® Quick Reference	by Greg Harvey	ISBN: 1-56884-007-1	$8.95 USA/$11.95 Canada
UNIX			
UNIX® For Dummies® Quick Reference	by John R. Levine & Margaret Levine Young	ISBN: 1-56884-094-2	$8.95 USA/$11.95 Canada
WINDOWS			
Windows® 3.1 For Dummies® Quick Reference, 2nd Edition	by Greg Harvey	ISBN: 1-56884-951-6	$8.95 USA/$11.95 Canada
PCs/HARDWARE			
Memory Management For Dummies® Quick Reference	by Doug Lowe	ISBN: 1-56884-362-3	$9.99 USA/$12.99 Canada
PRESENTATION/AUTOCAD			
AutoCAD For Dummies® Quick Reference	by Ellen Finkelstein	ISBN: 1-56884-198-1	$9.95 USA/$12.95 Canada
SPREADSHEET			
1-2-3 For Dummies® Quick Reference	by John Walkenbach	ISBN: 1-56884-027-6	$8.95 USA/$11.95 Canada
1-2-3 For Windows® 5 For Dummies® Quick Reference	by John Walkenbach	ISBN: 1-56884-957-5	$9.95 USA/$12.95 Canada
Excel For Windows® For Dummies® Quick Reference, 2nd Edition	by John Walkenbach	ISBN: 1-56884-096-9	$8.95 USA/$11.95 Canada
Quattro Pro 6 For Windows® For Dummies® Quick Reference	by Stuart J. Stuple	ISBN: 1-56884-172-8	$9.95 USA/$12.95 Canada
WORD PROCESSING			
Word For Windows® 6 For Dummies® Quick Reference	by George Lynch	ISBN: 1-56884-095-0	$8.95 USA/$11.95 Canada
Word For Windows® For Dummies® Quick Reference	by George Lynch	ISBN: 1-56884-029-2	$8.95 USA/$11.95 Canada
WordPerfect® 6.1 For Windows® For Dummies® Quick Reference, 2nd Edition	by Greg Harvey	ISBN: 1-56884-966-4	$9.99 USA/$12.99/Canada

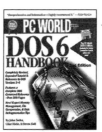

Macworld® Mac® & Power Mac SECRETS™, 2nd Edition
by David Pogue & Joseph Schorr

HOT!

This is the definitive Mac reference for those who want to become power users! Includes three disks with 9MB of software!

WINNERS 1994-95 TECHNICAL PUBLICATIONS AND ART COMPETITIONS OF THE SOCIETY FOR TECHNICAL COMMUNICATION

ISBN: 1-56884-175-2
$39.95 USA/$54.95 Canada

Includes 3 disks chock full of software.

NEWBRIDGE BOOK CLUB SELECTION

Macworld® Mac® FAQs™
by David Pogue

HOT!

Written by the hottest Macintosh author around, David Pogue, *Macworld Mac FAQs* gives users the ultimate Mac reference. Hundreds of Mac questions and answers side-by-side, right at your fingertips, and organized into six easy-to-reference sections with lots of sidebars and diagrams.

ISBN: 1-56884-480-8
$19.99 USA/$26.99 Canada

Macworld® System 7.5 Bible, 3rd Edition
by Lon Poole

ISBN: 1-56884-098-5
$29.95 USA/$39.95 Canada

NATIONAL BESTSELLER!

Macworld® ClarisWorks 3.0 Companion, 3rd Edition
by Steven A. Schwartz

ISBN: 1-56884-481-6
$24.99 USA/$34.99 Canada

NATIONAL BESTSELLER!

Macworld® Complete Mac® Handbook Plus Interactive CD, 3rd Edition
by Jim Heid

BMUG SPRING 1995 CHOICE PRODUCT

ISBN: 1-56884-192-2
$39.95 USA/$54.95 Canada

Includes an interactive CD-ROM.

NEWBRIDGE BOOK CLUB SELECTION

Macworld® Ultimate Mac® CD-ROM
by Jim Heid

ISBN: 1-56884-477-8
$19.99 USA/$26.99 Canada

CD-ROM includes version 2.0 of QuickTime, and over 65 MB of the best shareware, freeware, fonts, sounds, and more!

Macworld® Networking Bible, 2nd Edition
by Dave Kosiur & Joel M. Snyder

ISBN: 1-56884-194-9
$29.95 USA/$39.95 Canada

WINNER

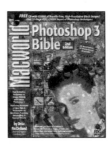

Macworld® Photoshop 3 Bible, 2nd Edition
by Deke McClelland

ISBN: 1-56884-158-2
$39.95 USA/$54.95 Canada

Includes stunning CD-ROM with add-ons, digitized photos and more.

WINNERS 1994-95 TECHNICAL PUBLICATIONS AND ART COMPETITIONS OF THE SOCIETY FOR TECHNICAL COMMUNICATION

NEW!

Macworld® Photoshop 2.5 Bible
by Deke McClelland

ISBN: 1-56884-022-5
$29.95 USA/$39.95 Canada

NATIONAL BESTSELLER!

Macworld® FreeHand 4 Bible
by Deke McClelland

ISBN: 1-56884-170-1
$29.95 USA/$39.95 Canada

Macworld® Illustrator 5.0/5.5 Bible
by Ted Alspach

ISBN: 1-56884-097-7
$39.95 USA/$54.95 Canada

Includes CD-ROM with QuickTime tutorials.

For scholastic requests & educational orders please call Educational Sales, at 1. 800. 434. 2086

FOR MORE INFO OR TO ORDER, PLEASE CALL ▶ 800. 762. 2974

For volume discounts & special orders please ca Tony Real, Special Sales, at 415. 655. 3048

Order Center: **(800) 762-2974** *(8 a.m.–6 p.m., EST, weekdays)*

Quantity	ISBN	Title	Price	Total

Shipping & Handling Charges

	Description	First book	Each additional book	Total
Domestic	Normal	$4.50	$1.50	$
	Two Day Air	$8.50	$2.50	$
	Overnight	$18.00	$3.00	$
International	Surface	$8.00	$8.00	$
	Airmail	$16.00	$16.00	$
	DHL Air	$17.00	$17.00	$

*For large quantities call for shipping & handling charges.
**Prices are subject to change without notice.

Ship to:

Name _____

Company _____

Address _____

City/State/Zip _____

Daytime Phone _____

Payment: ☐ Check to IDG Books Worldwide (US Funds Only)

☐ VISA   ☐ MasterCard   ☐ American Express

Card # _____ Expires _____

Signature _____

Subtotal _____

CA residents add
applicable sales tax _____

IN, MA, and MD
residents add
5% sales tax _____

IL residents add
6.25% sales tax _____

RI residents add
7% sales tax _____

TX residents add
8.25% sales tax _____

Shipping _____

Total _____

Please send this order form to:
IDG Books Worldwide, Inc.
7260 Shadeland Station, Suite 100
Indianapolis, IN 46256

Allow up to 3 weeks for delivery.
Thank you!

IDG BOOKS WORLDWIDE, INC.
END-USER LICENSE AGREEMENT

5. **Limited Warranty.**

(a) IDGB warrants that the Software and disk(s)/CD-ROM are free from defects in materials and workmanship under normal use for a period of sixty (60) days from the date of purchase of this Book. If IDGB receives notification within the warranty period of defects in materials or workmanship, IDGB will replace the defective disk(s)/CD-ROM.

(b) **IDGB AND THE AUTHOR OF THE BOOK DISCLAIM ALL OTHER WARRANTIES, EXPRESS OR IMPLIED, INCLUDING WITHOUT LIMITATION IMPLIED WARRANTIES OF MERCHANTABILITY AND FITNESS FOR A PARTICULAR PURPOSE, WITH RESPECT TO THE SOFTWARE, THE PROGRAMS, THE SOURCE CODE CONTAINED THEREIN, AND/OR THE TECHNIQUES DESCRIBED IN THIS BOOK. IDGB DOES NOT WARRANT THAT THE FUNCTIONS CONTAINED IN THE SOFTWARE WILL MEET YOUR REQUIREMENTS OR THAT THE OPERATION OF THE SOFTWARE WILL BE ERROR FREE.**

(c) This limited warranty gives you specific legal rights, and you may have other rights which vary from jurisdiction to jurisdiction.

6. **Remedies.**

(a) IDGB's entire liability and your exclusive remedy for defects in materials and workmanship shall be limited to replacement of the Software, which may be returned to IDGB with a copy of your receipt at the following address: Disk Fulfillment Department, Attn: The World Wide Web For Teachers, IDG Books Worldwide, Inc., 7260 Shadeland Station, Ste. 100, Indianapolis, IN 46256, or call 1-800-762-2974. Please allow 3-4 weeks for delivery. This Limited Warranty is void if failure of the Software has resulted from accident, abuse, or misapplication. Any replacement Software will be warranted for the remainder of the original warranty period or thirty (30) days, whichever is longer.

(b) In no event shall IDGB or the author be liable for any damages whatsoever (including without limitation damages for loss of business profits, business interruption, loss of business information, or any other pecuniary loss) arising from the use of or inability to use the Book or the Software, even if IDGB has been advised of the possibility of such damages.

(c) Because some jurisdictions do not allow the exclusion or limitation of liability for consequential or incidental damages, the above limitation or exclusion may not apply to you.

7. **U.S. Government Restricted Rights.** Use, duplication, or disclosure of the Software by the U.S. Government is subject to restrictions stated in paragraph (c) (1) (ii) of the Rights in Technical Data and Computer Software clause of DFARS 252.227-7013, and in subparagraphs (a) through (d) of the Commercial Computer—Restricted Rights clause at FAR 52.227-19, and in similar clauses in the NASA FAR supplement, when applicable.

8. **General.** This Agreement constitutes the entire understanding of the parties and revokes and supersedes all prior agreements, oral or written, between them and may not be modified or amended except in a writing signed by both parties hereto which specifically refers to this Agreement. This Agreement shall take precedence over any other documents that may be in conflict herewith. If any one or more provisions contained in this Agreement are held by any court or tribunal to be invalid, illegal, or otherwise unenforceable, each and every other provision shall remain in full force and effect.

Microsoft End-User License Agreement

Important — read carefully:

This Microsoft End-User License Agreement ("EULA") is a legal agreement between you (either an individual or a single entity) and Microsoft Corporation for the Microsoft software accompanying this EULA, which includes computer software and associated media and printed materials, and may include "online" or electronic documentation ("SOFTWARE PRODUCT" or "SOFTWARE"). By opening the sealed packet(s) OR exercising your rights to make and use copies of the SOFTWARE PRODUCT, you agree to be bound by the terms of this EULA. If you do not agree to the terms of this EULA, promptly return this package to the place from which you obtained it.

Software product license:

The SOFTWARE PRODUCT is protected by copyright laws and international copyright treaties, as well as other intellectual properly laws and treaties. The SOFTWARE PRODUCT is licensed, not sold.

1. **GRANT OF LICENSE.** This EULA grants you the following rights:

   - **Installation and Use.** You may install and use an unlimited number of copies of the SOFTWARE PRODUCT.

   - **Reproduction and Distribution.** You may reproduce and distribute an unlimited number of copies of the SOFTWARE PRODUCT; provided that each copy shall be a true and complete copy, including all copyright and trademark notices, and shall be accompanied by a copy of this EULA. The copies may be distributed as a standalone product or included with your own product.

2. **DESCRIPTION OF OTHER RIGHTS AND LIMITATIONS.**

   - **Limitations on Reverse Engineering, Decompilation, and Disassembly.** You may not reverse engineer, decompile, or disassemble the SOFTWARE PRODUCT, except and only to the extent that such activity is expressly permitted by applicable law notwithstanding this limitation.

   - **Separation of Components.** The SOFTWARE PRODUCT is licensed as a single product. Its component parts may not be separated for use on more than one computer.

   - **Software Transfer.** You may permanently transfer all of your rights under this EULA, provided the recipient agrees to the terms of this EULA.

- **Termination.** Without prejudice to any other rights, Microsoft may terminate this EULA if you fail to comply with the terms and conditions of this EULA. In such event, you must destroy all copies of the SOFTWARE PRODUCT and all of its component parts.

3. **COPYRIGHT.** All title and copyrights in and to the SOFTWARE PRODUCT (including but not limited to any images, photographs, animations, video, audio, music, text, and "applets" incorporated into the SOFTWARE PRODUCT), the accompanying printed materials and any copies of the SOFTWARE PRODUCT are owned by Microsoft or its suppliers. The SOFTWARE PRODUCT is protected by copyright laws and international treaty provisions. Therefore, you must treat the SOFTWARE PRODUCT like any other copyrighted material.

4. **U.S. GOVERNMENT RESTRICTED RIGHTS.** The SOFTWARE PRODUCT and documentation are provided with RESTRICTED RIGHTS. Use, duplication, or disclosure by the Government is subject to restrictions as set forth in subparagraph (c)(1)(ii) of the Rights in Technical Data and Computer Software clause at DFARS 252.227-7013 or subparagraphs (c)(1) and (2) of the Commercial Computer Software — Restricted Rights at 48 CFR 52.227-19, as applicable. Manufacturer is Microsoft Corporation/One Microsoft Way/Redmond, WA 98052-6399.

Limited warranty:

NO WARRANTIES. Microsoft expressly disclaims any warranty for the SOFTWARE PRODUCT. The SOFTWARE PRODUCT and any related documentation is provided "as is" without warranty of any kind, either express or implied, including, without limitation, the implied warranties of merchantability, fitness for a particular purpose, or noninfringement. The entire risk arising out of use or performance of the SOFTWARE PRODUCT remains with you.

NO LIABILITY FOR CONSEQUENTIAL DAMAGES. In no event shall Microsoft or its suppliers be liable for any damages whatsoever (including, without limitation, damages for loss of business profits, business interruption, loss of business information, or any other pecuniary loss) arising out of the use of or inability to use this Microsoft product, even if Microsoft has been advised of the possibility of such damages. Because some states/jurisdictions do not allow the exclusion or limitation of liability for consequential or incidental damages, the above limitation may not apply to you.

Miscellaneous:

If you acquired this product in the United States, this EULA is governed by the laws of the State of Washington.

If this product was acquired outside the United States, then local laws may apply.

Should you have any questions concerning this EULA, or if you desire to contact Microsoft for any reason, please contact the Microsoft subsidiary serving your country, or write: Microsoft Sales Information Center/One Microsoft Way/Redmond, WA 98052-6399.

Installation instructions

Well, almost. *The World Wide Web For Teachers CD-ROM* contains software for Windows users, software for Mac users, and plenty of things for *both* Windows and Mac users. The installation instructions for each program are too long to summarize here. Just turn to the **About the CD** section (Appendix D) at the end of this book to find detailed instructions on all that you get on the CD . . . and how to put these wonderful things on your computer.

Note from Microsoft Corporation regarding the Internet Assistant® for Word for Windows®:

This program was reproduced by IDG Books Worldwide, Inc., under a special arrangement with Microsoft Corporation. For this reason, IDG Books Worldwide, Inc., is responsible for the product warranty and for its support. If your diskette is defective, please return it to IDG Books Worldwide, Inc., which will arrange for its replacement. PLEASE DO NOT RETURN IT TO MICROSOFT CORPORATION. End users of this Microsoft program shall not be considered "registered owners" of a Microsoft product and therefore shall not be eligible for upgrades, promotions, or other benefits available to "registered owners" of Microsoft products.

❏ YES!

Please keep me informed about IDG's World of Computer Knowledge.
Send me the latest IDG Books catalog.